WARRIOR
IN THE GARDEN

ROB EASTMAN

WARRIOR IN THE GARDEN

Copyright © 2023 by Rob Eastman

Inspired Legacy Publishing is a division of (DBA) Inspired Legacy, LLC
PO Box 900816
Sandy UT 84090-0816.

Changing Names & Medical Advice

Some names and identifying details have been changed
to protect the privacy of individuals.
This book is not intended as a substitute for the medical advice
of physicians. The reader should regularly consult a physician in
matters relating to his/her health and particularly with respect to
any symptoms that may require diagnosis or medical attention.

ISBN 979-8-9888553-0-9 (paperback)
ISBN 979-8-9888553-1-6 (hardcover)

Printed in the United States of America.

WHAT PEOPLE ARE SAYING

"*Warrior in the Garden* is a lifeboat for those in similar despair and their families."
—**Michael O. Leavitt, Former Secretary of the US Department of Health and Human Services, Former Administrator of the US Environmental Protection Agency, 14th Governor of Utah**

"Eastman's journey shines a light on transforming challenges into triumphs, offering hope and inspiration. His emphasis on mindset shift and strategic determination showcases how such shifts can redefine life's course."
—**Maresa Friedman, Chief Strategy Officer at Strategy Solved**

"This book leaves the reader with a sense of inspiration and motivation, showcasing the realization that the only thing keeping you from being the best version of yourself is you."
—**Kedma Ough, CEO Superb Maids Portland**

"WOW!! What an amazing story of strength, perseverance, self-awareness and growth."
—**Gentry Jones, Certified Life and Recovery Coach**

"I laughed! I cried! When a book can elicit emotions like that, then it's a winner in my book. But most of all, I loved the honesty in Rob Eastman's powerful story."
—**Misti Mazurik, Director of Operations at RHG Media Productions**

"Rob somehow found the inspiration and rock-solid determination to overcome addiction. Now he teaches others how to avoid or recover from what he went through. A painfully candid but compelling story of redemption. I heartily recommend it."
—**Greg Bell, *Former Utah State Senator and Lieutenant Governor***

"This book illuminates mental health and mastery over life's challenges. It shows us how to be warriors of self-discovery and not lose ourselves in the face of life's battles."
—**Baron Baptiste, *New York Times Bestselling Author of Perfectly Imperfect (Hay House) and Journey into Power (Simon and Schuster)***

"Raw and authentic, this book delves into the author's vulnerabilities, revealing a side we can all empathize with. . . . Through personal transformation, the author poses a profound question: 'Is this the role model I want to be?' It's a testament to overcoming one's dark side."
—**Deborah Wiener, *Intuitive & Inspirational Business and Life Coach***

"*Warrior in the Garden* takes its readers on an emotional rollercoaster of joy and frustration as the protagonist finds his path and inspiration. A powerful read."
—**Maureen Ryan Blake, *Bestselling Author, TV Show Host, and YouTube Expert***

DEDICATION

I want to dedicate this book to the two women who have been my rock:

To my mother, who showed me that everyone is deserving of love, and who has shown me unconditional love even when I didn't deserve it. For that, I'm forever grateful.

And to my daughter Sophie. You are my life saver and showed me that I was capable of unconditional love myself. This book and my vulnerability and strength come from your love for me.

I am forever your son and dad.

TABLE OF CONTENTS

NOTE TO THE READER

I'm honored you have picked up this book. Before you jump in, I want to share that I have learned through the years that perception constitutes each individual reality. The saying goes: "there is my truth, there is your truth and then there is what actually happened." If I've learned one thing writing this book, and interviewing friends and loved ones, it's that how I perceived things and felt things in my life wasn't always how everyone else perceived and felt them. In saying that, please understand that my story is just that: MY STORY.

The deep lessons and understandings of my experiences are where I was able to develop my conclusions and opinions. I've spent the last thirteen years studying mental health, addiction, family dynamics and human behavior, but I am not a doctor or therapist. I'm a boots-on-the-ground coach, often in the trenches with people as they find their way to the light. I speak of my journey and those I've witnessed in powerful ways. In my book, I also speak about my experiences with school, religion and relationships. I hold no anger and in no way blame my fails on anyone or anything else but me. In fact, I honor all the deep and beautiful lessons. With that being said, I hope my story will help you see you're not alone, that there is a light at the end of the tunnel. It's not just a saying; it's the truth. As long as you have hope for your life or a loved one anything is possible, and you are worthy of love.

CHAPTER 1

"DAMNIT, ROBBY" AND COWBOY BOOTS

Terrified screams of other children surrounded me, but I couldn't move. The screech of metal tearing from metal was my only warning as the big chains and tires lurched under me. My tiny body could move almost as fast as lightning. At least that's what stunned adults often said. Yet at that moment, I could not climb off the swing fast enough.

CRUNCH!

I fell violently to the ground. I didn't know what happened except a pain shot up my foot into my leg as if I'd been stabbed. Pain was something I knew, but I'd never felt agony like that before. Clutching my leg, I lay helpless, my ankle caught under the huge rubber tire. Some kids ran past me to tell their teachers that the tire swing on the playground had broken from its frame, but then, the bell rang.

Oh no! I'm gonna be in big trouble . . . again!

I gritted my teeth and wrenched my leg free. Tears stung my eyes from the stabbing pain racing up my right leg. I felt sick to my stomach as I limped as fast as I could to my kindergarten class. I dreaded talking to Mrs. Rose, my teacher.

I just want Mommy. She makes it all go away.

Unable to help the silent tears, I wiped them away hurriedly with my jacket sleeve. Oblivious to the rugged mountains tipped with snow and our school nestled up beneath them, I focused only on getting to my classroom.

Mrs. Rose's sour face greeted me at the door. "You're late, Robby," she breathed scathingly, paying no attention to my red face, nor my limp. "Get to your seat right now."

"I got hurt on the playground, Mrs. Rose! It hurts, bad."

"Are you bleeding?" she asked dismissively, not looking at me as she watched the kids sitting at attention at their desks. They were now eerily quiet, and although I didn't look at them, I knew they were staring at me.

Glancing down, I was confused. No telltale blood was oozing from my leg, but something was *wrong*. It wasn't like the times I'd tripped on something or played tag with neighborhood kids three times my size and got run over. No, my leg hurt like a wolf or something had torn it off.

"No blood . . . but Mrs. Rose, the tire swing fell on me! I think maybe I broke someth—"

"Stop it, Robby! Now be quiet. I already told you to go sit down," she growled. Her words cut as she sat at her tall desk, her hard, beady eyes peering out from behind glasses, golden chains at her temples swinging in her fury. "Stop making a mountain of a mole-hill and go back to your corner, now! You know what *that* means."

I really wanted to cry now as I trembled in pain while the whole class stared at me. Standing, I was the same height as they were sitting; their eyes were level with mine. One or two faces were wide with worry, but most of them smirked at the teacher's comment. "Your corner."

Yes, I do know what that means.

A humiliated red rose hotly to my cheeks, competing with my bright red hair for

attention. No one in my class and hardly anyone in my school had red hair. Kids already teased me about it, and it didn't help that my ears stuck out a mile wide from each side of my face.

I knew what they were thinking, because I'd heard all the taunts a thousand times already. I was the runt, the pipsqueak who couldn't sit still, the Tasmanian devil. But I knew, as my chin trembled and my leg still burned and throbbed . . . if I let one tear fall, I would break down and sob in front of the whole class. Then I would be a crybaby.

That can never happen. The torture would be endless.

Mrs. Rose's deep scowl and the children's snickering followed me as I limped back into the corner. It was my job to stand there, all by myself like I had so many times since starting kindergarten a couple of months before.

As I reached the corner, lightheaded, I knew I *had* to pay attention, or I'd get in worse trouble. "Damnit, Robby!" I breathed to myself, even as I stumbled, trying to turn my body around.

Apparently I hadn't spoken soft enough.

My teacher was on me in an instant, ramming the dunce cap onto my head where she said it should be sewn on permanently. It didn't matter that this was the '80s; her '50s-style punishments ruled the day here. Not one second later, she shoved the large and dreaded bar of Lava soap into my mouth. Bits of rough pumice and soap immediately mixed together with my saliva, making me choke.

I couldn't help it any longer. As she fumed her way back to the front of class, tears of pain streamed down my face. Fortunately, the kids' attention was fixed on Mrs. Rose. She completely dismissed me, leaving me to gag quietly on the soap and the snot that I wiped away from my nose with my shirt.

I didn't catch a single thing taught in class that afternoon. My brain wasn't working. As soon as the bell rang, I numbly spit out the soap and tried not to throw up. Normally the first kid to bolt out of the classroom, that day I was the last. Mrs. Rose didn't look up as I hobbled out her door. I missed the catcalls and the yells in the hallway. Kids I usually raced down the steep ravine had already run ahead, stampeding down the hill to build the momentum needed to race as far up the sharp incline on the other side.

It took me forever to limp down. Trying to catch my breath at the bottom, I looked up. *How in the world will I get up there?* Gritting my teeth again, I took one step, and then another. I didn't remember cresting the hill, or the last couple blocks home, or moving into the new foyer of our beautiful home in Bountiful, Utah, nestled along the bench of the stunning mountains I loved so much.

"Robby!" exclaimed my mom as I came in the door. "Where's your jacket and hat? Where's your backpack?"

I looked at her numbly. *Jacket? Backpack?* I tried to take another step and stumbled. Mom caught me, and her eyes grew wide. "Robby, you're all pale and clammy! Are you sick, honey?" Without waiting for an answer, she scooped me up into her arms.

I did feel sick. I could hardly breathe, and my heart was beating dully. I could only concentrate on the one thing Mrs. Rose had ignored. "My leg," was all I could manage out loud, though I was screaming inside.

Then I was on the couch, my pant leg pulled up, hearing my mother's horrified cry. Without another sound, she whisked me into our car along with my little brother Drew. I didn't know where my three older sisters were—probably at some dance, gymnastics, or after-school athletics. Mom drove fast but was careful around the corners so I didn't whimper.

She believes me.

Next thing I knew, I was in some place with white hallways and crisp, noisy paper sheets on an exam table. The doctor told my mother I wasn't communicating much because I was in shock, and the nurses soothed my mother as she tried to soothe me. One nurse had me lie down while she elevated my ankle on a pillow and put some ice around it.

After some time, my brain started feeling like it was coming back. The pain was finally lessening with the ice. Getting bored, I started to fiddle with the knobs on the medical table below me.

"Well, you must be feeling a little better, Mister," Mom said, relieved as she held little Drew on her lap. She had that warm look on her face that I knew so well. It was like she was always torn between loving me to death and wondering what the heck I'd done. That was the look I usually got when she had to take time out of her busy schedule to tend to something I'd broken. Mom didn't have much time between five kids. She was always helping my dad with all kinds of business stuff, things at home, plus she and Dad both were leaders and teachers at our church. Some days, she told me, her biggest job was trying not to tick off the neighbors with our family's wild ways—especially mine.

Even when she gave me that look, I knew she loved me. I loved her fiercely, too, with every ounce of my being. She was Mom! She and Dad were my superheroes. They could've worn capes around their shoulders and fit right into my estimation of them, because they could fix *anything*. Dad was cool and brash at times but extremely popular in our community. Mom, on the other hand, was dignified and held her head high. She was also the one who remedied *me*.

Every night, she had to "tickle" the skin on my face, arms, and back to get me settled down for sleep. If she didn't do it, I couldn't sleep, plain and simple. However, she awoke anxious every morning because I was never in my bed, despite her rising early. I was already out of my room and often out of my house before the sun. Full of uncontainable energy, I'd curiously take apart anything I could find, leaving a dangerous trail in my wake at our house, our yard, or the neighbors'.

My three older sisters teased me unceasingly about my antics. They would often tell strangers the story of me and the meddlesome woman who still lived across from us. She always had her nose in our family's business and seemed to take a particular interest in me as soon as I learned how to walk. When I was just a toddler, that same nosy neighbor called my mother.

"Do you know where your boy Robby is?" she demanded.

"Well, yes," replied my mom defensively, looking around. "He's right here—"

"—Oh, no he's not!" the neighbor cut in. "He's up on top of your ROOF, walking around in his diapers and cowboy boots!"

Mom didn't even bother to hang up the phone before racing outside and up on the roof to rescue me—diapers, cowboy boots, and all. My sisters would end with, "Robby's always being too big for his britches!" I didn't really know what they meant, except I seemed to have an innate sense for sniffing out trouble, even when I moved out of diapers into underwear.

It scared Mom that adventure and danger were not distinguishable for me. The result? A few choice words spoken about me in our family . . . and far too often.

In fact, the year before kindergarten, when I was introduced to my lovely and amazing preschool teacher, Mrs. Wing, she bent down and asked me what my name was.

"Damnit Robby!" I said proudly, grinning a little shyly at the pretty woman.

She looked up in surprise at my proper, now very embarrassed and stuttering mother.

I looked at Mom curiously. I didn't know that "Damnit Robby" was not my name. I knew that I had heard that word so often in conjunction with "Robby", especially from my dad, that it naturally seemed it was my full, given name.

I didn't even know *damnit* was a swear word until Christmas of that year, when Dad had all of us write down our personal goals for the year (Mom helped me) and family goals. All my sisters wrote the same one: "I wish that Robby would stop swearing!" Some words I'd obviously picked up from Dad, but I also paid attention. On TV, at his car dealership, and the multitude of sporting events we attended, I noticed people really meant what they said when they were swearing. I wanted people to know I meant what I said!

Mom didn't know what to do with my language or my insatiable curiosity. I often overheard her on the phone, exasperated, talking to Dad or other family about the fact that I couldn't sit still, that I didn't understand—or didn't care to understand—the rules. That meant I was always, *always* in trouble.

Now, in the doctor's office, the doctor announced I would have to come back when the swelling was down so they could diagnose my ankle properly. I stayed home for a day or two until the swelling was alleviated enough to have X-rays. Sure enough, my ankle was fractured. My mother drove me to school with a cast on my ankle, and some crutches.

I was suddenly popular, and I sucked in my first brief moment of glory. No one was laughing at me! But while all the students "oohed" and "aahed" over the molded cast and wanted to sign it, Mrs. Rose sniffed and brought class immediately to order. The woman never apologized to me or even looked at me like she was sorry—not even once.

I wanted to glare up at her. I had been punished for telling the truth, and I got the same excruciating, embarrassing punishment I did all the times I hadn't listened to her, the times I got something wrong, or when I didn't follow the rules in the exact moment she asked.

I understood her being angry with me when I lied to try not to be in trouble—but when I told the truth? It didn't seem fair.

Surely this had to be an outright break in some code of teacher ethics! I had an ingrained sense of right and wrong, because even my dad—tall and charismatic and with a wild streak of his own that only the people closest to him saw, usually up on the ski slopes—if *he* did something wrong or punished me but later found out I'd told the truth, he always said he was sorry. Mrs. Rose? She was another sort of character altogether. I had tried my best to be polite and worked very hard to please her. The tire swing incident proved that although she was an adult, she was untrustworthy.

I begged Mom to get me a new teacher. However, no matter how much clout my mother and father seemed to have in our community and our church, they didn't like to "make waves." I didn't even know if my mother had tried to call the school. She hugged me, kissed the top of my head, and made sure I got to the classroom okay. She told me to be good, as she always did when sending me off to school, but there was no further discussion.

I am going to have to deal with this monster for the rest of the year.

I began to hate Mrs. Rose with a passion. Instead of anything getting better, it only got worse for me in her classroom. It didn't matter what I did! Her treatment of me worsened over time. Using that spiteful voice, she would make fun of me—and even of my best work on paper. I knew my alphabets, numbers, and beginning-reader words did not have the crisp, strong lines of everyone else's, but I did my best.

"Robby," she would say, "if your As look like Ds and your Ms look like . . ." She snatched the paper from me, squinting. ". . . whatever this garbage is, you will never amount to anything! You're only halfway through the exercise, and the rest of the class is nearly done. I will not have the class waiting on you again, you hear me?"

Mrs. Rose's bullying rubbed off on a couple of the boys and one girl in my classroom. Because she said and did certain things, *they* thought they had the right to do the same. They sneered at my papers when we handed our assignments to the end of the row. When assignments were handed back, they noticed Mrs. Rose's red marker was brighter and more frequent on my unfinished pages than on the others.

As time progressed, the bullies got braver because they didn't get called out. They shoved me out of line in class and the hallways, trying to get me in more trouble. They were wicked in the lunch line, where I couldn't escape them, and I avoided them on the playground. Then the older kids got in on the razzing. By the time my kindergarten year nearly ended, every bully in the elementary school seemed to have me as a target. My fear showed up in our class picture, where the kids all lined up, sitting nice and tall. I was at the end of my row, deliberately spaced away from the others, trying to hide.

Finally, when the last day of school arrived, I could not wait to get out. Mrs. Rose was droning on, but I couldn't concentrate, wishing for the bell to ring. I was daydreaming of the freedom that summer would bring. Maegen had been keeping me and my little brother Drew busy in the warming weather, mesmerizing us by building fairy houses around our wooded property. She ignited our imagination with her stories about them, and we brought the fairies cookies and milk to stick around our magical yard.

Maegen had also taught me something fun over winter break; it was a different form of magic I couldn't get out of my mind. Surrounded by deep snow, she and I jumped super high on our trampoline, then launched into the forgiving branches of the pine trees cloistered near the back of our property, hoping the combination of snowsuits and deep snow would protect us from being smashed and obliterated to bits. That activity kept me grinning and my heart pounding. Even Dad joined us a couple times, laughing loudly as each of us hit the snow-laden limbs of trees with a vengeance before falling into the soft drifts below.

I had an idea to do that again, as I sat gripping my desk. I wondered if a new combination of the water hose, the trampoline, the pine limbs, and the large bed of needles underneath could keep me unharmed.

I watched the clock. Only thirty seconds until I was finished with Mrs. Rose forever.

20 seconds . . . No more dunce cap.

10 seconds . . . No more Lava soap.

5 seconds . . . No more wicked, mean Mrs. Rose.

I couldn't help it. I busted out of my seat two seconds before the bell rang, grabbed my backpack, and bolted out the door on my fully healed ankle before anyone else in my class had even risen from their seats.

"ROBBY!" I heard Mrs. Rose yell as I blissfully ignored her and darted down the hall, her voice ringing in my ears as I burst out into the fresh, early summer afternoon. The bell had rung, and Maegen promised me that meant Mrs. Rose was no longer my teacher. *I don't have to listen to her. I don't have to have any more consequences from her.*

Besides, I didn't hear, "*Damnit, Robby!*"

In my mind, that meant I didn't have to stop.

CHAPTER 2

THE DISEASE OF INATTENTION

At the smallest hint of gold outside my bedroom window, my eyes popped wide open. *So much to do!* I loved mornings, before the breathtakingly hot summer afternoons of Utah stole my energy . . . and before my skin would turn even redder—making my friends' parents send me home out of concern.

Within seconds that morning, I was out the door and playing in the yard. The back perimeter of our property was practically a forest. I loved the pine trees and birches; I could climb them and jump into the neighbor's pastures. I fed the beautiful horses with apples in my pockets stolen from Mom's basket on the counter. Late summer brought free apricots from the fruit trees here that the horses loved. At times I smuggled sugar cubes from the coffee counter at Dad's car dealership into my pockets, knowing how popular it would make me among my giant friends.

It only took one horse to notice me, and they all came to greet me. Neighing softly in the soft morning light, sniffing my pockets knowingly, they nosed my arms and hands, begging to be scratched between their ears and petted down their long, soft foreheads. Despite the fact that I wasn't as tall as the horses' flanks, they were quite gentle with me. They listened to me when I talked to them. I noticed my frantic energy calmed around them. I walked along the fence for a bit, and they followed.

We came to a place where the apricot tree reached over the top of the fence. There, I climbed to the very top of the wood pole fence, swaying a bit, bolstered only by the gangly tree limbs. Using my treats as bribes, I positioned the horses just so, and then hopped onto one of their backs. I knew I looked like a beetle on top of an elephant because I was so small, but even though my legs barely reached the horse's upper flanks on both sides, this one, like the others, let me ride around the pasture on him.

I wasn't exactly supposed to be out here. I hadn't asked permission to leave the house—or to be on the horses, but my day didn't seem complete without a visit. Mom had told me the night before I wasn't to leave the house, but that if I did, I had better get back before we had to take my sister Danielle to her gymnastics meet. My mind wandered like the horse I was riding, all across the field, each of us eating an apricot and the other horses following us.

Mom won't mind me spending time with horses. After all, when she and the girls moved to Nevada before I came along, she was famous for racing dune buggies and winning. As dignified as she tried to hold herself when Dad bragged about her to others, I always saw the corner of her lips curve up. I guess she had a little wild streak to her, too. You would never know it by how prim and proper she made us sit in church!

I enjoyed riding the beautiful horse I was on that morning. He was a bay, with deep coppery brown hair and a black mane, and I marveled how his flesh rippled when he moved or whinnied. The golden light reflecting on the dewy grass disappeared. The sun grew higher in the sky without me noticing.

"ROBBY!" a sharp voice called out.

Oh crap! It was Mom, her face livid from what I could see. Packed beside her in the Cherokee on the side of the road were all my siblings. I hadn't even heard them coming.

"What did I say about you being *home* this morning?" she yelled, extremely flustered. "You're not even dressed yet! And what in the Sam Hill are you doing on top of Mr. Murray's horse?" She looked carefully up and down the street, seeing the Burninghams and others were not out watching. "Get your bum down here, young man. We're going to be late! You have to change into something suitable—fortunately I grabbed some shorts and a T-shirt with your flip -flops."

I looked down at myself. Sure enough, I was still in my summer jammies and smelling like horseflesh. Erin, the oldest, was shooting daggers at me with her eyes, and Danielle and everyone else were screaming at me to hurry up. I slid off the horse and dropped to the ground and galloped faster than the horses into the Cherokee.

Mom drove off before my butt was fully in the seat. Swiftly, she barked instructions to everyone about seatbelts and to help me change out of my pajamas into the clothes she'd tucked in the back.

As we sped from the top of the bench of Bountiful straight down the hill into the main part of the city, Mom informed us we would do some school shopping after Danielle's meet. The girls all cheered, excited, but my stomach dropped.

I'd had a glorious summer. We'd moved into our fully expanded house. It felt brand new once it had been added to, and Mom's friends all gushed about the tall, vaulted ceilings and the windows that let in tons of light and looked down on the city in one direction and up into the stunning mountains behind.

I'd loved swimming, playing, roughhousing with friends, and even dressing up and singing on stage at Lagoon, the wildly popular local theme park. I spent time riding my horse friends, biking up and down the hills in the neighborhood, having races, and so much more. We'd gone boating and camping, and I'd been pawned off on Aunt Marsh and Uncle Wayne to explore boring historic sites in the middle of nowhere.

But that was all over. Like every kid, I had to go to school by law. I knew because I'd even asked Dad.

Fear now stabbed up and down my spine. Nightmares of kindergarten filled my nights and made me shudder during the day. The good news was that I found out that Shawn would at least be in school with me. Our parents were friends, and I'd started to get to know him and his family a little through skiing over the winter. My parents were both avid and skilled skiers, and Erin, Danielle, and Maegen were getting pretty good, too, at least in my eyes. I'd been skiing since I was three and a half, and Dad said I flew "like a bat outta hell" down the mountainside. With so little weight, I didn't have to have a lot of skill, but I could handle my own and had a blast.

Shawn and another friend, Dave, didn't treat me like other kids from school the more we hung out together. That summer, the three of us also started baseball together, our folks hanging out on the bleachers, talking as we practiced and hollering during games. Our folks worked hard to be present during all their kids' activities, which meant track, gymnastics, soccer, cheer practice, swim lessons in the summer, and ski lessons in the winter, and this season for me and the guys, it was baseball.

As we sat in the bleachers during Danielle's gymnastic meet, I got bored between sets. The judges compared notes, timers were reset, the girls were warming up on the sides, and the music was prepared. I climbed up and down the bleachers, playing hide and seek with Drew until Dad, who had met us there, gave me "the look."

The music started and everyone hushed. It was awesome to see my sister Danielle competing so well. She was six years older than me but looked like a teenager since her face showed a little makeup Mom had put on, and she held herself with such confidence. She was hoping for a national qualifier performance. Like Mom, she could capture the attention of a crowd, and the boys seemed to think she was pretty.

As she did her balance beam routine, it looked like she was going to bring home another couple of trophies to place proudly on the mantel. She was getting close to the moment of her dismount, which I knew she'd practiced a thousand times. I stopped watching her and watched Mom's and Dad's faces all lit up, as they held their breath and then cheered from the crowd.

I want them to look at me that way, I thought. *I want them to be proud of me.* I promised myself I would try. The thought was fleeting, and soon enough we left for a late lunch and some school shopping. My oldest sister, Erin, was being obnoxious to Mom. She'd been having an attitude with her for weeks. Now for school clothes she was insisting on all black jeans and black or gray concert-style T-shirts, while Mom pointed out that Danielle and Maegen's clothes piles were full of "more appropriate" colorful assortments. Erin glared stubbornly.

I hated conflict. All I could think of was getting away from the tense energy. I forgot my promise to make Mom and Dad proud and started spazzing out, running in and out of the clothes racks and hiding from Drew. Once Dad caught me roughly around my shoulders and gave me a stern lecture, it was decided that he would drive Drew and me home while the girls stayed out and shopped. *Fine with me*, I thought. *He'll take us to McDonald's.*

The next morning after my ride around the pasture, I went next door to my best friend's house. It didn't matter that Tyler Burningham was four years older than me. It felt like we'd known each other forever. He was the kind of kid who would play strategy games, hike into the mountains, and race bikes; like me, he didn't care what we were doing as long as we were doing *something*.

Ten hours later, I came home for dinner, exhausted and happy. I didn't even fight Mom when she made me get a bath before I went to bed. I was filthy, and it was fun for a hot minute to see the dark stains and smudges run off my body in waves.

Later, after Mom had tickled my face and arms and I had fallen asleep, suddenly I sat bolt upright. *First grade. It's one week away.*

A terrible feeling rose up inside of me. It made me want to either throw up or punch something. *What if my first grade teacher is just like Mrs. Rose? What if the kids are just as mean as they were last year?* Tyler promised to walk with me to school and walk me home, but for the hours in between, I was on my own again. I stayed awake most of the night.

My neighborhood friends and I took advantage of our final days of freedom, but all too soon school was upon us. After Mom took the first-day-of-school pictures of everyone, I ran to Tyler's and picked him up. We rounded our corner and walked down the steep ravine. As we were walking up the other side, we were both panting, but I started shaking and had to hide it with every step.

I said goodbye to Tyler, trying to hold steady. Only one person laughed at me in the hallway, an older kid who sniggered at my large ears and pointed as he and a buddy shoved me and walked away. I lurched into the classroom, darting my gaze everywhere for a friendly face. Shawn waved at me and pointed to a desk beside him. I sighed a little in relief. *So far, so good.* I saw my friends Jenny and Ryan from last year, and with Shawn there, too, I felt like I could breathe . . . a little.

The woman at the front of the class introduced herself. She was younger than Mrs. Rose by a few years, and I couldn't help but notice that she smiled more in the first hour of school than Mrs. Rose had all the previous year!

Maybe it's going to be okay.

Miss Kosen was kind. In fact, she ended up being so much kinder than Mrs. Rose that my classroom experience over the following weeks was like night and day——at least in most respects. As much as I tried to please Miss Kosen, my work was most often not complete when we passed it in, and I still struggled in reading and writing. From time to time, I caught Miss Kosen watching me curiously. Within another week or two, she brought my parents in to speak with her, and everyone was tense. *Oh boy. What have I done now?*

"Robby is one of my favorite students," she said. "He's so kind and respectful to me and very polite. He listens to me, and I see him doing his best, striving to do well in the classroom."

I stared at her. That was opposite of what Mrs. Rose had told my folks at Parent/Teacher conference last spring. I began to love my new teacher at that moment. She didn't treat me like I was broken. Until her next words.

"Have you ever noticed Robby having a hard time sitting still?" she asked them.

"All the time," said Dad quickly, nodding. "At home, church, school—he can't keep still to save his life."

Mom nodded, and Miss Kosen went on. "That's what I've been seeing. Honestly, I think Robby has ADHD."

ADHD? What in the heck is that?

"It's called attention deficit hyperactivity disorder," explained Miss Kosen. "It's similar to ADD, but we've recently learned through research of children who suffer with it that some, not all, are also suffering with hyperactivity. It's a double whammy when it comes to kids like Robby. It's difficult to concentrate when they hear every sound in the classroom. The scratching of pencils, for instance, or someone coughing or giggling can throw them off focus. But add to it the body's inability to regulate itself, to monitor and inhibit impulses . . . well, that certainly can add to the challenges in the classroom. Robby is smart but definitely struggling, and we need to do something now, or we'll have to hold him back a grade."

I didn't understand all she was saying, but I could tell it was bad by my parents' faces. I did understand the words *we'll have to hold him back.* They played over and over in my head.

"Here's the good news," said Miss Kosen. "There are some medications that have been proven to help children with ADHD. A product on the market that has proven effective for a decent percentage of children is called Ritalin. Of course, we need to get Robby in and have him tested. Then a doctor would need to prescribe the medication—if it is what I think it is."

She turned and looked directly at me. "It means, Robby, that we think something can be done to help you! You could more easily catch up on class and wouldn't have to feel in trouble all of the time. Would you like that?"

I nodded, still feeling frozen, but with a spark of hope somewhere inside, reinforced by what I saw on my parents' faces.

I can be fixed! There's a pill out there that can fix me!

CHAPTER 3

THE MAGICAL GHOST

The doctor placed a black circle on my forehead that reminded me of a mood ring, of all things, because when it touched my skin it changed colors. He studied me carefully but spoke to Mom.

"So, he's been giving you a lot of trouble, this one? At home and at school?"

"Well, I wouldn't say a lot of trouble," said Mom cautiously, looking at me to see how I would respond. "He has difficulty concentrating on a task, like assignments in school and homework. He can't sit still long enough to do it."

"I see," he said, only I didn't know what exactly he was seeing. I felt like an ant under a magnifying glass out in the hot sun.

This sucks.

"Hold out your hands, please, Robby," Dr. Belnap said. His voice was kind, but it had the air of one who was used to being obeyed.

I held out my hands the way he taught me, and he placed a napkin over them.

"See how they are shaking, Mrs. Eastman? This is because Robby's disorder keeps him from managing his nervous system. Each time you come in, we'll conduct tests like this to see if Robby's dosage is working or if we need to increase the amount."

"I'm so glad your teacher recommended this, Robby," sighed Mom on the way home. I couldn't help but hear hope in her voice as she added, "You're going to be better now, you'll see."

Only I began to hate that place—the dark room with no windows and the medical table. I felt like a rat in a cage; the doctor's white coat made me feel weird, and all I could think of the whole time was *I hope the napkins don't shake. Shit, I hope the napkins don't shake. Am I going to be in trouble again?*

The good thing was that the Ritalin did settle me down, and I ended up having two loving teachers. Miss Kosen continued to treat me like a normal kid, praising me whenever I did something right. We bonded, and it helped to heal some of the old wounds. Tyler still walked home with me. We could joke and laugh, which was good, because the bullying at school was only growing worse.

Miss Kosen didn't allow bullying in her classroom, but she couldn't control what happened outside of it. Before school, at recess, and at lunch, it was never-ending. Kids continued to tease me for things I could not control: my bright red hair, and my skin that would match when I got upset—which made them want to do it even more. I was the scrawniest kid in school, and they made fun of that, too. Now, along with calling me a puny runt, they called me a mouse. I tried to act bigger and bolder and got made fun of for acting out. I felt like I couldn't win—ever.

The worst was when they made fun of my ears. They were large, and they stuck out from my head on both sides like elephant ears. I hated to look at myself in the mirror. All I could see was something to detest.

One day as Tyler and I were walking home, another older kid named Robby called out from behind.

"Hey, Rob-by!" he taunted.

I ignored him. He'd been causing a lot of problems for me on the playground.

"Look, everybody," he yelled in a voice that now echoed down the valley. "It's DUMBO! Can you *believe* those ears?" The entire crowd of kids started laughing, and I could feel their eyes and their pointing fingers. My face grew hot and my body ran cold. I wanted to run away and never come back to school.

Suddenly Tyler stopped, right on the road heading away from the elementary school. I stopped, too, and watched as he turned slowly and deliberately. On his face was the nastiest look I had ever seen—and this was my best friend. Suddenly everyone stopped walking and giggling and stared as Tyler stalked up to the other Robby. He had to be a head taller than the kid.

"That's *my friend* you're talking about," Tyler said as he glared down, jaw tight and fists clenched. "You'd better shut up! And if I ever hear you talking about him again, you're a dead man."

The other Robby's face went pale. He looked like he was going to cry but only nodded, then slithered around Tyler and walked away. Robby never said one more word to me. I had never been more grateful for Tyler than at that moment. He had never treated me like I was a struggle or a problem. He just let me be his bud.

Unfortunately, Tyler could not silence all the bullies in school, as much as I wished he could. Even though I loved my teachers, I began dreading every day of school, and I lived for every precious second after the bell rang. I couldn't wait for weekends, if only to get away from the ridicule and be with the people who loved and accepted me—although they often didn't know what to do with me, either.

Sports were the only place I could truly be myself. Mom had signed me up for soccer, which I loved, and I began to play it year-round. I loved anything and everything where I could run around to my heart's content, chase a ball, chase people, steal the ball, and not get into trouble. I was fast, and because I saw that look on Mom's and Dad's faces when I scored a goal or nailed a ski slope, I made sure to do it all the more.

In sports, I excelled like crazy, and Mom and Dad started getting me into special camps and training that helped me develop better skills than my Tasmanian-devilish "rip up the court" behaviors. I began to learn to fine-tune.

With sports, weekends were mostly glorious, except for three-hour blocks on Sundays. That's when my family went to church. We belonged to the Church of Jesus Christ of Latter-day Saints, sometimes referred to as "Mormons," and it was the most prevalent religion in our area.

That should have made me feel like I belonged, but I had the same struggles to sit still at church as I did at school—and for three hours! One hour we would be in a small class with the teacher, where we got a lesson and often a treat. I liked that part and didn't get into too much trouble if I liked the teacher. Another hour was all the Primary kids together, from three-year-olds up through age eleven, so I got to see my sister Maegen.

Maegen and I participated in Primary every week, and Mom made sure whenever we were supposed to prepare a lesson or a song to share with the class that we had it all memorized, practiced, and ready to perform. That was how I was invited to sing at Lagoon, complete with white suit and pink tie.

Still, if I wasn't performing and having to listen in Primary, it made it harder to hold still. I would get anxious and sometimes bolt out of my seat or do something stupid. I didn't know why I would do it, but the energy in the room, with all the moving little and big bodies and shrill voices, built up inside of me until I felt like I had to move or explode. I got in trouble often—and sometimes Mom had to come get me.

The last meeting was the worst. That was when the chapel was filled with everyone from crying babies to strict dads with somber faces to elderly men and women I had to watch out for. I was so small and so fast Dad said to be careful because I was like a little dog under their feet.

For that meeting, Mom lined us up proudly in one row: Erin, seven years older, Danielle, six years older, and Maegen, four years older with just as much energy, sitting by me, and then Drew, two years younger, who most often sat next to Mom. Dad was either up on the stand with the leaders or playing referee. Either way, it was a madhouse.

I didn't get teased as much in church as I did at school, but I hated being in trouble there even worse. There seemed to be strict rules—more strict than in school—about how we should act. We heard two words in Primary all the time: *obedience* and *reverence*—two things I naturally sucked at.

As I grew older, however, it seemed there was something that could be my saving grace. It was called *baptism*, which our church did at eight years of age. The way it was spoken of, with such excitement from the kids and reverence from the adults, it sounded like something I could look forward to, like it might be the answer to all my problems.

And boy, did I need answers.

Not only had I survived first grade, Miss Kosen announced she was getting married toward the end of the school year. Quietly, she even asked me and a couple of other classmates to be a part of her wedding reception. I was so excited that I got dressed up in a little suit without complaining. She was beautiful, and I didn't get in much trouble that night.

The hard part was now having a new teacher. My second-grade teacher did not treat me like Miss Kosen had. While not nearly as bad as Mrs. Rose, she still acted like I was broken and in constant need of repair. Worse, one day when I was getting out of hand, she yelled out in front of class, "Robby, stop! Did you take your medicine today?"

Total silence fell upon the room. And then the whispers began. *As if I didn't feel different from all the other kids already!*

I did not want to be different from the other kids. I knew the Ritalin was working. My grades were improving, and my attention span was improving, but I detested those visits to Dr. Belnap with his freaking napkins.

Screw that medicine!

That very next morning, I began taking the medicine under my tongue and not swallowing it. When Mom wasn't watching, I spit it out. I refused to be different from the other kids. Mom took me back to Dr. Belnap, over and over again, but it didn't matter: my behavior worsened at school. I was getting into fights on the playground. I seemed to be angry all of the time. The vice principal of the school quickly knew me by name, and my mother was at her wits' end. Finally, Mom realized I wasn't taking my medicine at all. At first she threw a fit, but I threw one bigger, and so she let it go.

Me? I was counting on another kind of magic, but not of the pill kind. I was counting on my baptism. It had become a magical thing in my mind, and as I moved from second grade into third grade and my January birthday approached with my baptism the first of February, I suddenly just *knew* that my whole life was about to change.

First, I was going to be washed clean of every sin. *Wow, are you kidding me?* For me, that was a big deal. That meant every time I'd messed up in school, every fight I started or finished, every rule I broke, every time I'd roughhoused and hurt Drew or Maegen, every time I knocked some lady's cane over in church, every bad grade—plus all of the things that were out of my control—all washed away.

I was going to be a new person!

Then there was this mysterious force that everyone talked about that was going to be a gift, that was going to become my best friend. I heard that, upon arising from the waters of baptism all shiny and new, I was going to be given *the gift of the Holy Ghost.* That meant that I would know right from wrong and wouldn't make mistakes again. I would be accepted and renewed. I would never be bullied again. I would be able to sit still. Most importantly, I would be able to be like everybody else. I couldn't wait.

My baptismal weekend came, and it was a big deal in our household and our church. Lots of our neighbors came to watch me—surrogate grandmas and grandpas because we didn't have any around, Dad's mentors, mom's friends, and a few of my friends and their families.

The day was even better than my birthday because all of these people were in the big stake center—a larger church for big gatherings and for baptisms. It had a baptismal font like a small but deep swimming pool of warm water. My dad and I were both dressed completely in white: white pants, white shirts, belts, and ties. It was time for us to step into the water and complete the spiritual ordinance. I looked around at everybody. It made me feel seen and important. I felt a true joy inside of me, one I had not felt in a long, long time.

My dad said some words and dunked me under the water. I popped my head out, grinning. We dried off, a bunch of people taught lessons to me, and then I was confirmed with the Holy Ghost. I had rocked it. I didn't do anything wrong. The next day at church was magical, too. I only had a bit of a hard time sitting still but not bad because everyone was beaming at the new me. *They noticed!* I was glowing, and I knew it.

The next day was Monday. I walked excitedly with Tyler to school. As he walked off to seventh grade, we said goodbye and I strode with confidence into the big doors of school, headed to my third-grade classroom.

"Hey, Dumbo!" sneered a voice above all the others in the hall. "Did you take your whole family on a flight this weekend? With those ears, you could have flown them all to Disneyland!"

It felt like every kid in the hallway snorted with laughter at me.

In that instant, life went from Technicolor to dull gray again. By the time I trudged into my classroom to sit down, I knew it.

They all lied to me. All my church leaders. Lies.

My heart shattered into a million pieces on the floor.

CHAPTER 4

SOULMATE AND SURGERY

WHOOSH! I cruised through the fresh powder at a breakneck speed. Whenever my friends came skiing with us, none of them could keep up. My dad could, though, and my adrenaline was high knowing he was close behind me today.

Is today the day I will be faster than him?

It wouldn't be long, both of us knew, before I'd blow by him on the mountain. Dad loved it when we pushed our limits in all physical adventures. He was always getting my siblings and me to overcome our fears and try new things.

I was becoming a skilled menace on the slopes. Speed, however, was only one skillset. Dad wanted us to master greater abilities than scaring the shit out of other skiers as we whizzed past them at a hundred miles an hour. Adventure and bravery were one thing, but Dad's highest praise came when we were *the best* at any sports endeavor.

It wasn't enough to play basketball; Dad introduced us to the best coaches so we could shoot hoops with the greatest accuracy. It wasn't enough just to play soccer; we had to manage the ball, steal the ball, kick more precisely, and protect the goal at all costs.

That's why I didn't gripe too much as Dad passed me near the bottom of the mountain. The snow kept falling softly, and the wind wasn't as biting as usual. If that wasn't celebration enough, Dad had picked Maegen and me to go with him to Park City for Jeep's King of the Mountain Tour that day. We were getting the opportunity to ski half-day with an Olympic gold medalist!

With our sponsor badges on, we bypassed others and took a lift to the top of the mountain, where Dad slid expertly to a stop near another guy with a different kind of badge. I looked up into the face of a larger-than-life guy in a cowboy hat, who Dad said was a giant in the world of Olympic slalom.

The stranger—who had killed it in the '64–'68 Winter Olympics—looked us over, and I'm sure he thought, *Oh great, I'm here to babysit.* After a run with us, however, William Winston Kidd, known as Billy the Kidd, was impressed enough to take us up on the big slalom course. By the time we were done, I'm sure I was as exhausted as Maegen looked.

"You two certainly surprised me," William said, his eyes twinkling. My sister and I perked up. He looked at our dad. "Dan," he said, "I'd like to invite these two to my ski team and camp in Colorado when they're old enough. They can already ski circles around half my team there."

Dad beamed with pride, and I soaked up every second. *Wow, me on a ski team in Colorado? That could be damn cool.* I knew I had to tell my friends.

I fell asleep on the drive back to Bountiful from Park City. I only had two speeds: go, and go faster. So when I stopped, I was out. It made it hard to get my homework done on school nights when my body and brain were exhausted. Over the last few years, however, I had come to count on the fact that Mom would help. *God bless Mom.* Part of that freaking knot in my stomach that never went away would lessen a little. But only a little.

It didn't matter how much I dominated a ski slope or a soccer field. I was good at that stuff, but lately school was only getting worse. The bullying that I thought was unbearable before my baptism the year before never went away. I felt like I was living a horror movie every day at school. Sure, I was prone to telling wild stories, but I wasn't making up the shit these bullies did to me.

I discovered that a family within our school's boundary took on some foster kids with the intention to adopt. Sounded nice. But quickly I noticed even the adults were afraid of these kids. They came from difficult backgrounds and carried dark and even violent attitudes. Over the next few weeks, other students were experiencing issues as well.

At lunch one Friday, I was with my small, tight group of friends: Shawn, Ryan, Jenny, and a kid who always snorted Jello to make people laugh. I was boasting an epic story of a ski jump I'd attempted that weekend. Suddenly everyone froze, and all the color left my friends' faces. I felt it drain from mine, too, realizing a bully called Monster was right behind me. He was a big kid for a third grade—solid muscle, and athletic—who wasn't afraid of anyone, even adults.

Monster's shadow hulked over our table. Without a word, he swiped Shawn's chocolate milk and mine with one hand, and from the corner of my eye I saw him pocket them in his large orange coat. Ours were the only milk cartons that hadn't been opened yet—I had been focused on my fries while they were hot and tasty. I hadn't even gotten to the delicious burger on the homemade buns we'd been smelling since recess that morning.

I glanced around wildly to see if one of the lunch ladies was watching, but they'd turned their backs on our table. I knew why. This kid had already thrown a couple of violent tantrums in the lunchroom within a week of arriving here, and now, as long as no one was crying or getting hurt, they turned a blind eye.

Help us! I wanted to scream at the lunch monitors. *Can't you see what he's doing? What he does every single day?*

"Hey, Dumbo!" Monster said casually. "You want that burger?"

Of course I wanted my burger. While I didn't eat much, Mom said I had a high metabolism, even for a growing boy. By lunchtime every day I was starving and needing *something*. I nodded my head. That burger was supposed to be for *my* stomach, not his. My hands clenched into fists. I was getting so sick of his bullshit. Lately, I'd started talking back to him. It was better than lying down like a dead carp as usual.

I felt every kid in the cafeteria's eyes on me, frozen in time. It was the shrimp against the monster. Every time I didn't agree with whatever he wanted to take away from me, I was pummeled. Not right there in the lunchroom, of course. Monster would lay in wait until he could get me out of the eye of any adult, but he would find me before the end of the day.

"Too bad," he snapped, referring to my hamburger with an evil grin. Then Monster did the unthinkable. He picked his nose. Out came a large green-and-yellow booger, crusty on one side and oozing on the other. As my friends and I gasped, I was astonished and wanted to throw up when he took off the top bun of my burger and placed the boogie squarely in the middle. It sat on the once-appetizing ketchup, mustard, and pickles I had meticulously piled on.

Setting the bun back down on the patty, he was sure to squish it in for all to see. "Still want it?" he demanded.

Sounds erupted from the tables around us. I noticed as long as Monster's attention was focused on me and not them, the other kids egged him on. But no one laughed at our table. Everyone just stared at me. The moment felt like forever.

Hell no, I don't want it now. I didn't think I would ever want a hamburger again in my life. I shook my head.

"I didn't think so," Monster cackled. And he walked away, munching on my hamburger.

I glanced up to see most of the kids in the cafeteria smirking at me. There were a few looks of compassion, but only one or two amongst the sea of delight in my misery. I had never even thought about smiling when bullies were picking on other kids . . . so why would my "friends" be happy when Monster treated me like this?

I took my tray up to the garbage and dumped the rest of my food. I headed in the opposite direction that Monster did, not bothering to go out onto the playground, my favorite place at the whole school. Instead, I stalked away from the lunchroom and into the boy's bathroom, climbed into a stall, and punched my fists up to my eyes, willing away the hot tears of rage, humiliation, and sadness. I couldn't afford anyone to see me cry.

I don't want to be here anymore. I don't want to go to school. I didn't want to be home. If this is how painful life is going to be every day, I don't want to exist.

A few weeks later, I heard about a kid who was in our region sent to a juvenile detention center called Moweda. He ended up hanging himself with his bedsheets. For some reason, I couldn't get that image out of my head. I felt bad for the kid, and yet there was a sense of freedom there, too. He didn't have to be in trouble or picked on anymore.

Without thinking, I tied a bedsheet onto the top bunk in my and Drew's bedroom and tried to experiment with it. I wanted to feel what it was like to take my life in my hands. Only I got scared, pulled it off my neck, and didn't do it again. The thought, however, stayed.

Over the next year, I went deeper into survival mode. In order to make it through without being beaten and humiliated every damn day, I did what I had to and changed tactics: I *befriended* all of the bullies at my school. I was getting pummeled so much, it felt like my one option to stay alive.

As the months progressed, I even became friends with Monster. It worked sometimes, although his mood swings meant at times he still beat me up. Then I noticed a pattern. If I hung out with Monster and the other bullies in a group big enough, Monster wouldn't touch me. *He is afraid of numbers.* So now, I kept my close friends during class, at my house, and on the weekends, but otherwise I was never far from someone bigger than me who liked my confidence and wasn't afraid to get physical on my behalf.

I learned how to "posture up" and act like a badass even though I was trembling on the inside, simply too tired of the beatings. Those days, I got really mad when I saw bullies picking on other kids. It started to become my thing to go after other bullies, although *never* Monster.

I'd heard the term "shit runs downhill," and I saw this to be true. Hanging out with those bullies changed how I acted at home, too. My poor mom and Drew had to take my daily temper tantrums. Mom was at her wits' end, and Drew? Well, Drew was just surviving. For all the years he had wanted to hang around me and would follow me and my friends, now they all avoided me like a disease—for good reason. All the rage and frustration I was holding in at school, I let out when I got home. I didn't see that I was actually becoming Monster.

Another year passed, and I entered the fifth grade with the same patterns. I was either getting bullied or being the bully. I hated my life.

Then, nothing short of a miracle entered in a most unusual and unexpected way. I busted out of the cafeteria early one day to claim the area of the playground where we were planning a hot game of dodgeball. I heard a commotion on another side of the field and went to see what was happening. There was a guy up on top of the soccer goal.

What the hell . . .?

Some older kids were throwing rocks at a new kid. All I knew was that his name was Danny. He was tall and lanky, like his body was growing too fast for him. I could tell he was kind of nerdy, but I knew that look on his face. He was scared to death of these kids and was shying away from every rock they were throwing at him as they laughed. As usual, no one was going to help.

I felt a sudden but familiar rage build up inside of me. No one deserved to be treated that way, not even this nerdy-looking dude. I gathered all my fiery Tasmanian-devil energy and erupted, racing across the rest of the field. As I sprinted, I hurled swear word after swear word and literally scared the group of older cowards away.

Danny stared at them running away, not believing what had happened. Then he looked down from his perch at me.

"Well, get your ass down here!" I yelled. "I didn't scare those stupid jerks away for you to stay up there all day."

He jumped down, and there we were, the tall nerd and the runty pipsqueak with a formidable temper. From that day forward, Danny Low and I were the best of friends. Despite me first being embarrassed to be seen with this shy, awkward dude, he joined our little gang of misfits.

Danny was smart and the kind of guy who would save a flea instead of kill it. I quickly discovered that if I protected him during recess, he would do my homework so Mom didn't have to stress about it not getting done. We started hanging out a lot. As we entered sixth grade, he was almost 5' 10", and I was still a foot shorter than that.

I started calling Danny my soulmate because he *got* me. We were yin and yang to each other—so opposite, we got along great. Tyler still walked me home from school, but each day Danny would already be at our place, ready to read Drew and me crazy stories. He was a bookworm and engaged me for hours in his storytelling and reading—yet he loved scouts and loved the outdoors. Danny was a great student, and he loved and protected animals with a fierceness. Maybe most importantly, Danny was the first friend *ever* to listen to me when my walls were down. He never teased me, no matter what other battles I was facing. I had a guy in my court, in my arena. The guy was not a rule-breaker, unless he was with me.

That was often a problem. Danny wasn't equipped to fight. He ran away from every battle. But as I protected him, he protected me in his own way. Emotionally I felt like I could survive most anything that came my way.

That summer, my friend Tyler and I came up with an ingenious plan. We were always figuring out ways to get money for our mischievous schemes. One of the big things we wanted to do was to put on a neighborhood play. We came up with roles for everyone in the neighborhood, but we needed money for props and costumes.

One morning, we sat up in our massive pine tree where Tyler and I had trimmed the branches up to make a fort where we remained completely hidden. The sun was barely rising, and as we peeked out into the sidewalks and streets we noticed the paperboy slinging newspapers along all the neighbors' driveways.

"You thinking what I'm thinking?" I said to Tyler with a grin.

"Yup!"

We raced down to our bikes, maintaining a careful distance behind the paperboy. Then we picked up all the papers. From there, we set up a newsstand. Well, that move worked for a hot minute. Unfortunately, neighbors went to our parents and demanded their papers back.

"What else can we do?" we asked each other at the same time.

All of a sudden, a brilliantly diabolical idea entered my head. The guy across the street was the only house on our block with a trampoline. Of course, all the kids wanted to play on it, so Bob made red, yellow, and green flags as signals. Red meant no one could jump. Green meant any neighbor kids could come. Yellow meant you had to stop in and ask for permission.

Bob was generous despite being ex-military, so, often, the green flag was up and his little fridge was filled with sodas for neighborhood kids. With that in mind, we took off, looking like wannabe ninjas with every dip and swoop on the way to that fridge and away from it. We set up our own official pop stand. In no time, as the temperature was sweltering, people stopped by in droves for a cool drink.

Our only screwup? Tyler and I had set up the pop stand at the *bottom of Bob's driveway*. It was the perfect place for traffic coming and going, with none of our parents close to ask where we got the drinks. Neither of us thought much about it, reveling in the money in our pockets until Bob pulled up for a chat.

"Hey, ya little entrepreneurs! This is such a great idea—look at how many people are stopping by." Then his face darkened. "But you are not to use *my* pop. Are you clear?"

"Yes, sir!" we both said quickly. He spoke to our parents, as we knew he would, and we were nixed from selling anything else in the neighborhood. That meant our plans for the play were nixed, too.

The next day, my friends and I rode our BMX bikes down to the dirt lot behind my dad's Jeep dealership. This lot started to make me very popular, and I learned the power of both persuasion and manipulation to get the attention I wanted—without getting targeted for bullying. I found I loved it, although I used it quite differently than my father, who was a master, and whom everyone in the community adored.

Sometimes . . . okay, way too often, I would be bragging about something, making a big story gargantuan when my sister Maegen would walk by, shaking her head. "You don't have to try to impress people, Robby," she'd murmur as she privately took me aside. "Quit trying so hard. It's irritating, and it pushes people away. I promise, friends will like you just as you are."

I glared at her. I knew she was wrong. People did not like me just for me . . . *not really*. I was nothing to look at, I was simply entertaining. My only redeeming quality despite my puniness was that I could kick ass in almost every sport, thanks to my fiery determination not to lose, and Dad providing us with the best coaches in the state. Outside of sports, I needed power.

No, my sister is wrong. I have to prove myself. I have to make people like me.

I was nothing without sports and Dad's cool cars and his BMX dirt bike trails. In my estimation, I had to *buy* love and loyalty. If I didn't do it enough, I would lose it.

That year, I started football. Most of my friends were growing by leaps and bounds, but I was still small. I got started playing center, even though I only weighed forty-five pounds, because I could hike the ball shotgun. I got my ass kicked over and over. It left a bad taste in my mouth for that sport.

But I loved soccer and had been playing full-out since I was six. Out on the field, I was tougher than nails. I wasn't afraid of the ball or any opponents because none of them were as scary as Monster. I could take anybody. Dad saw my determination and had me join a competition league.

The older I got, the more "Dumbo" was slung around the halls and out of Monster's mouth. I tried to tell my parents how awful my ears were, but they blew it off. I dreaded going back to school even more, because I was headed into Millcreek Junior High, where there were sure to be even more bullies.

At the end of the summer, my parents were cheering me on at a track meet where I was kicking butt and taking names. In fact, I took everyone's name. I WON!

I jumped up into the air and was looking for high-fives and chest bumps from my friends and family.

Suddenly a parent catcalled, "Hey, kid, you're fast!" Before I could revel in his praise, he added, "If your ears weren't so big, you would've lapped them!"

Although I had been telling my parents for years how humiliating my big ears were, this was the first time they saw that humiliation firsthand—and they *felt* it. Panting, I glanced over to see Mom and Dad's faces were nearly as red as mine, but not from exertion. It was fury. They were too conservative to lash out at people. Instead, Dad's face remained tight, and Mom swooped in to whisk me away.

Within a few days, they got me scheduled for ear-tuck surgery. That way, they said, I would be able to heal before school started.

I was so relieved. *Now, maybe, the bullying will stop.*

CHAPTER 5

ALL TUCKED IN

Horror was written on my face as I looked into our bathroom mirror. My whole head was wrapped in thick, white gauze bandages, clear down below my chin. It was so padded, it looked like I was wearing a helmet!

Crap! I look like a mummy, and Halloween is months away! Dread started to seep through me when I thought about the teasing I would get for looking like such a freak.

Suddenly a grin stole over my face. Wait a minute! I couldn't be ignored with this thing on. *Cool!* Any attention from my friends these days was good attention in my book.

And just like that—in a split second—my thoughts changed. My mind was like a jackrabbit, and so was my body, off and running. Shoving on clothes, I bolted for the door. Only then did I slow enough to quietly slip outside. It was my first day home after the ear tuck surgery, and Mom said I was supposed to be "recovering." But the sun was shining, and I could hear dogs barking in the distance and kids playing. If I was going to be dressed in a helmet, I might as well make use of it.

Ten minutes later, I met a couple of friends at the top of our hill who held their stomachs at the sight of me. I grinned, loving that it was me that was making them laugh that hard. We all shot downhill on rollerblades, going so fast the wind tried to whip the bandages off my head. They held, but not enough that I missed the screaming as I whizzed by our house.

"R-O-B-B-Y!"

Oh crap. I knew Mom wouldn't like that I was outside, but I'd hoped to get at least two more runs in before I heard her screech at me. However, now I could guilt my buddies into hanging out at my house instead. Relegated to something more mellow, like board games, we had fun for a while, but both friends were gone after an hour.

It was one of the things I faced every day. I was too high-rev, and even my friends could only take me in small doses. Fortunately for me, I had quite a long list of friends: it ranged from Dave to Craig to Danny to Tyler to the girls, and then to the bullies. Each of them would hang out at least for a little while as we schemed some new, wild adventure.

When I wore out friends at the top of the list, I kept going down until *someone* said yes. I'd have to wait as long as a day or two before I called them again. Today, Maegen was watching me from the stool in the kitchen. She stared with such pity in her eyes that I hated it. I ignored her as my third invitation was declined, and I made another call.

That afternoon, the yes came from Dave. He had a pool and a massive yard and paintball guns. I slipped over to his house without Mom seeing. I didn't bring a swimsuit because I couldn't chance the bandages getting wet, so we ran around like *Lord of the Flies* little shitheads, shooting each other up and gaining fifty bruises from the paintballs. Only my head was off-limits.

Wearing the paint like badges of honor, we rode our bikes up and down the hills. I completely exhausted myself but didn't forget to change my paint-stained clothes before Mom saw me. I nearly fell asleep at dinner, without even fighting with Drew or Erin.

I spent the next two weeks like that, especially as I wasn't allowed to play soccer or any sport where there was a danger of something hitting my head and splitting open the healing sutures. I was going stir-crazy. Mom and I finally arrived at the clinic to remove the sutures. The nurse looked taken aback at my dirtied bandages. Mom shrugged her shoulders in defeat. She had kept me from all contact sports but couldn't keep me from coming into contact with *everything and everyone else* around me, as usual.

Hesitantly the doctor removed the bandages, and everyone breathed a small sigh of relief. My ears had healed well. They took out the stitches and cleaned both sides of my head.

"Oh, look at you!" said the nurse happily. "Handsome Robby, you've healed nicely."

I grinned and whipped toward the mirror, almost expecting some good-looking guy to stare back at me.

Now it was my turn to shrug in defeat. As much as I hated my big ears, now that they were tucked back like "normal" people's were, they seemed . . . weird. *Are they too close to my head now?* People certainly couldn't call me Dumbo anymore, but now what would they find instead?

I still felt helpless and stupid. All the taunting words I'd heard throughout my life screamed across my brain. I had grown a couple of inches over the summer, but I still was short, and I still had red hair and red skin. I picked at every feature in my reflection, wishing it was different. *I could bleach my hair, maybe,* I thought, as if that would help. There was another checkbox on my list I couldn't complete: living with myself.

Just the thought of going back to school sent tremors of fear through my body. Within seconds I shot off the table, my adrenaline in hyperdrive. "Mom, can we go now?" I asked, annoyed and ignoring the nurse's wide-open mouth and my mom's scowl.

I couldn't hold still long enough for Mom to finish chatting and pay the bill. I grabbed her keys from her and went out to the Jeep. After slamming the door, I turned up the music, *loud,* so Vanilla Ice blared through the speakers. Mom turned down the music to drive, and we didn't say anything in the car on the way home. As soon as we stopped in the driveway, I lunged out the door and raced away on my bike. It took two hours of nonstop movement to settle my adrenaline.

The following day I discovered my next step: braces. I had two teeth missing: the incisors on either side of my front teeth had never grown in. We were going to see if we could bring them in. *Oh great—forget the ears, I'll be Metal Mouth.* At least a couple of my friends were getting braces, too, so we could complain about them together, but no matter what the nurse said, I wouldn't be smiling much when I went back to school.

My only comfort was that I would soon be on the field. I couldn't wait. The sound of the ball hitting the net as soon as I could play was music to my ears. *Another GOAL!* Screams from the sidelines meant that both my parents were there, right where I liked them, yelling triumphantly.

I took a moment to breathe in the soccer field; the smell of sweet summer grass made the early-morning game even better. Heat was quickly hitting the field. I flicked the sweat away. I was here to dominate.

I growled and got the response I wanted from my opponent on the line. He swallowed nervously as we got ready to start the kickoff for the second half of the game. It didn't matter that I was barely half his size. On the field or the court, I supercharged my anger and distraction into intense focus upon the enemy. I was there to slaughter, and opponents knew it. I was determined to win at all costs.

It amazed my siblings and the adults around me that in one area of my life I could be that focused. Even on the sidelines I stirred up trouble for my teammates. But the moment it was my time in the spotlight, I became the Tasmanian devil, as so many still called me to demean me. Here, I counted for something, winning praise from coaches and my parents—and even other kids' parents. I could block out all the demons in my own head and just . . . perform. I wasn't perfect, but I was most definitely a force to be reckoned with.

I had great teammates, too. There was only one comp team per area if you were in AAA soccer. It was the best and the busiest. These kids and parents meant business. We had to travel quite a bit for games and tournaments, from an hour and a half all the way to Idaho and Colorado and even Texas. I also played comp basketball and baseball. I dominated there, too, but soccer was my jam.

The next half of the game whizzed by in no time. For 90% of it, I was the smallest and fastest dude on the field. I mostly played striker (also known as center forward) and sweeper. I loved watching the sidelines light up every time I stole a ball, set up a goal, or scored one.

We were taught by our coaches and especially my dad to have good sportsmanship. For me, that meant it was balls to the wall when I was running toward the net! I didn't get carded much, because, magically, I only used foot stomping and elbows when no one was looking. Soccer was my sanctuary. I didn't want it to end.

"Robby!" barked Coach. "Goalie. Now!"

Sure enough, it was a shootout. He usually sent me in because of my speed and because I wasn't afraid of the ball. No goals were scored by our opponents this time. I ripped off the goalie jersey with a scream of satisfaction, then flew back to my space as the forward, noticing with sheer satisfaction how the team was pleased with my performance and the opponents looked nervous.

There was something about seeing the looks on my parents' faces when I'd come off the field or court after a game. It was about the only time I saw it—their faces more relaxed and glowing, without the tight lines of grimace and sternness to their voices. I knew I was hard to handle, hard to control, hard to mold. It wasn't like I wanted to be—I just . . . Couldn't. Sit. Still. I was too loud, too fast, too grumpy, too violent, too . . . *everything.* But during a game, there was affection and the words I craved:

"Way to go, Robby!"

"Great goal."

"Go, son!"

"That's right, Robby! You show him who's boss!"

"That's right, Red, go get him—Yes! That's the way!"

As if that wasn't enough frosting on my cake, I was making bank during games. Gone were the days when Dad would buy me one Nielsen's frozen custard for every goal I scored. He quickly realized that wasn't going to work any longer when the goals far exceeded my ability to hold and eat custards. He started offering me cash instead.

That meant I could buy things—food and toys, mostly, so more kids wanted to hang out with me. Even better, comp teams meant the parents at these games could afford to pay for coaches, training, travel, and tournaments. Comp teams meant fathers who wanted us to win so badly *they* would also offer me cash on the spot—$5 for the next goal, and today I discovered I could earn twenty bucks for a game-defining moment that would take us to state and on to nationals.

By the time we were driving home, my pockets were filled with cash. Who needed a job? I took home more than most older teens did working jobs after school every day and on weekends. That made me even more smug about it. It added to feeling superior on the field.

Entering the halls of Millcreek Junior High a few weeks later, however, I wasn't smug or confident and certainly not superior. I quaked inside, hoping no one knew how terrified I was. Walking these new halls, I was no longer a big dog at the elementary school—I was a small runt again, and this time in a very big pack.

Several elementary schools funneled into this one school, with 7th, 8th and 9th graders, many of whom looked like giants. I felt lost and alone. It took less than sixty seconds for older kids to start the familiar name-calling, pushing, and shoving. The lockers were tall enough to shove a kid into them, so within minutes, I had to learn how to open them from the *inside*.

By the time I got to class, I felt I must have had a "kick me" sign tattooed on my forehead. While no one seemed to notice my surgery except friends, and people couldn't call me Dumbo anymore, I was in trouble already on the first day—despite my efforts at careful control. It seemed like all the older boys were looking to strike first, establishing their territories. Here, there were seven classes and seven teachers, and the worst of the bullies from our area, somehow related to Monster, ruled the classrooms—and the lunchrooms and the hallways. I couldn't get away from them. Their power seemed concentrated.

The stakes have changed, I realized long before I headed home. If I thought those bullies had frightened the adults in elementary school, it was nothing compared to what they did now—boys built like men, towering over teachers and administration. I was no longer afraid someone was going to steal my lunch money or my hamburger right out from under me—although that happened already. I was now worried for my life.

Monster seemed to have grown a foot over the summer. As I watched him torture some poor kid the first day of school, I took my own mortality into consideration.

I could die in these hallways.

While Monster and I had hung out occasionally during the summer when my friend list grew thin, by the second week in school, I joined forces. It was better to be on his good side than to wonder if I would make it home alive. What that began to mean, however, were fistfights with upperclassmen bullies at least two to three times a week.

I wasn't always a part of the fights like he was, but now the big dog was establishing his territory. The payoff? If I sided with him, yelling at opponents and celebrating his victories, I was picked on less. Eventually we became like a little gang. Others joined us as we roamed the halls, now looking for prey instead of becoming it. My other friends were all doing well in school. They were going to class when we weren't.

Within another week, the older bullies were mostly leaving me alone. They knew who my protectors and buddies were. It would have surprised them to know I was still friends with Danny, Dave, and the others. I was seeing them in Sunday school and several nights a week for church activities and church sports or in my neighborhood. School, however, was an alien battlefield that I was forced to enter every day. It made everything else seem like a cakewalk. My grades, which were never very good, began tumbling down a dark hole of no return.

Within two months, it wasn't enough to have Mom and my buddy Danny helping me with my homework or doing it for me. I was going to flunk out. As the weather turned frigid, I came home one Friday afternoon to find both of my parents in the living room. I thought someone had died, but it was my own mental-health death sentence.

"Robby . . ." Mom began carefully, "Dad and I hired a tutor for you."

"A what?" I shouted, flying off the handle. "No! I don't want a tutor!"

"Robby, you have to have a tutor," said Dad firmly, his face tight in that stressed look I was growing to hate because I caused it. "You're failing in all your classes. You're struggling to pass a single quiz, much less tests."

I knew it was true. Whenever a teacher would hand out a quiz or a test, I sat in sheer terror, looking at each page as if it was written in a foreign language; there were words I couldn't read or comprehend.

My dad was good at making things sound like they were a privilege. He added, "We found a lady who really wants to work with you. She wants to help you polish your math skills."

I couldn't even add.

Yeah, but damn . . . more school after school? That sucked rocks. Starting the following Monday, I was to go straight from the classroom to the trailer next to the school to see that tutor until my grades improved. My anxiety and ADHD were already at a nasty breaking point, and now they skyrocketed to an all-time high. I didn't relax all weekend long.

The following Monday I didn't want anyone knowing I had more school—that I was that stupid.

"Where you headin'?" asked Monster as he towered over some of the students who steered clear of his long arms or legs to get out to the pickup area.

"Oh," I said casually as my heart was pounding out of my chest, "I've got an interview with *World Champion Soccer Magazine.*"

He smirked like I was full of shit, then nodded before I strode away. He never knew what my real story was, and I was glad for it. With mounting anxiety, I climbed the metal steps to the trailer in the back lot. *Here goes nothin'.*

The door squeaked open, and behind it I found a teeny woman with glasses. She seemed older, but every adult just seemed older to me. She smiled broadly.

"Welcome, Robby!" she said warmly in a soft, sweet voice. "I'm so delighted to be working with you."

Mrs. Avis already seemed good, kind of sweet, and I could tell that while I would be getting away with nothing, emotionally she might be a soft landing place.

"Your parents are asking me to work with you on math and some other subjects you may be struggling with—just until you get caught up," she reassured me at my stricken look.

Other subjects, too?

Mrs. Avis turned out to be an amazing tutor. Every day that I entered that trailer, I knew that she cared for me and wanted the best for me. She was one of the nicest people I had ever met. I felt like she cared, when I could tell other teachers couldn't care less—especially when I pissed them off in the classroom.

Mrs. Avis didn't give up on me. She sat beside me and was patient, even on the days I zoned out and couldn't handle one more thing. In class, there was only *one way* to learn something, exactly how it was spelled out in the textbook, and when I didn't get it, teachers rolled their eyes and gave up. The pattern had to be followed, or I was too "stupid" to be taught. Or at least that's how I felt.

Mrs. Avis looked me in the eye and assured me that there actually *were* other ways to get to the same solution for every problem. "Not everything is cookie-cutter, Robby," she said, her voice kind—even after two hours of working on one assignment. "Don't give up. Let's try it this way instead . . ." It helped.

To everyone's disappointment, I still fought against Ritalin for the social stigma. I lied and never went back on it. I never ended up getting "caught up." Getting caught up meant catching on completely, and for some reason, I didn't seem capable of that at all.

CHAPTER 6

RUSSIAN ROULETTE

"Flippers! Oh my gosh!"

The crowd was laughing, and I was soaking it all in. They were gathered around me in the lunchroom, eyes peering over each other's heads to be in on the local entertainment: me. I flipped my retainer again, and my two side front teeth popped out of their spaces. The braces hadn't been working, so the dentist designed it so I could look like I had normal teeth like everyone else. That would have been fine had the retainer not been necessary to take out every single time I had to eat.

Now the girls screamed and the boys guffawed. It must have been quite a sight. I didn't know because I avoided looking in the mirror those days. Like the famous *Star Wars* line, "There's nothing to see here; move along," I felt some invisible repellent force pushing people away from me constantly—and me away from myself.

This antic with my teeth, however, was drawing them in, in droves. Sure, most intelligent kids who didn't want to be picked on for one more weird thing about them would have hidden the fact that they were missing some teeth, but not me. Like a freak, I loved the attention.

"All right, kids, get back to lunch. You don't have much time," rasped the principal against the roar of the crowd. Then he threw a look at me that I knew all too well. *You're doing it again, Eastman. Knock it off.*

It seemed I annoyed Assistant Principal Nelson at least six or seven times a week. I was either going on or coming off of In-School Suspension, or ISS. I was often attracting crowds, and it was rumored that I was fighting with other kids across the street at the church parking lot, where the administration had no say, no suspension rights, and no other way of punishing me—not that any of their punishments worked for long. Just like the last two and half years with Mrs. Avis were proving, I didn't seem to be teachable, moldable, or penetrable. No one except Danny and a small handful of people could ever talk sense into me once I got an idea.

I experienced my first girlfriend, but we had a strong difference in morals. Strangely enough, it was me who broke up with her when she wanted me to touch her chest. I had promised my mom I wouldn't engage in sexual behavior, nor drink alcohol, so that was that.

At least for one hot minute. Alcohol was in short supply as a 9th grader, but girls weren't. Within months of my first girlfriend, I had a second, and this time my hormones were so high that I didn't keep my promise to my mother. The only problem was that this girl and I had absolutely no idea what we were doing—none! And to make it worse, we got caught by dear old Mom as we were trying to do what we didn't know how to do. The door flew open, meaning that was the end of that.

Fortunately, besides the bullies, I had loyal friends. Craig, Dave, and Shawn would hang out with me in choir that no one wanted to be in, and in drama, starring in plays together that everyone wanted to be in. I wasn't shy about being in the spotlight since I was that kid in the suit, singing at Lagoon. I ate it up.

I tried wrestling in the seventy-eight-pound division and enjoyed that as well as comp basketball and baseball, but it left no time for skiing, nor for the love of my life, soccer. The comp league was so intense that it took most of my time. Since the payoff was so great, I kept at it. Mom and Dad went to every single game. I didn't know how they did it, with Dad's dealership being so busy and Mom having all the girls and their sports, dance, and cheerleading to deal with. Still, somehow, they made it, and I felt their love.

By that time, Mom was done fighting with me. It was all she could do to make it from day to day in her expectations of me as her son. It must have sucked, but her being tired meant I had freedom—freedom from homework, from chores I didn't want to do, and certain behaviors. For Dad, however, it was harder. I didn't like letting him down . . . but I found myself doing it all the time.

Even in soccer, if I didn't watch my temper, I was a huge disappointment to Dad. Despite this, my parents were never negative. They'd get frustrated with me, but they'd never talk down to me in public or private. Still, I could tell it nearly killed my dad when I pulled something that embarrassed myself, my family, or my team.

It sucked how often I embarrassed my folks. In fact, even though soccer had been my refuge, I blew it. Mom and Dad had traveled a couple of hours for the state championship. We were down to the last few minutes of the game, knowing if we won state, the team and I were headed to nationals. It was a vital, close game, and we were tied. Suddenly, the opposing team scored a goal with only thirty seconds left.

I knew we had one chance to steal the ball and score a goal for overtime where we might overtake them. With just thirty seconds on the clock, the guy bringing up the ball on the field was taking his sweet time. I grew more and more furious. *That rat bastard is stealing from us our state title and our chance at the national title!* I flew forward and blasted him, barreling into the guy with all the brute force I could muster. I let him know every ounce of fury in my body, forgetting the ball and taking it out on him.

I felt one glorious moment of heated triumph before the booing of the crowd reached my ears. I looked up to see cold disappointment on my father's face.

That was it. I was done. I didn't want anything more to do with soccer.

It didn't matter that soccer was year-round and a new season had started. No, I would give everyone a break from the bullshit I constantly put everyone through. Even my girlfriend had given up on me, and we broke up. Life would be better for everyone if I wasn't around.

I started fixating on that. *What if I really don't have to be here anymore?* I'd thought about taking my life once before. Now I tried to push it out of my mind, struggling to fixate on other things without soccer.

We had a club for young teens where we could hang out and dance. It was in a strip mall, and kids came in from neighboring areas and schools. We loved to pick up girls there. Only these were *our girls*, and we were very territorial. Fights ensued every weekend, especially as our reputation spread, and other arrogant dudes wanted to rule the henhouse. Of course, I was always right in the middle.

One cold fall evening in September, instead of getting in a fight, I was invited to a party. NWA and Run-D.M.C. were pumping on the stereo, the beats and the violence of the words amping up my already high adrenaline-lit mood. Like all the other teen boys in the room, we thought it would be cool to be in a gang. The tension was made higher when I brought out my dad's revolver. I had carefully stolen it from his gun safe earlier that day, in the closet of our home, and Dad had no clue.

All eyes got big and round as I dared the other kids to play Russian roulette with me. I laughed heartily as the color left their faces. First I pulled the trigger on myself, not caring if the chamber was loaded or not. The crowd of about eight kids jumped back, scared as hell. When I pulled the trigger again, they all freaked, and more than one called the cops. Minutes later, the place was swarming with police and all hands were up.

No one else got in trouble—only me, and rightly so. I went for a ride in the back of the patrol car, handcuffed and strapped in. They didn't take me to the police station. I relaxed a little as they drove up the long hill to our house.

That relaxation left the second we pulled into the driveway. Dad met the cops at the door, said thank you, and led me straight into the garage. I had never seen such intensity on my father's face as I did now. I began to shake as I watched him place his gun—the one the police handed back to him—onto the cement floor of the garage and pick up a sledgehammer.

I backed up. My father had never hurt me, but I didn't understand that look in the big man's eyes as he raised the sledgehammer. Then Dad proceeded to annihilate the revolver at his feet with violent intensity.

"Do you know why you don't have grandparents?" he asked me, raising his voice. He'd already flattened the barrel, making the gun useless, but he kept on going at it.

I shook my head, afraid to look at his face. I'd hardly ever known our grandparents. I overheard Mom on the phone once telling a friend that Dad's mom had made him feel like she didn't want him. She'd had her own trials when she lost her first husband. We would have all been Cobbs, but my grandma remarried Robert Eastman shortly after my dad was born. She truly fell in love with him.

"You know about Grandpa Eastman?"

I nodded lamely. Grandpa Eastman had been a good guy, but Dad would not have the chance to know him well. Grandpa drove his truck off a bridge. I knew because we talked about that part as a family. There had been a terrible ice and snowstorm. A car next to my grandfather's truck on an icy bridge kept sliding into him. He had a choice: preserve his life by making them go off the bridge, or he would instead. The family in the car involved told my dad if Grandpa wouldn't have done that, their entire family with little ones would have died.

"Robby, a year after Grandpa Eastman did that terrible, *noble* act to save that family, my mom committed suicide." Dad's voice was bitter and sad. "She left a note saying, 'I'm sorry, I love you, sorry I can't do it. Bye.'"

I gulped. That one act left my dad with no parents and us with no grandparents except tottering Great Grandma Bowen, who had only enough life in her to sit on a couch, staring off into space. That's why our family loved the "grandparents" in our neighborhood so much.

"My mom committed suicide, Robby!" Dad cried as shrapnel from the destroyed firearm flew across the garage floor. "She is not here anymore because she chose to take her own life!" he shouted as he blasted the last pieces to bits. "I don't know what I would do if you died. Robby, I would die."

I stood shaking as I watched a tear fall. I had only wanted my father to feel proud of me. What I did at the party was stupid with a capital S. I could not bring myself to do to my dad what his mother did to him.

Head hanging low, I went into the house and went to bed. The next morning, I crept into the garage, picked up all the destroyed pieces of the gun, and threw them away. I was tired of Dad having to clean up my messes.

Later that day, I got a call from my soccer coach, begging me to come back to the team. I agreed, and it was probably one of the wisest decisions I'd ever made. It saved my mental health, my sanity, and my life over the following months and even years, giving me someplace to shine and something to look forward to.

It only saved me on the field, however. Just like the stage lights shutting off after the play, the moment I'd walked off the field, the limelight was gone. Somehow, I had to find something else to take away the pain of the other 90% of life.

CHAPTER 7

ANARCHY AND ECSTASY

I'm killin' it!

I strutted the halls of my new high school like a badass in my long, bleached-blond hair. I certainly had more confidence my first week of high school than in all of middle school—but it was all an act. I wanted to be Kurt Cobain, but not just in looks. I still hated myself. Even after I promised my father I wouldn't take my life, it didn't take away my desire to die as the musician had.

Groups of kids in the hallway moved out of my way even though I was smaller than most of them. In a few months, I had built a reputation to the point even older boys didn't mess with me. I'd grown close to Monster throughout junior high, so no one tried to touch us anymore—not even the seniors. The unfortunate ramification was that I wasn't sure how long any of us would be able to stay in school. Our freshman academics were already in danger of collapsing.

That's why Mom and Dad didn't let the grass grow under my feet. I could no longer take studies from Mrs. Avis, yet I needed help. An after-school regimen would interfere with my competition soccer and other activities. So, instead of taking LDS seminary—a class unique to Utah, where we studied our religion—I was relieved to be let off the school grounds for that hour to be taught by another tutor who lived across the street from the school. While no Mrs.

Avis, she came to care for me, and I had to learn to step up my negotiation skills when I didn't complete an assignment.

What my parents didn't know was that I was hanging around a lot of rebellious kids outside of school, sports, and church. We were cutting classes, driving up into the canyons when the weather was nice, and hanging out wherever when our parents weren't home.

That's when I smoked weed for the first time, too. As I held the smoke in my lungs, a profound feeling overcame me. Everything else in my brain melted away. All the anger, hatred, and bitterness at my constant anxiety disappeared like the smoke.

Peace. This is peace!

I couldn't remember the last time I'd felt this way. Never, maybe? It slightly reminded me of the soft euphoria right before falling asleep on the way home from the slopes, finally warm and triumphant, and the bone-weariness of a warrior slipping into well-deserved rest. I'd found it—the stuff to save my life.

The next time I tried marijuana, I also drank alcohol. I was now officially "bad" in my LDS, black-and-white culture. *If I'm evil, I might as well be evil all the way.*

A month later, I experienced my first real injury during a soccer game. Surely weed would help with the pain after, but I was in the middle of the game and had hurt my ankle pretty badly. *Damnit, I'm a star player! I can't be benched.* The coaches wrapped me up in a blanket on the sideline, and the doctor gave me something for the pain called a Percocet.

Within minutes, I stood up with weight on both my cleats. I was feeling fine again. Actually, I was more than fine: I scored two more goals, not feeling any pain. *What was that stuff? Give me more of that!* Plus, I didn't take a fall—I just ran through people. It was what I needed to be able to go no matter what. Even better, to coaches, parents, and teams, it was *acceptable.*

I stopped thinking about suicide. I started thinking that drugs had saved my life.

One day before Christmas, I was in the hallway, talking trash about hockey players. "They aren't athletes! They're just ice skaters with sticks. It's so stupid."

"Oh yeah?" said Wade Caldwell, one of several guys I hung out with that was a member of the school's team. "You ever been to a game?"

My face turned red. "No," I admitted sheepishly.

"You come with me to see a real game—a live school game, not on TV. Then you can talk trash all you want if you still believe it."

It only took one game to open my eyes. *What the hell? You can be as aggressive as you want, pick fights, and it's all good on the ice?* I was all for it.

Even better, I discovered that the common factor in the hockey world was weed. It was a ritual to get high before practice (and it probably saved a few lives), but we built up a tolerance that was not normal, and I became dependent. I experienced mood swings. As an active athlete when I added painkillers, I became dependent on those, too.

Danny was the only reprieve from the sheer intensity of my anxiety-to-adrenaline-paced life. Coming home from school and practice, often half lit, wound up and a bit beat up, I'd find him hanging out in my room. Danny was like my rabbit's foot. No matter how awful the world was outside, how many mistakes I'd made, or what failing grades I was having, his presence as I walked in the door was a healing salve. I could be myself. I could listen to him as he engaged my brain in extraordinary ways with unheard-of (for me) ideas, more stories—and he always, always made me laugh.

Sometimes other friends didn't understand him, but I sure did. The yin to my yang, a dose of Danny settled me for a time—even if only a few minutes. My parents adored him, especially compared to some of my other friends. Danny was welcomed every day and treated like family.

By my junior year, it was becoming harder to hide my intense, partying lifestyle and choices from my parents. They, of course, did everything they could to prevent me and squash any of my illegal and "immoral" activities at home. At first, they were furious when they found bags of marijuana or empty beer cans, but that didn't get anywhere. Mom was already so tired of the fighting, but Dad . . . he got creative.

I thought I was clever to hide my chew and cigarettes up under the dashboard panel, the lip of plastic that tucked away the wires. Unfortunately, that hiding place wasn't as smart as I thought it was. One day he added a little "treat" to my chew container to show his displeasure with using tobacco.

I drove down the road, my windows down and music blasting from the subwoofers I'd "borrowed" from Dad's home stereo. Grabbing my chew from its hiding place, I went to put in a dip. Suddenly I let out a curse that would have made old Mrs. Folsom across the street wish I was still in diapers and cowboy boots on top of the roof.

I stopped my Jeep and jumped out at the smell of my chew. He had added dog poop to the chew, and I had taken that plug in, hook, line, and sinker. I was furious.

Another day, Dad found my cigarettes. He took them out, one by one, and inserted them in between the weather stripping of the driver's side window, an inch apart, busted in half. Then he just left them there! He simply smirked at me as I was trying to play it cool. That brand-new pack? Useless.

My parents' antics with my beers, cigarettes, and chew were infuriating in the moment but made my friends laugh out loud for hours later. I knew Mom and Dad loved me and didn't know what to do with me. I still wanted to please them, but they didn't understand. Drugs and alcohol were the only thing keeping my feet on the planet. Without them, all those horrible thoughts would come back and I wouldn't want to live anymore.

Instead, my friends and I got craftier at hiding all of our substance abuse, the sluffing, and the bad grades. If we would have set our minds to making money instead of chaos, we'd all have been billionaires by our early twenties.

As for me, I was committed to the anarchy of my own life.

CHAPTER 8

SLAPPED WRISTS AND SUCKER PUNCHES

THWACK! The ball hit right in between the goalie's outstretched arms and the uprights.

I screamed in triumph, my adrenaline over the top. *This is better than any drug.* I flung my body high up in the air, my fist raised amongst a group of my teammates. The red-faced players we'd gone up against from London were good—really good, in fact—but not good enough to match our tight, highly trained competition soccer team.

Having flown all the way from the US to the UK, we were winning this "football match" by two points now. The whole time we heard the loud groans of the opposing team's fiery sideline, I grinned, especially when I noticed the cheers of our parents on the opposite side. They had flown here with us to enjoy the matches and the local flavor.

Thanks to Coach McNichol, we had been invited to play matches against teams in both England and Scotland! Our comp team was made up from multiple schools. It was crazy because the two best forwards were my buddy Brian and me from Bountiful High, while the two best halfbacks came from Woods Cross High—normally our biggest rivals. Even our two badass defenders played for another high school.

I had to laugh thinking about it while we celebrated our latest point. It had been an extra special treat this spring season meeting all these guys—not as teammates but as school competitors with bragging rights on our respective high school soccer fields. We'd all talked a lot of smack when we lined up on opposite sides. "You'd better watch yourself, Eastman," I'd heard again and again. They wanted to shut us out, and we wanted to shut them up. Even our coaches participated, riling everyone up! Brutal on the field, Brian and I got great satisfaction the times our high school team annihilated our opponents—all depending on how good the rest of their players were.

As soon as our junior year high school season ended, we switched allegiances. We'd all gone back to working together, the competition team full of kids like us, raised by Coach McNichol, having risen in the ranks to create Team USA, prepared for this trip abroad.

During the last three years of school soccer, I had stayed off drugs, my grades went up, and drinking was only for weekends. Once the season was over, as much as I loved the comp league and trained hard for it, I wanted alcohol, girls, and partying. I craved it—even here.

Apparently, in the UK, it was almost impossible to get drunk. Alcohol was all around us, but there was no way for us to *get* it. Besides, there was so much to see, yet no time to see it. Our time was thoroughly scheduled by Coach, and he had a reputation to protect. We were not to let him down. We were there only to "eat, sleep, and shit soccer." My parents added a few suggestions too: "Don't you dare embarrass us."

After we had already played a match or two in England, my parents suddenly announced they were going to take my brother to France on the Chunnel. For them the timing made sense, and it seemed the safest time to leave me. After all, my teammates and I should be exhausted after endless games and training, locked up tight in the chastity belts of small rooms in a castle, behind stone walls and thick gates.

Immediately, even before my folks left, ideas lit up my mind. I desperately wanted to drink. Second, the boys and I had all heard about the notorious "red-light district" in London. Castle walls? No problem. As athletes, we could easily jump the barriers quietly enough not to alert anyone. From there, we figured we could find a way to our desired destination via taxi.

We were supposed to be overcoming jet lag and the seven-hour time difference to be in top shape to play, but I was easily able to talk a small handful of my teammates into the escapade. Just as planned, we scaled the stone walls easily and wandered into London across cobblestone sidewalks. Fascinated, we maneuvered streets where people drove on the wrong side. We stopped a taxi.

The driver looked us over, then took us into an area with red lights and the unmistakable flashing signs of girls everywhere. At the entrance to one club was a massive doorman, who quite possibly caught onto the fact that we were a bunch of dorky, seventeen-year-old Mormon boys who didn't know one lick about this seedy world. Most of us hadn't even had sex. The doorman led us down the skinniest, steepest stairwell I'd ever seen. We tried to sound braver than we were as we took step after step, down and down, chuckling, "Who's going first?"

In the basement, we were not greeted by what we expected at all. There were no girls except the waitresses, and the only other occupants were five guys sitting on a long couch.

"Have a seat," said the doorman, although the bench he led us to was too tight for all of us to sit comfortably. We elbowed each other as a waitress brought us "menus." We stared at them, wide-eyed; the language was Greek to us. Once again, we clearly didn't know what we were doing; our faces were even redder in the crimson lighting. One thing we did understand was that it was £110 minimum per person!

I gulped, and so did the guys.

"Oh n . . . no," stammered one kid. "We're sorry, but we can't do that. We didn't know. We didn't bring enough money."

Suddenly whistles started blowing, startling us as the other men in the room stood up. It dawned on us that they were not there to peruse the menu, like us. These were bouncers.

"You'd better pay us, and pay us now," one large and hulking figure growled. I gulped and looked at the other guys. *Oh crap! They are expecting us to fork out more than four hundred dollars that we don't have!*

"Uhh . . ." I backed up and tried to explain apologetically. "Look, we just need to go. We really don't have that kind of money."

That's when the men charged, grasping our limbs with iron grips, no matter how charming their accents.

"Yeah, that's not happening," they demanded. "You're not even going home if you don't pay. Give us everything."

These thugs in their mid-thirties intimidated us so badly that we poured out all our money from our wallets. As soon as we hit the fresh air again, we fled back to the castle on foot with our tails between our legs. Climbing the walls once again, we had to admit to our eagerly awaiting buddies that not only did we not see any girls, we also hadn't had a single drink. Worse, now, we were going to have to explain where all of our pocket money had gone. My shoulders fell.

What a major fail! One night on my own, and I screw up that trust again. And now I have no money for food. Dad is going to kill me if he finds out.

I felt especially bad because I was the one who talked the group into something sketchy and less than smart. Seemingly fun and adventurous, sure. Wise? Absolutely not. I borrowed a bit of money and thought I got away with it all until my family came back from the Chunnel.

"Mrs. Johnson said you had to borrow money from her, Robby!" Dad shouted at me in their room. "That you were robbed while we were gone. What's this all about?"

No way was I going to tell him about the red-light part of our screwup. However, I did have to admit to the sneaking out and getting robbed part. Mom and Dad looked at one another, furious. Then Dad bitched me out.

"Really, Robby? We're barely away, with you locked in a castle supposedly resting for your team, and you couldn't stay put? Not for one night?"

I'd rarely seen him so angry and so embarrassed. The guilt set in again. But, like always, Dad would get angry but there were no major consequences. I was allowed to go play the next day, and I worked hard with my teammates. My parents' constant fury mixed with ongoing disappointment wasn't enough to keep me from sketchy situations.

My friends, however, had taken to watching me like a hawk, even in the day. They had to. We were playing soccer in some areas where our coach warned, "Hear me now: if you get in a fight, no one will make it back to the bus. Don't you dare start anything." So,

I focused all of my heightened anxiety onto the field and watched my p's and q's on the sidelines.

Our team played well together and won another game. So far, we were completely unstoppable. Everything could have proceeded forward smoothly if it were not for me. We won all of our matches in London and landed in Edinburgh, Scotland, a place of breathtaking historic beauty. Even the soccer fields seemed fancy. As we kept winning, I became more arrogant and felt untouchable.

On one of our final nights in a post–World War II high-rise building, I talked a small group of teammates into sneaking out again. We were so much wiser this time. Being in Scotland, we meant to get our hands on some Scottish whiskey. We succeeded and immediately snuck back into our room, safe and sound. No one saw us coming or going. Feeling proud of ourselves, we pounded the whiskey.

The problem was, I always had to push the limits. As soon as we made too much noise, one boy in the room turned out the lights to quiet us so we wouldn't get into trouble. The moment everything turned dark, my head and my world started spinning.

Ohhh, crap. I'd consumed too much. Fortunately, I could see the faint outline of the window. I scurried across the room, tripping over teammates and the empty glass bottle. I reached the window just in time to point my face out of it and puke.

As my entire stomach spewed out, I was blind to the finer points of Scottish architecture. In this twenty-story, glass-towered building, the old windows didn't open as expected. Instead of hinging from the top to open at the bottom . . . they opened from the *top*.

Moments later, there was a loud banging on the door, and Coach McNichol's voice screamed bloody murder. We tried to scramble into beds and closets, but he bolted in, raging like a lion.

"You bloody fools!" he barked. "Here I was, working on game plans for the next day, when puke begins pouring into my open fuckin' window!"

We were supposed to be representing the best of Utah, and I had deeply humiliated everyone. I wanted to bury myself in a hole. For a little while, at least.

Once we were back stateside, Danny and Katie, my girlfriend, were there to greet me. It felt like a reunion, and instead of acting sorry I boasted all about our team's triumphs and my arrogant stupidity. They laughed so hard that it took the sting away. Soon I was telling *all* of my friends the stories, although my comp teammates were not speaking to me. I found I didn't care. Like my list of calls to make when I wanted to party or hang out, I always made sure there was another person who could handle me, for a time.

Katie and I had met in St. George over spring break. She was a soccer girl, more wild than I had dated previously. So fun and adventurous, she often joined me in my not-so-bright adventures and ideas. Danny, along with a bunch of other guys, often met me at the beaver ponds above Bountiful, to go "fishing and motorcycle riding." Sure, we did some of that, but, as cops and parents left us alone, we most often went up there to party.

Danny started going along with me wherever I went outside of school and games. At first, many of the guys couldn't figure out why I hung around this guy who was my opposite. He was so bright and happy all the time, cracking jokes. Danny was still that same nerd, talking about books and stories and stuff no one else my age cared about.

To my delight, I noticed that once Danny came along a few times, the guys loved having him around as much as I did. For one thing, girls flocked to Danny, reading his gentle energy. They never dated him, but they trusted him and liked him. For another, late into the night at the beaver ponds as we were wasted that summer, staring into the fire under the sky full of stars, Danny would read from an Arthurian novel called *The Winter King*.

Crazily enough, the nerd would hold us hostage with his interpretation of each character's voices and mannerisms. Danny was a hoot, and for a time I could put away all my irrational fears, my anxiety, and my self-loathing. Those nights, before drifting off in my sleeping bag with my buddy creating a world I could escape into, all seemed right in the world.

When my senior year started, I was still struggling and worried about graduation. With no soccer again until spring, I had a hard time maintaining grades and had no reason to keep clean or sober. I was the big man on campus again, with everyone else either younger or knowing better than to mess with me. Monster had dropped out of school by that point. I mostly saw him at parties.

Soon, my parents were digging me out of scrapes on a weekly basis. I already knew cops, and they knew me all too well. Every weekend it seemed I got pulled over by the same dude. I didn't know if my dad had him on me, but I got warnings all the time. I had speeding tickets as well as alcohol tickets, and I put way too many miles on the dealership's Jeeps, but that was the least of my parents' worries.

By late fall, my buddies and I who were attending (or pretending to attend) school often ended up at a party before going back to school late or not going back at all. One day, I suddenly heard a loud sound outside.

HONNNK!

Aw, no! It sounded familiar. Sure enough, when I peeked out the window, it was Dad. *How the hell does he know I'm not at school—and that I'm here?* I rolled my eyes at my friends and swore up one side and down the other. Still, I knew I couldn't stay another minute. Dad had joined the local school board. Lately he seemed to have a pulse on when I was attending class, and especially when I was not.

That day was the first of many where Dad seemed to find me to remind me to get my butt back to school. It was annoying. I felt like dropping out like the others, but Mom and Dad would not let me even consider it. I didn't see what the big deal was. I'd been working a little bit here and there at my dad's dealership for extra money. I wasn't making a lot of cash, but I washed cars and got into a lot of trouble. I took Dad's dealership for granted, checking out the newest vehicles, test-driving when I shouldn't have been, and taking friends for rides when I also shouldn't have been. Except for yelling at me, Dad did little. Whenever I got into trouble, like Mom he would make it better. He would fix it.

That January I did have something to be proud of. Our competition team played in the Junior World Cup in San Francisco at the 49ers' practice stadium, then at the Coaches' Classic tournament. There were at least a hundred college coaches in attendance at Cowboy Stadium in Texas. We went undefeated. I was pretty sure that every kid on my comp team was getting a Division One soccer scholarship, including me despite my really lousy grades. I had to continue to play damn good, and they would come calling at our local school championships, too.

Immediately, we launched into spring training at our various high schools. I got serious again, more on a natural high than anything else. The boys and I were on the varsity high school soccer team, practically commandeering the tryouts team. We wouldn't go to practices except to heckle and haze the new recruits. I saw the looks of disappointment and disgust on the faces of the coaches and the junior varsity players, but I didn't give a crap.

One day, the JV captain tried to call me out.

"Eastman, you're so full of yourself! You suck at teamwork, and everyone knows it."

I scoffed in his face. "Do you see *your* picture in the school newspaper and the local paper this week, Miller?" I taunted back. "What about Channel 4 last night?" I gave him a sarcastic look. "No? Well, when you can start pulling up your own big-boy pants, then maybe you can talk to me about teamwork!" And I walked away, knowing I was the star of the show.

In two weeks was our last game of the high school season. This one would be against Woods Cross High, the team my comp buddy Jason Coombs played on. There was sure to be a lot of posturing. I was counting on soccer getting me out of my small town where everyone knew my dad and it felt like I was living in his shadow— where I could never live up to the family name. My sisters were doing well, having gotten married with successful husbands. Drew was getting good grades and was a star athlete that everyone knew for *positive* things. I was the family screwup.

I was ready for the partying college life. Plus, who knew? Maybe I would get my shit together and do well in a new place.

One of my friends, Levi, came up to my house where I was hanging out with Danny. "Hey, I need to talk to this kid, Alex, up at Maple Hills condos. It's really important. Can you give me a ride?"

"Sure," I replied, too easily. We all hopped into my Jeep. With the windows down and the top off, we all drove up to Bountiful Boulevard with music blasting out of my stereo system, feeling on top of the world.

Parking a couple hundred feet away from the front of a condo where Levi popped out, Danny and I sat out on the street, heads bobbing to some Bob Marley.

Suddenly we heard a loud BANG! We jerked up and saw three people outside the condo. One of them must have been the kid, Alex. He looked like a small wannabe-gangster, like us. There was also an older guy, lean, and maybe 5' 10" and 180 pounds. *He must be Alex's dad.* I could have cared less, except the jerk had Levi pinned up against the hood of a car.

"What the hell?" I yelled, and we ran down there to separate what looked like father and son ganging up on my friend. I got Levi free and was about to walk off when the dad looked at me.

"You're eighteen," he assumed smugly. "You're free game." Then he punched me in the face.

For a moment, I saw stars. Then I shook my head to clear it and launched myself at the two perpetrators. Suddenly, Alex had Danny on the ground. Danny had never been a fighter, but worse, Alex was beating him with a mag flashlight. That really pissed me off.

Within ninety seconds, we beat up the dad and Alex. *I'll teach you to go after my gentle friend.* Then we ran back into the Jeep. We had only made it a couple hundred feet over the hill when we were surrounded by cops. After some extensive questioning, they let us go. I asked Levi a bunch of questions, wondering why it had all blown up so fast, especially involving an adult, but he didn't have a lot of answers.

Later we discovered the adult, who was indeed Alex's dad, was a highway patrolman. Alex's mom was a dispatcher. That was *not* good news. The guy knew my dad, and he had done some special investigation into break-ins at Dad's dealership. While the police let us go that afternoon, charges were brewing.

Fortunately, Dad cleaned the whole mess up for us, especially when I told him about what had happened from start to finish. Even though I rarely told the truth to stay out of trouble, I didn't need to embellish a single thing on this one—it was so bizarre that this guy had up and slammed me in the face with no provocation.

Dad relayed the deal that had been made. I had to keep my nose clean. I was not to speak to Alex. *Don't make his life any harder, then nothing will happen.* I avoided the kid and forgot about it.

At the massively crowded home game the following day, I felt back on top of the world. I kicked in two goals during that crazy, adrenaline-filled game because half my comp team was on my school team and the other half was on the Woods Cross team—our main rivals! I was grinning from ear to ear when I left the field. "When you beat your buddies, it's extra special, eh?"

"We pummeled them!" my friends cried triumphantly, although we were limping a little. The competition had been intense on all sides.

I met my congratulatory parents and my little brother on the way out. We were leaving the field with the entire team in the one spot where the whole crowd had to funnel off to the parking lot below. Suddenly, flashing police lights filled the entire lot.

"Rob Eastman? You are under arrest for assaulting an officer."

I stared at the two cops in front of me, wide-eyed, as one of them read me my Miranda rights.

"What the hell?" I cried, my voice getting higher as that cop roughly cuffed my wrists behind my back—right in front of the massive crowd that moments ago had been cheering my name. I looked at Dad, bewildered. All the color had drained from my face, and his. The crowd was staring. Due to our school rivalry, some were sad and a lot were happy. As a cop shut the back door of the police car, my wrists were still in cuffs. I saw my dad turn away, a trickle of a tear streaming down his face. He took Mom's hand to walk her to their car. As I watched them go, all I could think about was my dad, who never did anything but good for his community—the guy serving on the school board, serving in Scouts, serving on other business boards and nonprofits—the all-around service guy and the dad who only wanted to steer me in the right direction.

I'm his son, and I keep displaying the exact opposite of what I was raised to do.

And now everyone knew it. Camera flashes fired off as we drove away, and, with more fear and guilt, I realized that any chance I had of keeping *this* secret from college recruiters was out of the picture. My shooting star had been kicked out of the sky.

CHAPTER 9

NUCLEAR FRENZY

The atomic bomb dropped. Obviously, I'd sucked at being a great student—or any sort of student at all—but since my sophomore year, soccer had always been my golden ticket to college. It was what my mother and father were counting on, my bright future, and the surest way to get me out of their hair. It was what I lived for, what I dreamed of to get me out of our uptight town, and the only thing that kept me halfway on any straight and narrow path before I wandered off into the thorny bushes.

Now I was in deep trouble. Dreams of a Division I scholarship were history. I was completely lost. I shoved my deep feelings of failure down like I did all the previous pain and misery and tried to pretend it wasn't happening. Everyone around me knew it. My anxiety skyrocketed to high adrenaline 24/7.

Two weeks after my arrest for assaulting an officer, I was training for Nationals in Seattle, Washington, with my team when I got a call.

"We worked something out with the courts, Rob," said Dad, "but it wasn't pretty." His voice was somber—although not as somber as when they first thought I might go to jail or prison no matter what.

"The judge is allowing you to go abroad. This is kind of like a plea in abeyance. If you do well with this and keep your nose clean, they'll drop all the charges." Before I could get too excited, he added, in that same warning tone: "But you will have to be on your best behavior. We're sending you to Israel. The program is sending you a packet up there where you're training." He paused. "You *have* to fill it out completely, Rob. This is the only thing keeping you out of prison. They're also sending a book, and you *must* read it and send back a report. It's about Yasser Arafat and the Middle East."

I didn't breathe a word, except "Yes sir." It broke my heart that he was disappointed in me, and I knew he must have pulled some strings for me not to be incarcerated. I thought about his high position on the school board, and I recognized that not only was it the reason I'd felt like I could strut the halls of the high school without fear of any teacher, it was also why they were afraid of *me*. I didn't like to admit it, but I had realized it probably was the only reason I had graduated. Now I was being given a second chance—a third chance, really.

I hung my head, although he couldn't see it from the other end of the phone. I listened as he told me some other details, like the fact that the study-abroad group was leaving in three weeks. I would have to head straight back to Utah after this training and Nationals, then head out.

Damn, too little time to party with my friends, I thought miserably. *Most of them will be off to college in the fall.*

I couldn't let myself feel sorry, however. I was so lucky. I didn't have to do jail time, and I could party while I was away, anyway. *Isn't this what I want—to be away from Bountiful where no one understands me, and have the freedom to party how I want, when I want, where I want?*

"Oh," added Dad. "By the way, the program is through BYU. Church standards only."

That was the second atomic bomb. I choked on the phone. *Are you freaking kidding me?* I bit back my answer. "BYU?" I croaked out, hoping I had heard wrong. The private, religious university sponsored by the LDS church was huge in our state.

"Yes," Dad replied. "They have an active campus there. You'll be expected to act like all the other students there." He waited for a blowback by me, but I didn't know what to say.

I choked again, this time managing a faint "Thank you" before hanging up. *Crap. BYU. They are all about those freaking ridiculous church standards that I haven't lived since junior high, even when I tried so hard.* How the hell would I survive this next chapter of my life? I took a breath. Then another. *One thing at a time, starting with the book report.*

It wasn't easy for me to read a whole 300-plus-page book, but still I read the material on the Palestinian leader as best I could when I was in Seattle. I did what Dad asked and filled out all the paperwork and then wrote the report. It certainly gave me a deeper understanding of the culture.

Israel. I was going to Israel. I couldn't believe it.

The one good thing that had happened was that Dad had come to believe my story about what happened with me and the kid Alex and the cop-that-we-did-not-know-was-a-cop. At least Dad and I were on the same page. I felt so helpless, but Dad was my hero. He had wielded his enchanted wand, but I couldn't get out of my mind that it was BYU. I knew exactly what that meant.

We played really well in Nationals. I was happy for my team-mates, and I fell into a state of nostalgia, realizing that it was my last game. I made every second count, dreading what was coming. Several of my classmates from well-to-do homes were going to

Europe or the tropics with family to celebrate their graduations. I was going to the desert, a place that I learned in the book had been at war for centuries. And I was being thrown into the mix in a Mormon setting. I wanted to puke.

By that time, I hated church. I had a long and awful history with it. Just like at school when I was young, I was always in trouble at church. Most of my church friends that I'd hung around with and played church ball with since I was itty-bitty wouldn't talk to me any-more, either. I felt abandoned by them—that I wasn't good enough for them. I didn't realize they were protecting themselves from me.

On the ride back from Seattle, I looked at my copies of the expectations sent by BYU. The biggest thing that stuck out was the standards for conduct, and I ticked off each column as a failure:

Be honest.	*Oh, boy.*
Live a chaste and virtuous life, including abstaining from any sexual relations outside a marriage.	*Uh-oh. Too late for that.*
Respect others and avoid pro-fane and vulgar language.	*Are you kidding? I've been get-ting into trouble with my lan-guage since I was five.*
Obey the law and follow cam-pus policies.	*Okay. I'll do my best.*
Abstain from alcoholic bever-ages, tobacco, tea, coffee, and substance abuse.	*Not okay.*
Participate regularly in Church services.	*Not okay at all.*

There were certain dress standards, too. I didn't fit any of the criteria. I had earrings; I had bleached-blond hair. People would comment.

Dad already knew. "You have to cut your hair—above your ears," he ordered when I'd made it home.

I glared at him but didn't say a word. As lucky as I knew this situation was, I didn't want to go, and I sure didn't want to cut my hair. I was so upset, I went down to my room and slammed a bunch of stuff around. Then I went into the bathroom and looked in the mirror. My longer, grown-out hair which often obscured my face and eyes had become a way for me to hide. I didn't have to see or be seen, especially my emotions, unless I wanted to. *But now I have to have a little Mormon haircut. Instant bad karma.*

Still, I didn't argue. It would have been stupid to, anyway. The problem was, I could fake who I was for a few hours at school or at church, but for six months? Not to mention *living with them,* of all things, and having to go to school. What scared me, but I didn't tell anybody, was that I wouldn't have Danny or my parents to help me in school or have any of the material things I was comfortable with—like my rockin' ride, my Jeep.

All I could think of was that I would fail.

CHAPTER 10

CULTURE SHOCK

I sucked in the hot, desert air. It shouldn't have been such a big deal to go from one desert to another—the desert of Utah to Jerusalem. But I stood there, completely out of my element.

It wasn't just the climate that was different—a little more humid. It was a massive cultural shock. First, there were the smells that floored me from the moment I stepped off the plane. People in the region didn't use deodorant or aftershave. Not being used to this, when we went out to market I felt like I could smell every person before they came into view—that and whatever camel or goat or petrol car they'd rode in on. It was definitely shocking to my senses. Same with the markets with the incredible spices and colorful fruits and vegetables that I didn't recognize.

The extremely bright colors in the market were indescribable, a huge contrast to the Israeli white sandstone. It was crazy to me how all the buildings blended into the landscape. Even gorgeous buildings seemed carved from the land itself. The Jerusalem Center was one of those.

I didn't use the word *breathtaking* much in my vocabulary, but that was the one word that came to me as I looked up at the building before me with curving arches reaching to the sky. It was built into the Mount of Olives on five acres of gardens. When I stepped in at ground level, I realized there must've been ten or fifteen separate levels. Some of it was inside, and some outside. The living areas' hallways were outside. Our dorm rooms were small and enclosed, but each room had its own balcony. Our dorms were simple, but the outdoor living compartments looked out onto city views that stunned me. *Dorothy, we're not in Kansas anymore.*

Even after the trip from the airplane to the center, I couldn't wait to shower. Every time I'd walk outside the building, the intensity of heat and humidity were hotter than hell. Out of respect for the local culture, all of us—teachers, students, administration, and even janitors—had to wear long, modest clothing, even longer than I was used to in Utah! It was so nasty, even for an athlete used to guys' locker rooms. All the smells would have knocked me out of the water had there been any! *Girls stanking and guys stanking . . . just get me to the shower!*

I was still angry and disgusted at being forced to be somewhat sober. I faked it well, but underneath I had a huge chip on my shoulder. It was kids like these who had shunned me back in Utah. I had a roommate—another redhead, of all people—whose name was Eric. I liked him right away, but he was one of *those* Mormons.

Administrators gave us the first seventy-two hours at the Jerusalem Center to get adjusted to the time change. For me, it was the first time truly away from my parents for more than an overnight or so in the mountains. *Mommy is not going to the store for you.* I'd been off of drugs and alcohol since leaving the US. I was uncomfortable and anxious, and intense feelings started coming back up.

I need to find a fix to survive this place. Every time we walked into Jerusalem, there was a gas station with a taxi cab parked across from it. I got the idea that this guy would know how to take me to what was needed. Finally, I stopped to talk to him and asked him about his job.

"I work during the day and drive a taxi at night."

My brain started calculating. I knew that about an hour away from Jerusalem was the ocean. *Hey, I could take my new friends to the beach, teach them how to surf. And . . . I know the bars and pharmacies are there, too.*

Within a few minutes of arriving, I found muscle relaxers on my way to the only bathroom in a bar. I had a shot and came back out. Suddenly I felt like I could focus and do this thing called Israel.

The classes I ended up taking weren't as bad as what I first envisioned—at least not there, thrust into another culture entirely. We had lessons focused on the New and Old Testaments, as well as ancient Near Eastern studies and modern studies. I didn't touch Hebrew or Arabic. Not my jam.

In the meantime, sometimes we would hear machine guns, see missiles in the distance, and see the result of explosions on TV. We even spent a little bit of time in lockdown when tanks were on the border of Lebanon. It was sad. Gaza was being lit up a little. We thought we were religious and understood what was happening, but we only got a small fraction of everything that was in play.

What was crazy for me was witnessing my first miracle. In the midst of the height of the tension, Sabbath started Friday night. In an instant, one million people shut everything down. Four million cats, honking horns, bumper-to-bumper traffic, and Middle Eastern music all went quiet. Even the battle, the guns, and the explosions stopped. There was only the eerie, quiet hum of a Friday evening.

One Sabbath, a group of us walked down into Old Jerusalem when there was no one about. We started to hear chanting and singing on our way to the Wailing Wall. My eyes were opened wide. Here were all these different religions and hundreds of thousands of people kneeling, praying, and worshiping. Writing prayers to tuck into any little nook and cranny were Orthodox Jews, Muslim Palestinians, and others. I had never seen anything like it.

Within a short period of time, another miracle happened. Without the drugs and alcohol, I was seeing firsthand how other people thought about things. It was crazy—these guys would share creative thoughts and feelings, and I saw a different way of thinking than I was used to. My roommate Eric, plus Greg, a 6' 5" center for Utah State, and his little cousin Dave, were a few of those who would hang out together with me, along with a group of girls equally adventurous.

What was weird was all these kids were adventurous with *education*. They would think things through. It made me shake my head.

This came first in the form of my roommate, Eric, calling me out. I hadn't detoxed, and from my first week in Israel I had done whatever it took to secure some alcohol or weed. The taxi driver had hooked me up plenty of times, although I tried to hide it.

"I know what you're up to, Rob," Eric said simply, looking directly in my eyes. "From what I've gathered, you've already been in some trouble. I don't think this is a good idea."

"I don't know what you're talkin—"

"—Yeah, you do," he said bluntly. He wasn't going to let it go.

Looking into Eric's eyes, I realized I could dive deeper into my addiction, my rebellion, and my stupid ways that had almost gotten me into prison . . . or I could see what these people were about. From that day, I shut up and latched onto these young men and women who were there for the right reasons—not to flee charges. It wasn't easy, but I began to fill my time with other things. To my surprise, within a couple of weeks, I found myself happy and laughing . . . and *sober.*

Greg and Dave and the guys and gals we hung out with would invite me to go on adventures where we would have a blast, but it wasn't doing something dangerous or stupid. What a concept!

My thought process when thinking up a plan always began with A, then jumped straight to Z, like diving off a cliff before seeing how deep the water was below, or taking a new ski jump without testing it first. These guys, however, thought things through, from A, to B, to C—all the way to Z if necessary—and had a great time doing it. It was weird. I didn't admit it out loud, but I started to like it.

A few weeks later, our group took a trip. We wanted to find the actual place where it was believed that David faced Goliath in the Valley of Elah. All around, there were underground caves that ancient robbers used through the centuries—but also the Taliban would use some of them. The guys planned the trip more carefully than I would have, and we climbed around the caves for over an hour. I couldn't believe it: there were miles and miles of them, with bedrooms and living spaces and altars. It was cool—and no Taliban and no bombs, due to their careful research.

The biggest culture shock I received was being a part of these things—real things happening in real time—and not just reading about stuff in history books. These were worldly studies with lessons that I could utilize in my life. It blew my mind to read the stories of David and Goliath and go to where it's thought that happened to search around for perfect stones to fit in a sling. Suddenly the Biblical stories I never understood made sense. And I knew what my Goliath was. I looked around and recognized every single person had gifts. I knew everyone was smarter than me.

Even back at home, my certain group of friends were freaking brilliant. Yet each day we would only spend our brilliance on how we would get a few bucks and get high to get through the day. That was the sum of our brilliance. I realized. *Holy crap . . . imagine if we'd used our brains to actually do something, create something, build something.* These people I was around now, they were different, and they had hopes and dreams. How many times had my dad told me, "It's important to surround yourself with the kind of people doing and being what you want to do and be"?

Now I was listening. Suddenly, I was the first one to get to class, I was the one reading my scriptures, and I was the one asking if I could talk in church.

My group treated me like a little brother; they watched over me, and they still called me out on my other stuff, like my quick-to-anger tendencies. By their example, however, I learned I could be more observant. They were showing me how to lead the right way instead of the wrong way.

Little by little, as these model kids laughed with me, learned with me, and prayed with me, something began to happen. Among those clean-cut, hard-working, and, sheesh, freaking spiritual people who I had judged so harshly, this crazy thing began to happen . . . I began to soften my hard shell.

Oh hell. I think I kinda like these guys. I mean, they were not the adrenaline-filled, thrill-seeking, let's-go-endanger-our-lives kind of people I was used to—and the fact that they didn't party at all felt really boring to me at first. But, like Danny, they liked me for being me. They shared themselves with me like he would. They wanted to know my thoughts. I began to think that they maybe liked me, too.

A few weeks later, I was just out of class where a group of us had been engaged in a really intense and emotional conversation about spirituality and humanity. All of a sudden, I had sensations in my body I couldn't explain. A warmth filled me like I'd never felt before. It scared me. Energy was moving through me, and my heart was pounding so wildly I thought it was going to burst.

Then it didn't go away.

"What's wrong?" asked my roommate.

"Oh my God, Eric, get the nurse—I think I'm having a heart attack!"

Eric, who had been in on the conversation, chuckled.

"What are you laughing at, Bro?" I cried out. "This is freaking scary!"

"Robby," he said gently, "you said you've been happier than you ever have been in your whole life, and there have been no drugs or alcohol involved. Dude . . . you are being given the gift of the Holy Spirit and blessed with the gift of joy."

I stared at Eric. He had to be crazy.

But over the following months, I discovered it was true. Before the summer ended, there were new emotions that surprised no one more than me. I was the kind of guy who had done a lot of talking in my life and not taken a lot of action. I'd also done a lot of lying. It felt good to have my parents proud of me succeeding for once.

"Dad?" I said on a call from Jerusalem to Utah.

"Yes?"

"I think . . . I think I want to go on a church mission."

CHAPTER 11

PYRAMID UP, SPIRAL DOWN

"The Utah courts are not ready for you yet," said Dad over the phone, his tone matter-of-fact. Instead of bringing me straight home from Israel, my father informed me that he was sending me with the BYU students on some excursions. "It looks like you'll be visiting famous sites and learning history around Egypt, Jordan, and more."

I was stoked. "Wow, that's rad!" I replied eagerly, surprising him.

I meant my words. There had been a lot of buzz among those preparing to head out for these special cultural, anthropological, and spiritual study trips. "Like visiting the pyramids? And Ramses' tomb and the Sphinx?"

I couldn't believe it. No one I knew from high school had traveled there. It had seemed so out of reach as my new friends were talking about it. Israel had not been a part of my world months prior. Being clean had me thinking more clearly and appreciating my parents, these new friends, and my unusual situation.

Shortly thereafter, I was still excited as we crossed the Sea of Galilee, traveled into Jordan, and prepared to cross the border into Egypt with 110 students and some BYU faculty and guides. I found it was harder to look like such a badass when my mouth was open in awe 90% of the time.

It also felt good *not* being in trouble every minute. I didn't have to hide or escape inside, but I didn't have to use any bullshit bravado, either. It didn't mean I was perfect. Habits formed over a lifetime didn't disappear altogether. People were still watching me. It didn't help that my driven, sometimes rebellious or combative behavior would rear up.

My friends often came to my aid and smoothed things over, bringing me back under their wings. Some of my teachers knew why I was there, and initially they seemed strict, stern, and cold. Then again, at first I had not been going to church and was often late to class. By the semester's end, things had shifted so dramatically that, in my mind, it felt like a miracle.

It was a good thing, too, because being immersed in the culture created mind-blowing opportunities . . . and questions of consequences. At one point, our smaller group of five young adults was walking near our hotel in Jordan when we were asked by locals if we wanted to attend a wedding celebration. Hell, yeah! We jumped into the back of a pickup truck and rode to the celebration. It included splitting up the boys from the girls. The girls were whisked away and swathed in colorful silks from head to toe, veiling the lower part of their faces. They danced with other women and girls only, on one side of the area.

The boys and especially the men invited us into their circle. This included waving machine guns in celebration, shooting bullets into the air—and letting us do the same. It was exhilarating. There's that saying, "When in Rome, do as the Romans do." Well, when in Jordan, right? It wasn't until the next morning that I wondered where all those bullets fell.

As we crossed over the border into Egypt, our guides gave us two simple rules that would keep us alive:

1. Do not go out after dark.

2. Do not climb the pyramids.

Simple, right? Yet the massive, awe-inspiring pyramids and the backdrop of Cairo reminded me of my countless adrenaline-filled adventures in the Wasatch mountains. Of course, I had boasted to my friends about those times back in the States. In private, scaling those pyramids was *all* I could think about. The fact that it was forbidden made the challenge seem all the sweeter.

Egypt was shocking to me, and Cairo another world all its own. The city was gross. The roadsides were filled with garbage. Half the buildings had sheets instead of windows. That was a big eye-opener to me. How could a place at the height of civilization thousands of years ago be so nasty now? As one of the guys, I didn't like how the local men thought they could touch our girls.

Women walked behind their husbands. Veiled or not veiled depended on their religion. None of our girls could walk anywhere in the market or to the restroom without at least two of us with them. Even us guys had to have a buddy system for safety when nature called.

We were immersed in colorful markets and certain streets where I was shocked to see a helluva lot more camels and donkeys than cars for transporting people, food, and goods. We were warned about the corruption around us and learned how not to get ripped off in the markets—and not to hold judgments.

Aggressive haggling and lack of ethics were simply a normal part of their culture and survival. I quickly learned what a little money would provide: just about anything I wanted.

Fortunately, we didn't stay long in Cairo, and over the next several days we visited multiple sites I had maybe heard about in the news or dusty history books that held no juice for me. In this immersive experience, they all came alive, bursting with centuries of stories that made sense. Petra, Mt. Sinai, the Luxor Temple, Valley of the Kings, and Ramses' Tomb were some places, along with museums and markets.

Most of the time, I listened in on the guided tours, feeling rad, like we were in an Indiana Jones movie. As the week progressed, I found that the beauty, glory, and adrenaline of something so new and awe-inspiring only sharpened my fixation to be the main character, saving the day.

Upon our return to Cairo, my obsession to somehow scale the pyramids was *on!* It became heightened the sizzling-hot day that our large group went to see them up close and personal, despite the militarized police force guarding them from tourists and acts of terrorism. Our group took a couple of photos together with the giants in the background.

The pyramids were massive, nearly the color of the surrounding sand. It was hard to believe that they were built 4,500 years ago, until we went inside during one part of the tour.

BYU staff had turned us over to a local guide. Dressed in khaki pants and a collared shirt, and with sweat stains that matched the rest of us, the small but gangly historian was clean-shaven, unlike most of the men around us. He shared that Egypt's pharaohs were the highest-ranking members of Egyptian society. They expected to be treated like gods and believed they would actually become gods in the afterlife. They erected temples to prepare for the afterlife—but the massive pyramid tombs they built for themselves.

The moment we entered the underground chamber, the temperature dropped suddenly. The ancientness of the place got to me.

It was crazy that, housed within such a gigantic structure, the tomb itself was only about fifty feet by fifty feet. Our guides spoke of tomb raiders and slaves and what it took to chisel the Sphinx and Ramses' head. That pharaohs were so materialistic as to take thousands of men's lives just to get their portraits chiseled blew me away.

"Does anybody ever climb these?" I asked the guide.

He shook his head and pointed clearly to the militarized police.

"Is there any way to do this?" I asked him later. I was getting the hang of the culture. A couple days ago, we heard about a bus hitting a taxi, and they both paid the cop and drove off. We might consider it a bribe. They considered everything a mutual exchange. So I kept asking until it was almost time to leave.

Finally, my guide, worn away by my insistent questions, assured me, "If you grease my palms, you can have whatever you want—but it will have to be after dark."

It turned out that everything I needed was a tall order. First, we needed a taxi, then horses, so as not to make it obvious to authorities we were out there. We were then to be dropped off with a Bedouin who knew the desert in the dark and could point us in the direction we needed to go to make our climb.

I could not believe my good fortune. I made all the arrangements to leave in the middle of the night. I quietly talked three of my classmates on that trip into going. We could scale the pyramids and be back before BYU arose! They would never know, but we would have this secret memory. I had no idea how I would explain my spiritual conversion to anyone who knew me well, but I couldn't wait to share this story with my buddies back home.

We were staying at an American hotel with armed guards standing outside the entrance. Their job was to make sure we didn't get messed with. We found that they couldn't care less if we came and went—unlike any fellow students and faculty.

We took a taxi to a rendezvous point the driver knew, where two men met us with four raggedy-looking horses. There, we had to haggle with the Bedouin that our guide had sent us to. He took care of camels, sheep, and goats.

We were told, "Give him a little money and no problem." The taxi driver, who agreed to stay to give us a ride back, raised his brows. Dirty and unshaven, the Bedouin was fully armed—and unafraid to show it as he sized us up and down, an AK-47 in his hands.

At that moment, looking sideways at my uncertain friends, I felt like I had to show up. It was now or never. I had to be a leader. I had to be unafraid, or we wouldn't come back with a great story.

I nodded, my heart thudding against my chest, and the all-too-familiar wave of adrenaline surged through me. It was as if my body cried out in recognition, *Hello, old friend.* None of us was an avid horseman, but two of us knew our way around horses pretty good and showed the other two how to mount and control them. Then the Bedouin showed us which way to ride into the thick of night.

In my mind's eye, it was a perfect evening. It was dark enough not to be seen, and the occasional nicker of the horses swept into the vast desert as we approached opposite the main road where the guards would be looking.

At the pyramid, we had to go up to the shadow side. Quietly, my buddies and I started helping each other up on the massive stones that make each piece of this giant. When we got to the top square, it was like we were standing on the edge of a skyscraper looking down—*hell, if we slip, we'll get pretty banged up before hitting the ground.*

But the view was amazing! I felt like the hero, having provided a once-in-a-lifetime adventure. Then reality checked in as the sky was changing . . . when I saw a light blue color on the horizon, I knew it wasn't the dead of night anymore.

"Hey, we'd better get back before BYU wakes up." I was getting nervous. This forbidden excursion had taken longer than I anticipated. Now we had to climb down without killing ourselves.

But as we turned around, we found ourselves face to face with one of the officers, who'd climbed to meet us at the top of the pyramid. "Give us everything of value or we will kill you and put you in the desert."

My worst nightmare! My buddies and I handed over our money, watches, necklaces—whatever we had on us. They were shaking as badly as I was.

When they let us go, we ran like hell back to our horses. Galloping away from the pyramid into the desert on thundering hooves was an experience I knew I would never forget. My heart was in my throat, and I almost expected to be gunned down at any moment. We made it back to the Bedouin, who seemed to expect a payment to let us pass again.

He started yelling in a language none of us could understand, and one of the horses got spooked. With dread, I watched it race off into the abyss of sand, and I knew we could not catch him. A familiar flash ran through me, reminding me of my hairbrained scheme in the red-light district of London. The bouncers who had taken our money had roughed us up a bit, but they left us alive. I wasn't sure what was going to happen now. The guys who owned the horses were not happy with us. Arguing ensued between the guide and the horse owners.

"We gotta get out of here!" I whispered to my buddies. "This is getting out of hand."

They nodded, and we sprinted off to the taxi, which, at my urging, drove away as fast as possible. Soon, however, we noticed lights behind us, deliberately staying on our tail. The movie scenes didn't quit as we raced through the streets of Cairo and our driver tried to lose them. For the next ten terrifying minutes, we held on tight as a junky two-door pickup raced after us.

It was light by the time we ended up in front of our American hotel, with the tires of our pursuers screeching to a stop. The next thing we knew, there was shouting from all around as the irate horse owners explained to the guards what we had done. The guards quickly alerted the BYU officials. The shame was hot upon our faces as the desert sun finally rose.

My teachers were furious. BYU had very strict standards for a reason—one of them being international relations. Four of their students had desecrated one of the seven wonders of the world, lost an Egyptian citizen's horse, and created a high-speed chase through the streets of Cairo! In my stupidity, I blew up an international incident that put a blight on the whole school, and our religion.

Very quickly, word of my behavior got back to my dad—and to the courts. We only had a day or two before going home, but it was now total chaos. I had violated my probation. I took total responsibility because it had all been my idea. I had broken laws—and, worse, broken the tiny bit of trust I had built since leaving the country. The most difficult piece for me to come to terms with was how I had put our lives in serious danger.

"You're going to go to Europe," seethed Dad, "while I figure some things out! You are officially a fugitive, and I cannot have you back home."

With that, my father put money on a credit card and sent me away to find myself in Europe. Before I even got on a plane to Turkey, I retreated into the scared, insecure little boy I was when I left. The pyramids, which had once represented to me my direction of up and committed to God and my personal growth, now only represented the beginning of my spiral down—a swift descent into stupidity.

Now what am I going to do? I was all alone—a stranger in a very strange land.

CHAPTER 12

BOILING POINT

As I was flying into Austria from Turkey, I thought about how I never claimed to be the brightest grape in the bunch. My focus had always been on surviving and thriving as an athlete. As I sat on the plane, I realized that I hadn't once considered the pyramids—one of the seven wonders of the world—as a protected place. It was another adrenaline-filled adventure. And now, I was so ashamed. *Just a week ago I had been looking forward to proving myself to my dad and serving a mission! And now . . . I can't go home.*

Even as I sank deeper into my seat, I retreated into that terrified kid from Mrs. Rose's class. After all my dad had done for me, once again he had to fix my mess. But no one, it seemed, could actually fix me.

Still, I tried. I had learned a few thinking skills along the way. On the plane I began talking to a businessman from Japan, who turned out to be a full-blown VP of Sony. He appreciated my Sony Walkman. Soon, we chatted about my soccer experiences—the only positive thing I had to say. He told me his son, who lived with him in Austria, wanted to learn to play soccer. He asked if I would teach him.

I blinked back in surprise. *Me, teach someone something?* I had been a horrible mentor to other kids when I was in high school, as my big head made me hold my soccer prowess over others like a crown. But maybe I could do something different this time. Slowly,

I nodded, a grin spreading over my face. I could teach this kid soccer. And so I did.

In Austria, I was graciously invited into the family home. It was beautiful—stunning, really, and set against the backdrop of the beautiful Austrian mountains that reminded me daily of my own mountains back home. I spent a few days with my host's kid, who was ten, building up his confidence and his skills. I found I actually loved coaching him! There was something cool about watching his face light up when he could do a move or kick the ball with greater power and precision.

After about five days at their place, I was eager to get out and see as many places as I could. I went to Germany. My first day there was a struggle. As I got off the train I couldn't pronounce the name of the city, and I couldn't find anyone to speak English with.

I also couldn't find a hotel. With my backpack on and now desperately needing a shower, I found that the hotels where staff did speak English did not accept "backpackers." I was floored. What the hell did that mean? My money—or my dad's money—was as good as anyone else's! They suggested I try a "hostel" instead. I didn't know what the hell a hostel even was, but it didn't sound great.

As I headed back outside from the second snooty hotel, it began to rain heavily. In moments I was soaked, feeling the water trickle down my back and soak my pants under my hoodie.

Oh great. Homeless, lost, and now completely wet and cold and everything is shut down. This sucks!

Heading down one street, I saw a welcoming light in a doorway but a not-so-welcoming sight of a man screaming in it. I realized in a split second that the house wasn't his home; he was taking shelter in the doorway, like me, from the storm. As I hesitated and flipped some of the rain off my body, I looked up to see him motioning to me as he screamed words I did not know to someone who was not there. In his hand he held something I would recognize anywhere. It was a bottle, the liquid gold sloshing in the light.

I hesitated, but only for a moment. When he offered, I grabbed the bottle of whiskey and allowed the liquor to burn all the way down my throat. I didn't even grimace. I allowed the familiar, warm feeling to envelop me, taking away all the hurt, the fear, the ways I had screwed up my life, and the feeling of the cold in my rain-soaked body. I grinned at the stranger, took another swig, handed the bottle back, and thanked him. Maybe I could at least survive the night. As we continued to share swigs, his screaming lessened, although it never stopped until he slouched in the doorway.

As I stared at him, I thought perhaps now I could make it. I had been thinking all wrong. All I needed was some booze and perhaps a few recreational substances, and, thanks to those numbing agents, all would be well in my world.

That night began the downward spiral in Europe. I lost everything I had gained in sobriety at BYU. I found myself in a fun little town up in the mountains themselves, near a famous restaurant and bar that was known worldwide. As I ate one night, I thought about what my dad would do, and I made friends with the owner of the establishment. I told him a little bit about me—leaving out the bad stuff—but he seemed to sense I was a little lost.

"Why don't you work for me for a while?" he asked. "You have a great way with people. What if you were my host? You know, greet people at the door, get them to a table, and make them feel completely at home?"

It blew me away. I'd run into two opportunities in such a short period of time. I took him up on the offer, and for several weeks I hosted the front entrance to the establishment, meeting and greeting people from all around the world and hearing stories that made me take a wider view of the world. It was amazing, and it honed my skills as a communicator and even a salesperson. I could talk people into the special of the day, a great wine to go with their meal, and the chef's specialty dessert. It was fun.

Soon enough, it was time to move on. I found another traveling companion who showed me all the tricks of the trade of an addict. He was a good-lookin' dude, and the chicks loved him. We buddied up and went to France.

First there were the restaurants he and I would not frequent, but underneath were rooms catering to users and those on adventures to escape the world, like me. Just like that, I learned the underbelly of Europe through Germany and France.

I stopped working out. I stopped seeing the sights. I started lying to my parents about my desire to go on a mission. For two full months they were so excited, and I could still hear it in my mother's voice that she really wanted it for me and for them. We talked about how I would submit my papers when I was able to come home, and we spoke about where I would go—this fictional, unattainable place called a church mission.

I had to lie. I found I couldn't be another disappointment.

By the time I got to France, people wouldn't talk to me or be friendly because they thought I was a skinhead and looked so unhealthy.

Then I got a phone call. Dad said, "We made a deal. You can come home now."

I could tell by the shock upon my parents' faces that they could hardly recognize me upon picking me up from the airport. My gorgeous blond hair was gone, shaved to the scalp during a blackout in Switzerland. I was twenty pounds lighter, and from the dark circles under my eyes it was pretty obvious that I was once again an addict. I started back up with old friends, especially Danny, and a few others who still loved partying as much as I did.

Quickly, Dad and Mom sent me up to Logan, a small town in northern Utah to attend Utah State for fall semester. That was terrible because I couldn't take Danny, and we all knew I was horrible at school. It was better to try to forget how things had been different for a time: I had been excited when I was sober. I had been able to concentrate on my studies, and I'd learned a few important things from history and mythology and religion and people, especially my friends.

I pushed away the facts and promptly forgot that I had that ability, and it wasn't true anymore anyway. I'd only had that experience once, when I'd been completely sober and surrounded by support. Now I partied too much, wore a chain with a lock around my neck to feel like a badass so people would leave me alone, and couldn't concentrate on school.

One morning, when I sat in the massive auditorium with other students, I raised my hand when I was confused. The teacher told me right away, "If you can't keep up you don't belong in my class."

Every person started laughing. I glared, stood from my seat, and left. Right away, I made my way over to the admissions office and decided to take back all the money my parents paid for those classes, withdrawing from them.

The next day, it was easy to go up to Beaver Mountain and grab a season pass with my cash so I could snowboard any time I wanted.

But that didn't last: Mom was on the school's board of trustees, and when grades came in at the end of the semester, she knew exactly what I had done. Once again, it was time to go home.

I was now nineteen with no hope of furthering my education. I started laying tile, which I found I could do well, and my dad lined me and my older cousin up with our own house—a fixer-upper off of 1500 South in Bountiful. The upstairs of the rambler was like the movie *The Money Pit* with windows that wouldn't open or perhaps close, and broken shower heads and shower curtains.

It was an old place, built in the '70s, but not beat up. I found out it had only had one owner. Its carpet was worn down right in the middle, a trail that only ran from the bedroom to the bathroom to the kitchen. The front room was never used.

I knew we'd need to make some improvements when one morning a chunk of drywall ripped off the wall when I tried to grab my towel. I almost jumped when my heel punched right through the bottom of the shower floor.

Still, the downstairs had been fully remodeled, and there I felt like a king! There was a bar in it and plenty of room to party. There was a carport and a Tuff Shed, which became our hotbox. Out of all my friends who didn't go off to school, and including the ones that did, I was the only one who had a house of his own, a new and beautiful girlfriend, and a nice Jeep. I began to forget completely about my spiritual experiences at BYU and regaled my friends with stories of Europe that made their skin crawl as they laughed out loud.

I was so on top of the world that when I was laying tile in Wendover, I used my fake ID to get into casinos to gamble and drink. I thought I was managing it all and that I had the very best life until I partied too much, to the point that I wasn't showing up on time repeatedly, and I lost my job. I didn't let that little factoid matter much because Dad was paying my bills. I had more time to party.

Soon enough, within the second year, my cousin bought me out of that house since he'd had enough of me, my parties, and my attitude. I didn't blame him; he was fifteen years older than me and had been fighting to get custody of his kids. He'd been going to church, getting his life together, and working hard, and I was smoking and drinking constantly.

I found myself living back at home, and I thought my mom would go crazy. She didn't say much, but her body language and her eyes spoke volumes of her disappointment, worry, sadness, and frustration. I ignored it by leaving the house to go out to party with my old friends continuously, staying away for days at a time but always coming back to sleep and sweet-talk my folks into dishing out more money that I would blow on alcohol and drugs.

Things came to a head one early-summer day the year I turned twenty. My Jeep was full as Danny and I and two others headed to the spillway at the top of Bountiful City, hidden away amongst greenery. The area was slated to become a park eventually, but for now it was a nice green area with a dirt access road for workers. Often deserted, it was the perfect place to hang and have a couple of beers without having to go all the way up the canyon.

We'd all had about half a beer and were laughing and joking when a family suddenly came upon the scene. *Oh shit.* I knew them. I knew 99% of the folks in the area, and the majority of them were Mormon, like these folks. Worse, they had kids my age, and our alcohol containers were sitting out in plain sight on the Jeep's bumper. They gave us a funny look, then immediately turned around and headed back the other way, not wanting their younger kids to be influenced by us.

We were all underage. I tried to play it cool and shrug it off, but we decided to chuck the cans and knew we had to be careful if the family called the police. Suddenly an emergency warning came over our pagers. 5-0, 5-0.

Damn. It was the cops! Our buddy who had left earlier was warning us the police were on their way up. A cruiser came upon us in seconds. We didn't look as guilty this time, but they found a wine cooler a kid had left under my seat. Me and Danny blew something stupid, like a .002, but it didn't matter. We were underaged. We both got an alcohol ticket.

The cops took us to Danny's house first. There were certain things my father couldn't fix, and Danny's parents let us know they were getting frustrated with us. Finally, his dad declared sternly, "If you get into any more trouble, we're going to have to move. I mean it. Do you hear me?"

"Yes, sir," we both said to break the tension in the room. "We can't be without each other. We'll be good."

When his father left, Danny and I both started sobbing. We held onto each other, tears streaming down our faces. We were in deep trouble, and we both knew it. Mr. Low, Danny's father, was never in a position of making idle threats. He respected Danny, but he wanted the best for him, so he meant business.

I couldn't have my best friend taken from me. I always joked he was the yin to my yang. I was all sorts of unbalanced when I didn't have him around. I was uptight, fearful, and combative. Inside of Danny's presence, I seemed to mellow out. Stupid things didn't get to me. His stories soothed me, and his very presence calmed my red-hot reactivity. I needed Danny, and as I looked at his tear-streaked face, I knew he needed me.

We kept a lower profile for a few days, but then Danny's father's furious warnings began to fade in our minds. For me, talk was cheap. I was getting anxious. I would be losing Danny to his new summer job, and I had to get in as much time with him as I could.

Only two weeks after Mr. Low's warning, Danny and I were partying when I had a wild idea. His parents were out of town, which made it even more tempting. In our neighborhood, we strung fishing line across the street, between a light pole and a fence, so that when a car drove by it would break off their antenna. We hoped to upset some poor schmucks driving by while we laughed our asses off from behind the bushes.

But that didn't last long. When the cops got called, they were pretty pissed because someone else had done the same thing in another state and a biker almost got decapitated.

"What were you thinking? Don't you realize you could have killed somebody?" the officer yelled at us. "Your thinking is asinine!"

We hung our heads. *Damn. It was all my fault.*

I was shocked and heartbroken when Danny and his family actually moved to Provo, more than fifty miles and an hour away from me. I couldn't believe his father would take that kind of definitive action. We were both upset by the whole thing.

I was crushed, but I couldn't show anyone. With Danny gone, I found myself not knowing who I was anymore. I visited him when he got back from working for the National Park Service at the Grand Canyon, but at home we had little resources and support. We lived too far to see each other on a daily basis like we used to, and gas was too expensive. Now we had to plan carefully, and so we usually saw each other only for parties. So I made sure I could do that with him as often as I could.

CHAPTER 13

WHEN I LOST MY YANG

Working at Dad's new Suzuki-Chrysler-Plymouth car dealership was the coolest thing. Located right in the heart of the original Bountiful City, it was growing so fast. I thought I was hot stuff.

Instead of setting me up at the front counter to deal with customers, Dad put me at the back counter, working with mechanics as the rear counter parts manager. I felt right at home with that riffraff—although my father never treated any of us like that. We were a more rough and ready crowd.

I would arrive to work on my longboard, with my massive Great Dane, Thunder, at my side. He and I kind of scared people when we came out front, but I had a good time watching people's faces. I might not have been dominating any real soccer fields any more, but I still knew how to make an entrance!

Mike Bisch, my manager in the parts department, was the top sprint car racer in Utah. He married the other black sheep of our family, my sister Erin. She and Mike partied hard. I had a lot of fun with him, although I avoided Erin like the plague. We had never gotten along, and she had a temper like me.

Danny was back, and we would spend weekends at the sand dunes or up at a place called Pineview Reservoir with boats and jet skis, having a great time. I was constantly getting drunk, and there was always weed, but my brother-in-law introduced me to something that matched my revved-up personality even better . . . or so I thought.

I walked into his place one morning to find a line of white stuff on the counter. "Give it a try," he smirked, and as I did, I felt the whole world go away and my nose hurt like hell. Then an extreme amount of confidence and surety seemed to fill every cell. I felt like I had on the soccer field after a goal.

Wow! Some people might think I didn't need another drop of confidence, but since Egypt, I had been needing whatever I could to get out of my steep fits of anxiety. I couldn't let anyone see the cocaine. Only my close friends and girlfriend knew. I felt I was pretty smooth in covering it all up. This new white stuff sure was addictive. Mike could walk away from it—take it or leave it, essentially. I found that I started thinking about it more often, obsessing about it. For me, it became like my life's breath. I had to have it often.

Thanks to this brand-new addition to my drug arsenal, I could drink longer and more often. I continued my reputation as a badass; as time progressed, I became known for treating girls like crap. I didn't know how to find middle ground in a relationship. I either worshiped a girl and the ground she walked on, needing her within an inch of my life, or I wanted nothing to do with her. There wasn't anything in between.

The same was true for my lifestyle. I was either fighting with Dad or I was away from him, which meant we could actually get along. I was either working like crazy, or I was drinking, doing my drug of choice, or both. Unlike my previous tiling job, drugs were secretly sanctioned to use on the floor as long as I was handling myself well with the equipment and the mechanics and minding myself in front of the customers.

The following January, my best friend let me know he was planning a huge party for my 21st birthday. I was beyond thrilled. I hadn't seen Danny in a couple of weeks, and I couldn't wait to hang out with all of my buddies for a big birthday bash.

We had a blast clear up in the hills, and, as usual, after they sang me a drunken "Happy Birthday," I was the last man standing. That took away my chance to thank Danny one more time. I ignored my family as I finally went home to sleep it off. Fortunately, I didn't have to go back to work until Monday, and even then, it didn't take much for me to get up and go in to the work I loved so much, especially with a little leftover white powder in my pocket.

About a week after my birthday, the sky was overcast again, and the weather forecast on my car radio had mentioned more snow. I rubbed my hands together, even though the cold rarely bothered me. Warming up my fingers by the heater vents, all I could envision was time on the slopes with a bag of weed or borrowing a couple of my dad's new snowmobiles to share with my friends. I wouldn't drink on the slopes anymore. I had done that only once, hit a jump wrong, and landed like Bambi legs. It wasn't pretty.

A few minutes later I arrived at my friend Amber's house. She was just a girl I knew. I'd already knocked back a couple of beers as soon as work ended, and we were getting ready to party when suddenly I heard a ringing echo in her room. Amber answered and looked at me.

"It's your mom," she said, surprised.

"Hey, Mom," I started, "what's up—"

"Have you seen Danny?" she demanded.

I couldn't help but feel the panic in her voice. "Uh, no," I admitted. "The last time I saw him was for my birthday, over a week ago." I chose my language carefully. Mom and I didn't fight nearly as much as Dad and me, but she kept a finger on the pulse of my partying. Just like when I was in high school, I couldn't get away with much without her knowing.

"Well," she said more softly, "he's missing. It's been a couple of days, and his truck is gone. His parents can't find him. His brother found some notes he left to a few people about 'the last frontier.' They were really cryptic things that didn't make any sense."

Immediately, a dark feeling came over me. It wasn't like Danny to take off. He'd never been missing in all the times we were friends. Or, if he was missing, he was with me. Now I had no clue where he was, and apparently neither did anyone else.

Almost as soon as I got off the phone with Mom, a law enforcement agent called. "Hey, I understand Danny Low is a friend of yours. If he were to run away, where would he go?"

"Uhh . . ." It took me a moment to figure out what to say. "Up in the mountains, I guess, although the weather is piss-poor so that doesn't sound like him. He hangs out with me and my other buddies in the mountains a lot, though, so I'll check around here," I added, knowing the cops would be checking the Provo area. The more help, the better.

In an even voice, the man replied, "As soon as the weather calms down, we'll go check up the canyon. It's too dangerous to send a trooper up there now."

I got frustrated, even aggressive with the officer. "That's my friend! You'd better get your asses up there—"

The officer cut me off and threatened arrest if I spoke to him like that again. Still, he could tell I was feeling frantic.

By that time Drew had heard the news, and so I grabbed him and we immediately got into my Jeep and headed up into the Bountiful hills, in places we used to all hang out often—it didn't matter the time of year. Others joined, and we were radioing back and forth through the dark, rumbling weather. There was no sign of Danny.

What did I miss? He just threw my birthday party eight days ago. Did he tell me he was in trouble? Was I too wasted to pay attention?

As I drove, I was stunned. I kept the stereo off and was alone in my anxious thoughts, my hands tapping furiously against the steering wheel. It wasn't looking good. I couldn't help thinking back to what my mom said was on those notes Danny left behind. *What the hell does "the last frontier" mean? There's no way my best buddy would . . .*

It didn't matter. We had no luck.

When I arrived home, empty-handed, my dad called me into his room. "Hey, son," he said somberly, as he stood by his TV hutch. "I understand you're headed down to help with the search party." There was a long pause. "I, uhh . . . I'm heading down to help, too."

I stared at him for a second and then snapped my eyes back to his TV. *Dad is helping? But he hates anything having to do with . . .*

Dad cleared his throat. "I'm only doing this for you. And because . . . it's Danny."

That blew my mind. Dad drove with me down to Provo in his Grand Cherokee, and we started scouring every nook and cranny, especially up Provo Canyon near where Danny lived. There were bridges, abandoned mines, and old cabins that we checked, too.

Because of the snow piling so high, we had specific instructions of how to effectively search for someone. They said, "Look under trees, near rocks, check mounds of snow." And I was all for it, scouring even old tram houses that ran along the side of the canyon.

We searched for eight hours. Being missing in that weather was more than scary; it was life-threatening. I also realized it had taken Dad *everything* he had to offer his help. I remembered him losing his shit in our garage in junior high when he destroyed his own gun after I'd been playing Russian roulette.

He still badly struggled with anything having to do with some-one taking their own life. The only reason he was putting himself through this sheer hell with me was because of Danny—because of the son that Danny had been since the time he had befriended me. Because of the even keel Danny had been able to keep me on more often than anyone else.

I started fielding more calls from Mom, then Maegen. Again, this was my Danny, *our* Danny. The Danny who practically grew up at our home, who was there more than I was, who was a helluva lot kinder and more respectful to my family than I was, who didn't lose his temper with Drew and the kids in the neighborhood like I did, and who was sort of an adopted brother or son to my family. This was Danny, my life's breath.

"Good God, Danny, where are you?" I cried out when I hung up from the last call. Because of his passion and zest for life, this didn't make any sense to me.

The next day, the weather was turning into even worse of a mess; the quiet, thick snow was building up to the point that it was impossible to see anything and dangerous to be on the roads. By this point, I was the only one from Bountiful searching, although there were a bunch of people from the local area.

The blizzard wasn't letting up, but soon I got another call: they found Danny's truck in the first parking lot up Provo Canyon, near a popular summer park and close to a bridge. They couldn't find Danny anywhere, however.

I didn't want to listen when the police called off the search. I wanted to keep looking when it became too dark and too thick to see a damn thing. I started to cry as everyone was ordered home.

Danny, where are you?

And, God, where in the hell are YOU? I thought bitterly. *Why can't you make the snow stop so Danny can be found?*

Over the next day, I was completely inconsolable. Despite the snow, there was an ongoing search with volunteers and search-and-rescue teams and rescue dogs, but I was helpless to do anything. I didn't go to work and was always ready for a call that the search was back on. Early on the morning of the tenth day after my birthday, the blizzard had let off a little and I was intending to head down to the Provo area when I got a call. Despite the weather, a search-and-rescue dog had found Danny. He was 150 feet away from where he had parked his truck.

The sheriffs said that Danny had overdosed. His official date of death was nine days after my birthday. Walking my best friend's— my soulmate's coffin to the grave, I bawled. I didn't care who saw me. I would never be able to see him again.

Shortly after that, I heard through the grapevine that Danny's family held me personally responsible for his death. I believed the bearer of the news and was completely devastated. I accepted all the blame, letting myself fall to the bottom of a deep, watery hole.

Like a coward, I didn't go talk to Danny's parents. Instead, I still asked the same questions again and again in my mind, torturing myself in the most twisted ways possible after his funeral. I hadn't even been able to get a grip on my life, and I was drinking, smoking weed, and taking pills together as much as possible to hide from the pain I could not handle.

Danny and I began doing drugs because we thought they would save us. Fast-forward five years, and they took his life.

Danny and I had been a partnership. I was the dark one, the out-of-control one, the tsunami, the whirlwind, the Tasmanian devil. Danny was my light, my positive anchor, and my reason for holding on. I didn't know how to live without him, so I figured the drugs might as well take my life, too.

CHAPTER 14

OUTWARD BOUND, INWARD BATTLE

Dad and Mom watched me with growing concern. I didn't even have the energy to fight my father like I had before. I would go to work, do what needed to be done, and head home to sleep. Only the days of sleeping ended up being more and more frequent. I still was doing drugs, but not partying. That was my own internal hell—a cycle of enough drugs to get me up, then help me sleep when my dreams were constantly haunted by Danny and everything I did not do to save him.

It's *all my fault.*

Finally, Dad came to me after dinner one night. It was probably the thirtieth night in a row I didn't speak a word to anyone. "Look, son, I want you to consider this leadership training called Outward Bound. I think it would be smart for your career. It may be a good reason to get away for a while and think while you push your physical boundaries, as you love to do. It's all about thriving through adventure and learning leadership while rock climbing in the mountains, traversing rivers, trekking through jungles . . ." He looked at me, hoping I would respond.

Mountains, rivers, jungles . . . Something started to compute.

I looked up for the first time and nodded my head. "Sure. I'll take a look at it."

The materials he handed me were brochures with young people doing all kinds of active and extraordinary things—rappelling down cliff sides, exploring thick jungles with mist and mountains with snow, and paddling canoes past beautifully forested backdrops.

I noticed there were guys and girls, so that seemed one positive side to this thing. I was still terrible in how I treated girls. It was really hard for me to know how to be with a woman without abusing her or needing her full attention to feel whole. But at least the sight of them made the days go by faster. I also knew I was drinking and drugging way too much. My anxiety kept increasing, and I was having a hard time going to work.

I definitely needed something. Since third grade, I thought that I didn't want to be alive. That was before the drugs. Now I had drugs and didn't want to be alive anymore again. I didn't even want to get up in the morning, no matter how much weed, alcohol, pills, or coke I had snuck by my concerned parental guardians. I almost missed the days when drugs originally took away those dark thoughts, but now they made me worse.

As I looked at the pamphlets, I realized this was drug and alcohol rehab disguised like leadership training. People would be facing their greatest fears, completely sober. I wouldn't be allowed to take anything to numb the pain. If I wasn't so ready to change and do some soul-searching, I would have refused. Yet something about beautiful Costa Rica seemed like the perfect place to find myself again.

I told Dad and Mom I was ready. They scheduled me for a program that included three stages.

When I flew in for my first adventure, I discovered after the group shopped for supplies that we would be spending the next seven days kayaking from island to island, bringing fresh water to the inhabitants. We had two leaders. One was Steve, a survivalist, and the other was Michel from the Navy. We could only take what we could carry as a group, which meant fifty to a hundred pounds a person.

I started to get to know the other students, who all came from something miserable—bad marriages, addicted to internet porn, addicted to drugs or alcohol or both. *Good. We're all in this together*, I thought, only we weren't.

On our first day, I realized one guy was so overweight he was huffing and puffing even without a pack. He pouted all the time and wouldn't help. So not only did I have to take his extra weight on my back, but I also had to paddle for two. Luckily there were a few other guys willing to help.

Quickly I realized that this wasn't about following a leader. In fact, as we paddled so far out we could not see land, some of the group began to panic. We had to learn to work together. It was our job to navigate because the "leaders" were not going to do it for us.

So I decided to start showing up as a leader. I had learned from my dad how important it was to be a voice of reason—to really show up when people were losing it. It was easy for me to get everyone's attention and listen initially, but I found I lost my patience whenever I didn't get my way. That was not like my dad.

Over time I learned that whenever people shut down in high stress, I actually thrived. Besides the assigned hike masters, I became the guy in charge of the attendees when we would have to make decisions or push ourselves. Physically, without the drugs and alcohol, I was detoxing and had to learn how to gauge my strength, water intake, and more. I started doing lots of pushups so I could paddle faster and maintain that leadership.

With that group, I couldn't afford to grow tired. Most of them were thirty-somethings trying to find themselves, and I was the young pup twenty-something. I may not have been exactly a street kid, coming from a wealthy family, but I was certainly street-smart. I'd also been watching my dad and his friends since I was little. People looked up to them every day. I'd had examples without realizing it.

When that first excursion was over, I was physically exhausted, but, for the first time in years, I was mentally exhilarated. Danny still haunted my dreams at night on top of every waking minute, but when the crises were high and something needed to be solved, I didn't think about taking my life. I thought about leading people to safety. That was a welcome change.

For my second excursion, we were headed to hike from beach to jungle back to beach—the longest jungle hike in the world. We would be facing twenty-seven of the most poisonous snakes in the world. People around me became fearful of what they were about to face, but I was like, *Hell yeah!*

This time, I started out as a leader—which was pretty stupid, because as the leader you had to touch every vine to make sure it wasn't a snake.

We slept in individual tents each night, listening to strange creatures prowling and growling around us, including the unnerving howler monkeys and their constant raids. Our tents consisted of about four or five inches of height for sleeping room and the rest was necessary bug netting. With mosquitos the size of your hand, you didn't want to chance any of those mothers getting into your tent and feasting on you. It didn't help that snakes and things slithered across the tents at every hour. They seemed to like the feel of the vinyl.

One day, right in the middle of the jungle, conflict in the group developed. The cool, tough Navy guy, Michel, left early in the morning to hike on ahead to set up camp. Now, however, there was a lot of arguing, and I was shocked as I saw the survivalist—our Outward Bound guide, Steve—having a breakdown. All of a sudden, his backside vanished through the growth because he up and left us! I was trying not to freak out, since we were literally relying only on a map and compass.

This guy was not mentally equipped for such a crazy-intense hike. He also took off on his tantrum with nothing on his person. We had to work as a team to get to the next camp. It was a twelve-hour trek. Fortunately, we did reach the camp that Mr. Navy had set up, and I couldn't have been more grateful for clean water and the smell of food cooking as we prepared to lay out our tents in the dark.

"Hey, where's Steve?" asked Michel.

We told him what happened, and Michel's eyes widened. We had been the blind being led by the blind. In fact, Steve didn't show up for another three days.

He should be on our side, I thought, blaming him, *the side of the students.*

Then it hit me. *Wow . . . When you're the issue, you don't see what that looks like from a different lens.*

As I settled down for bed that night, I realized how many tantrums I had thrown in my lifetime, and how I dictated the sports I was involved in with those tantrums. It had been easier for coaches to give me a position so I didn't cry about it. Now, seeing someone like Steve losing it, I realized I must've been such a whiner and an embarrassment to my family!

By morning, I decided I needed to be better. Instead of trying to control everyone with the level of my voice or bullying people into what I wanted, l started looking for more opportunities to lead. Costa Rica is called The Land of Eternal Waters. I was about to find out it was covered with many lakes and streams. The first time we came to a river, I realized I was in another predicament as the leader. Before I knew it, I had to tie a rope around my waist and the others would watch for "eyes." Why eyes? They meant crocodiles.

Fortunately, dangerous things I liked. I got so much out of each leg of the trip, and when I called home to Mom and Dad, I was happy to be able to report good things. Because of my mental health crises, I found myself finding me. Who I really was came out in the ways I helped people. That meant being on our own and learning how to work with someone I might not like—and teaching others to work with people they might not like.

One thing I realized quickly was that if I was not challenged, I was going to create a challenge. I had to learn how to let the dramas we were facing be enough of a challenge to learn how to overcome. I was soon to learn that humans didn't need a whole lot to create drama.

For my third and final excursion with Outward Bound, we were climbing the summit of Mt. Chirripó, the highest mountain in Costa Rica at 3,821 meters (12,536 feet). We hiked up for a couple days. It meant a wake-up bell at 3:00 a.m. on the final morning to make it to the summit in time. That was when the internet porn guy and a few others started having doubts . . . and having some real discussions.

I was watching all of this drama take place, shaking my head. I did not want to get involved. We did not have time to buy into anyone's fears. Still, within hours of hiking, the group became divided. I got pissed when we got stuck on a cliff face for forty minutes, trying to talk people into moving. *It's freaking cold and no one's budging!* I forced myself to stay calm, and people finally began listening to me and some other positive voices.

We all made it to the top, finally. We took photos under the Mt. Chirripó sign that showed how tall it was. We visited villages on the way down and poured concrete. That particular project helped secure some bridges that would otherwise wash out during monsoon season. The little kids swirled around me. I think my red hair and red skin had them all freaked out and insanely curious. The moment I smiled at them, they wouldn't leave me. I found I really liked all that attention.

I also realized that these poor kids had mothers who were barely surviving, and their fathers were either absent or out on hunting trips or working in the city. They didn't have a lot of caring males around them. Something shifted in my heart, and I made sure to look each of them in the eye during those interactions.

After the final cement was laid I thought we were all done, but it was brought to my attention that we had a vital ten-mile run down to a bus stop. *Time to step up again and lead out front, or it will take us too long and we'll miss the bus!*

Hopping over logs and finding the best foot positions over streams for my team, I pondered how funny it was that back in Utah, my parents were always trying to get me to do service work. I hated doing yard work for some old lady whose kids should be coming by instead. But in Costa Rica, I saw firsthand all the benefits we brought with water, then with concrete, and then with kindness and communication. All of a sudden, I loved service! I saw how it benefited an entire community.

We made the bus. Finally, our team was able to take a few days to relax. When I prepared for a long, long shower in my room, I had a huge realization: *I haven't looked in the mirror for thirty-six days!* I ignored the wild hair, sunburn, and month's growth of beard.

I thought I would be completely changed, because by the end, I was feeling so good. I felt strong. I could go home, and I figured I'd kicked this thing with drugs. I hadn't handled a single haunting dream or thought of shame when it came to Danny, but I pushed it aside in my arrogance. I was fine. I was perfect now. And I didn't need to use any substances. I would go home, clean and proud of myself.

It was time for some of us to leave while a few stayed on for another night or two. We all shook hands and high-fived, and some hugged. I stayed behind with a guy from Brooklyn and one of the girls. Unfortunately, I was too easily influenced. Despite thinking I was somehow better and I was cured, I got drunk that night and completely relapsed. I was back to craving alcohol and looking for a fix.

By the time I arrived home, I fell right back into lying to my parents. "I'm clean now," I declared, but I wasn't. All the personal growth I made on the trip was lost. I couldn't stand to be a failure, so I moved back into the constant repetition of that lie.

I did my best to get back on my feet with work, with my relationships, and with dating. In Utah, most of my extended friends had gone out on church missions at age nineteen and were coming back and getting married by twenty-one or twenty-two. I was one of the last in any of my groups and any of my schoolmates not to be married yet. I started thinking it was time.

It might be time to ask my girlfriend if she wants to get married.

The only problem? She doesn't know I am an addict.

CHAPTER 15

ONE WAY TO CURB IT

And the Boyfriend of the Year Award goes to . . .

. . . *Yeah, not me.*

One morning after I had arrived to work at our new Honda motorcycle dealership, I laid out one big, white line of coke across the front of my desk to start my day. I looked up to see my girlfriend roaring into the parking lot in her truck. *Uh oh . . . why is she not at work?*

Stacie headed straight to my office, not giving me enough time to snort the line. Instead, I carefully placed my keyboard over the cocaine, wincing at the slight crunch it made. I posed at my PC, making myself look busy. I even placed a fake surprised look on my face when Stacie rushed in.

She was a whirlwind of luscious curves and a tear-stained face.

"Stacie, what's wrong?" I asked, genuinely concerned as I took a closer look. It seemed like she hadn't slept all night, and she hadn't even been at the party with me until 4:00 a.m.

"Oh, Rob!" she cried, and threw herself into my arms. "They found my cousin. You know he's been missing for a couple days . . ."

My heart fell. I'd forgotten! "Oh, uh yeah, that's right," I said as I led her to a couple of chairs. "I'm glad he's been found. Is he okay?"

"Not at all," she cried. Through her tears I could barely make out what she was saying. "They found him in a hotel . . . doing c-c . . . cocaine!"

"No way!" I replied, trying to keep my eyes averted from my keyboard. "Cocaine? That's bizarre." Feeling like a piece of shit, I held her tighter. "Slow down. Tell me everything."

As Stacie explained the whole story, my mind wandered. *How did I get to this place? Where lying to her is easier than the truth?*

Mom and Dad got me into a new (for me) house in Bountiful on Center Street and 228 East. My sister and her husband lived across the street, but I rarely saw them. Since *everything* reminded me of Danny, I plunged myself into the only thing that seemed to save my life: escaping pain by being busy and using some sort of substance to hide from my pain.

Dad and Stacie were about the only reason I kept my alternate lifestyle on the down-low as much as possible. He had retired from the Davis school board and discovered he really loved serving the public. He decided to try his hand at politics.

I was proud of my father. As much as we argued over my choices, he was always trying to show me a better life—and I would do almost anything for him. *Almost.* He had been Governor Mike Leavitt's right-hand man for a while, and he and Mike made me the cameraman to capture Mike's Road to Victory Tour all across the state, culminating in a banquet hall with a thousand cheering supporters watching the big screen for the results of vote night. I went to take a break when two pretty girls walked in. That's how Stacie and I met.

In 1999, Dad sold his auto dealerships and stepped fully into politics. I was even more proud as I saw his integrity. He nearly self-funded his campaign so he wouldn't be beholden to any individual or corporation for his votes as he was elected to the Utah State Senate in 2000. I could tell it was a big deal to him, especially as Utah was preparing for the 2002 Winter Olympics.

The last thing my father needed in public was a loudmouth son who was always in trouble. Yet I couldn't seem to help it.

By that time, Dad could tell I needed to put my energy somewhere or soon I was going to explode . . . or implode. It seemed he thought positions and labels might fix me—that all I needed was the right opportunity to mature from entitlement to earning my way. He was the one who brought me into the endeavor with Honda motorcycles and made me feel like a partner in the dealership. In fact, he said, I *was* a partner. My brother-in-law's portion was 40%, while Dad and I represented 60%. He warned me not to take my own 30% for granted.

I couldn't think of anything cooler and was actually excited to be involved. It was paradise to ride bikes all day and check out the latest and greatest motorcycles. I was a sales manager, and despite the fact that they hired Donnie as the GM, it still felt like I ran the place.

The bike dealership was on the farthest road beyond Fifth West in Bountiful. For the past century, that area past the freeway was little more than farmers' fields with absolutely nothing out there except an old tire change shop with concrete walls. My father renovated the old shop, installing three huge glass fronts and an immaculately painted showroom on one side, with a cubicle for a secretary. Outside the showroom floor, we put the Honda bikes up front and repaired bikes in the back. It was legit!

We were now the new, happening part of town. Other businesses started blowing up the area. At twenty, I had the keys to the kingdom. Bikes were selling like crazy. It was a hot market, and with two of my own tricked-out dirt bikes, people oozed jealousy as I buzzed up and down the street or up into the hills to ride. Soon, fellow trailblazers came into the showroom to trick out their own bikes or buy the newest, hottest ones.

Since part of my job was making a big appearance at Knowles or the sand dunes, it was fun to show off the Honda bikes, brought in by trailers hooked up to these huge diesel trucks blowing smoke and causing a ruckus—just the way I liked it.

Now I spent the next half hour consoling Stacie in my office while my body was craving the line of cocaine I couldn't access. I tried to soothe her as I listened to her wail about the family turmoil and embarrassment. Her pain made me feel twisted up inside, like my rib cage was shrinking until it would crush my heart. *How can I ever tell my girlfriend about my using coke?*

Long story short, all this emotion didn't keep me from carefully dusting off the undercarriage of my keyboard the moment she left, reestablishing a solid line, and snorting it up my nose before the loud sound of her truck even made it down the street.

My world was nearly identical to life in high school. I didn't have a sport anymore, but I had gotten really good at buying people to be my friends. The dealership and my new party house made me feel popular again. My father wanted me to feel responsibility, but I gained only an even grander sense of entitlement and had more cash to spend on drugs.

People couldn't understand that substances had become my oxygen. Trying to go off of them was like being held underwater—I would do anything to get some air. Your body says you're going to *die*, and even if that means you need to go and commit seven felonies to make this happen, you need to get those drugs just to *breathe*.

If I was not high, I would become super low. Needing to use daily meant that what was once my high had become my normal. Like a lot of my buddies around me, I now had to be high to accomplish anything, like showing up to work or carrying on any conversation.

I thought about how everything was so black and white—using drugs was either considered popular and cool *or* completely unspoken and unacknowledged, even though my buddies and I were living proof it was an everyday, growing occurrence among our community's most conservative population. I couldn't talk to anyone about it. I was suicidal, and Dad saw it getting out of hand.

First, my folks tried to ship me off to Connecticut to be with my sister Maegan and "clean up my act." It didn't work. I could find more dealers there than in Utah! Dad tried to take me to the family property near St. George to sober up, but that didn't work either. Drugs remained such a taboo subject among the whole community. Our family had no clue about any professional solutions.

I became so physically sick, irritable, and paranoid, I wanted to be left alone. All too soon, I lost my girlfriend, and 2002 passed by in a drug-induced state without Stacie. I didn't feel like dating anyone for very long, and I decided any girl I dated would have to know I was a party animal.

When an offer came in from a much bigger dealer to buy the Honda motorcycle shop, my father, brother-in-law, and I all agreed it was for the best. *But now what am I going to do?* I always got scared if there wasn't some sort of a conduit for my high energy. It was still there, buzzing around in my head, moment to moment. I needed something to focus on.

The new owner of the bike shop said he didn't want any bikes with miles, so my father thought about it and said he'd let me sell the used ones. With an inventory of forty bikes, he figured it would take quite a while to sell them. To everyone's surprise except mine, they were gone in two weeks.

Since I sold all the bikes myself, I considered the cash all my profit. With a big smile of satisfaction on my face, I settled in for a long night at a local bar where everyone knew me. Of course, I came armed to the teeth with some celebratory coke already up my nose and more in my pocket for later. I started to get hammered while talking to a friend, a local landscaper.

"You're unemployed now?" he asked me during our first shots of Wild Turkey. "Come work for us—you'll love the money and the hours."

Well, there was the problem: I didn't believe I should be an *employee*. I thought I deserved to be an *owner*.

As long as I was on coke, I could drink everyone else under the table . . . until the coke wore off. Then, too often I would go into a blackout state where I didn't remember anything. That night while talking to the landscaper, I made a radical decision. When I woke up from my celebration two days later, there was a bunch of landscape machinery in front of my house—a big construction trailer equipped with a concrete mixer and sandbox.

What the hell?

I called the guy to discover my blunder, hoping it was a moment like on *America's Funniest Home Videos* where someone does a blooper and it gets captured on film but at the end of the day, everyone walks away happy.

"Yeah, no, Rob, you bought a curbing company. The ink's been dry for two days. It's all yours. You came here to the dealership and bought a brand new curbing trailer and machine. You signed all the paperwork and called it Big Red's."

My mouth dropped open. I didn't know what to say for a whole minute. *I drove up in a blackout state and bought a whole company?* "Listen," I replied pleadingly, "I'm sure it sounded awesome on twelve shots of Wild Turkey, but it was all a mistake."

"Sorry, dude," he said firmly. "The check has already cleared the bank. It's a done deal."

That started my tenure in the concrete biz. Now I had to figure out exactly what that meant and how to do it! It started out utter chaos and mayhem. I hired a couple of friends, guys with even less of a clue what we were doing. Being a fairly proficient salesman, I got our first job and celebrated. But then I had to pay a guy to come complete our first job—because when we tried it, it was a mess.

Back to the drawing board. Over the next several days, we proceeded to practice how to mix cement properly and how to lay the curbing professionally. Both had to be done well.

Fortunately, I caught on fast and we got pretty damn good. We started getting jobs all over town and in other cities. That was a relief, because my finances had been drained with the purchase. I built my account back up to a safe level where I wasn't nearing bankruptcy at each moment, and I realized I could manage this beast.

Still, what I would quickly discover was how big a problem that was for a druggie who could easily pull in $3,500 by noon. My guys and I loved staying up all night partying, then working for only a half day, going home to sleep, then waking up at night to start partying all over again. It perfectly supported my lifestyle.

By that time, I was introduced to Oxycontin. My problem was not that I would find a substance I liked and then replace it with something else; the problem was that I would only add it to my already full arsenal. Oxy seemed great, and just like I did inventory on cement and labor, I purchased exactly what we needed for jobs and what I needed inside my body to complete a job.

Then I met a girl at a party, and I thought all my dreams had come true. Tasha was a brunette so beautiful she took my breath away. We started flirting with each other, and I felt I could be fully myself with her. That meant the world.

Just in case, I was sure to pull out some coke and do a few lines in front of her the first few times we dated. If she couldn't accept me, she couldn't have me. It still didn't stop the trembling inside when I looked up, not knowing if I would see approval or repulsion. Tasha didn't reject me. I felt like I could breathe again, and after that, we were inseparable.

Still, I didn't want her to know how bad I was. While I'd openly do drugs in front of her, I never let on to *how much* I was doing. I let disappearing to the bathroom or making a "business call" be part of our relationship. That worked . . . for a while.

I fell head over heels for Tasha. She was wild, with as adventurous a spirit as I had. I loved the fact that she was as into me as I was into her. I loved that she was outdoorsy and I didn't have to baby her in the woods. Through the years I'd found there was nothing worse than going camping and partying with a girl who said, "I have to go to the bathroom in a *bathroom*," and made you drive down the canyon.

Tasha was right at home in any environment, and she was my cheerleader. She built me up. If someone said anything derogatory to me, she was the first to shut them down. And while Tasha was not religious, she had a moral compass. It was pretty weird for me to know a righteous non-Mormon person! Not only was she spunky and feisty, but Tasha could hold herself together. She wouldn't put up with my shit when I was drinking, and she could hold her own. The girl was never in my shadow because she had her own light.

Tasha's parents also drank, so it was okay for me to do so in their presence—though I kept it to a minimum out of respect. There was something special about her folks. I didn't take for granted that they liked me, too. I wanted to keep it that way. I had to watch the amount I drank. It was a constant and dangerous game, the mix of chemicals in my system . . . I wasn't going to hurt this woman. She already meant too much to me. That's why I never, ever offered her drugs.

Too bad I didn't stop hurting me.

One weekend, Tasha, my friends, and my brother Drew were up at Snowbird. After a day of skiing, we partied hard. I went upstairs to use the bathroom and sneak some drugs where Tasha couldn't see. As I was about to come down the stairs, I could see everyone below in the open floor plan. Tasha had her back to me.

Wouldn't it be funny if I flew down and scared her like Superman? I wasn't stupid enough to think I could fly. I thought I could easily hang myself from the wrought iron railing on the top floor and lightly plop down beside her—the awesome athlete that I was. If I thought I was Superman in certain moments of delusion, she was my kryptonite.

Carefully I climbed over the other side of the railing, holding on tight inside the wrought iron until I was ready to make the jump eight or ten feet down on the floor. Only my foot slipped with my arm still inside the rail. My entire body plummeted, but the wrought iron caught on the muscle of my forearm. Had it not been right on the muscle, I would have broken my arm or possibly lost it, but in the meantime, I was in deep trouble.

I didn't remember my anguished yelling for help, how Drew disentangled me, or the flight down the ski canyon to the hospital. Somehow, my friends realized when they saw my quickly swelling arm that I might lose it if they didn't play the part of first responders. There was no time for the ambulance. All I clearly remembered was wishing someone would knock me out from the pain. I hated seeing the horrified look on a stranger's face as he saw Drew and Tasha rush me into the emergency room.

Fortunately for me, that stranger was a surgeon who recognized severe trauma—and that I had mere minutes to release the pressure or I would experience either permanent damage or death.

I woke from surgery hours later in a hospital bed, feeling like crap and my arm bandaged to the hilt with some kind of super-tight compression.

I have to get my shit together. It wasn't enough not to hurt Tasha. *Hurting me hurts her.* Somehow I had to stop doing drugs.

CHAPTER 16

MY FAIRY PRINCESS . . . AND I? THE TOAD

I was head over heels for Tasha, and fortunately, she was equally obsessed with me. Even though her father was a fire chief (which sat a little too close to law enforcement in my book), I really respected the man. I decided I would ask her dad for her hand.

Happily. Ever. After.

If she will have me, that is. I will have to make the offer something kick-ass, something she can't refuse.

Years prior, I'd met a senator who owned a hot air balloon down in the Provo area. I had an amazing idea. What if I took her on a date and asked her to marry me up in the clouds? My head was already there anyway . . . why not the rest of me? Why not her with me?

On an early summer morning, Tasha's eyes grew wide at the sight of the hot air balloon, with red and white stripes and a navy-blue star at the top. It wasn't just patriotic—it was stunning. As we climbed into the basket, the senator winked at me with a "Well done!" sort of look in his eye. I couldn't feel any finer, and Tasha, shocked and pleased with the surprise date, still had no idea of what was to come.

Tasha's family and my family were all in on it and ready to celebrate the moment we landed. I was super nervous, the diamond ring hot in my pocket. I was making enough money at Big Red's to pop for a nice one, although I had to pull back a little on the afternoon high for a few days. It was time I got my life and my act together. *Marriage is serious stuff.*

Up in the hot air balloon, I was holding Tasha's hand, looking out on the amazing landscape below—but I wasn't seeing any of it. My heart was pounding like the herd of horses thundering below us. Behind my hard shell and mental health issues, I was a romantic. I was smitten by this girl. *What if she says no?*

Suddenly the walkie-talkie at my hip went off, with some weird metallic sounds and clicks. Then I heard a voice as plain as day though filled with static:

"Rob . . .? Did she say yes?!"

You have got to be kidding me. Mom, way to ruin the surprise! My face turned the reddest it had probably ever been—and that's saying something. Tasha looked at me sharply, then started to grin.

"What am I supposed to say yes to, Rob?"

I fumbled around in my pocket, my hands trembling in my search for the ring. Then I tried to get down on one knee in the swaying basket of the balloon. "Tasha," I asked, my voice shaking the same as my hands and my heart, "will you marry me?"

My girl looked at me for a long moment, as if she wasn't sure. I had taken her to the opposite side of the hot air balloon basket for a little privacy, but there really was none. I gulped. "Listen," I added quietly, my eyes pleading, "I promise to cut way back on the drinking and stop the . . . the other. I'll clean up for you, babe. I want this . . . I want *you.*"

At that promise, suddenly Tasha threw her arms around my neck and kissed me passionately.

"Rob?" I heard my mother's voice again over the static of the walkie-talkie. "Did she say yes?"

Tasha and I burst out laughing. "Roger," I called back, and I could only hear cheers on the other side

Soon the balloon ride was over, and we landed on a street near the senator's home. The whole family came to congratulate us. It was beautiful, and I loved the joyful tears in my fiancée's eyes.

Plans were made, and details began to quickly unfurl. So quickly, in fact, that before I knew it, it was time to leave for our honeymoon at a gorgeous resort in the Bahamas. Before our wedding, I'd told Tasha that I stopped doing drugs. I didn't tell her the truth.

We checked into our Sandals Resort, and my hot, gorgeous wife was ready for sunshine, water, romance, and relaxation, dressed in a killer bikini and sunglasses. She was sporting a margarita and a great big smile just for me. I, on the other hand, had already started swigging from a large bottle in the hotel room, ready to scout out dealers on the beach. Once alcohol touched my lips, the craving for cocaine was so strong I couldn't sit still—and certainly not in a lounge chair. My eyes scoured the coastline until BAM, somebody popped.

You can always tell the dealers: all done up like it's Sunday, no matter how impoverished the local population. I spotted this one a mile away, with his brand-new hat, fresh tee, and sneaks, gold chains dangling, ripping it up on jet skis and hanging out with the girls.

"Honey?" I turned to Tasha, trying not to look too distracted as she lounged near the pool. "Look, I've got to run to our room. I'll be back in a few minutes."

I didn't go to the room. I didn't come right back.

When I did return, I was so drunk and so high. Even then, I could tell Tasha was pissed. I really tried; I just didn't know how to change. I also wanted to be honest, but if being honest meant losing her, I couldn't do it. I needed her almost as much as I needed substances. Just not more.

As soon as Tasha and I returned to the States, she moved in with me. Once we shared life together, however, I couldn't hide my drug use. Everyone who worked at my curbing business partied. We continued to work mornings and get high and drunk every afternoon into the evening. By the time I made it home to Tasha, I passed out, either on the couch or floor.

As the year progressed, every night after work, I was drinking 100-proof vodka, but that wasn't all. I had to be an extremist in everything. If your line of cocaine was two inches, mine was six. The amount of alcohol and drugs that would last most people a whole weekend lasted me only thirty minutes.

There was always a lot of love between Tasha and me, but soon there started to be a lot of screaming and yelling, too. To my shame, I engaged in verbal abuse, and then, less than one year into our marriage, tragedy struck. Late on a beautiful spring night, it turned ugly in a flash—what happened when you got in between Rob the addict and his dope.

"Robby, I *need* you to stop drinking. You're like the nicest guy when you're sober, but the moment that stuff passes your lips, you turn into someone else—someone I don't recognize."

"That's b-bullshit," I slurred.

"No, it's true. Look at you! Fighting with me every time I turn around. No matter how many times you 'quit,' you take one sip of alcohol and the drugs reclaim you!"

"No, they don't!" I protested, my face hot. "I have this under control." I started to stagger away from her, then began to jog more quickly.

Tasha stalked after me, refusing to back down. "Robby, they're making you dark—they're sucking away your soul!"

I said something horrible to her and stumbled down the hall to go into the kitchen to get away from the truth of her words, like lashes from a whip.

Tasha wouldn't accept me running away from the conversation again. In irritation, I reached back to swat her away like a fly, and her face hit the thermostat box. I heard her scream, and I turned around, then froze. Tasha's face was split open near her eyebrow. Everything got real. She was bleeding everywhere, and I could tell right away it was bad enough to need stitches.

Oh my God. What have I done?

We raced to Lakeview Hospital and then into the emergency room. Tasha held a kitchen towel up to her still-bleeding and rapidly swelling eye. Sure, we had our stories straight by the time we got to the hospital, but every gaze attuned to us knew the truth: this was domestic violence. To top it off, I was actually wearing a freaking wifebeater tank top.

I hated that I was the epitome of the drunk, raging husband. Thank God all the medical staff were great to Tasha, but their lack of compassion toward me hit at my heart. I deserved every cold look. Worse, my wife was now standing up for me with our "story." She was protecting me when that was *my* only job to do for her. I'd failed her.

We made it home around three in the morning. Tasha looked like hell, and we had Mother's Day brunch scheduled up in the canyon with her mom, dad, and siblings. *What were we going to say?* We tried to get a few hours of sleep, but she was miserable, and my mind raced with raging excuses and internal lashings.

Sitting down at a beautiful Mother's Day table a few hours later, the natural scene and setting was lost on everyone. The sun was out, so our sunglasses were on to hide my bloodshot eyes and her swollen wound, but it couldn't hide her stitched and bandaged face. The energy on the patio turned cold. Accusing looks were cast across the table. I was a piece of shit. I knew it. I was everything I promised my mother I would *never* be. Plus, I had let Tasha down and this family down—the ones I loved and respected. Everyone at that table hated me at that moment, but no one more than myself.

Even after that fateful morning, Tasha continued to try. She changed our schedule, engaged in more loving conversations, made us get out to do more things instead of "working" so much or partying too much. In time, however, the shame and pain became more than she could handle, and despite her efforts, I was not changing. The Mother's Day moment had passed, and I slipped back into denial about my problems. It was always someone else's fault. At her wits' end, Tasha tried to reason with me before I hit a party one night.

"Rob, we've got to talk." She led me onto our back porch where we often held parties and barbecues. "Look, something has to change. You spend more time at the 'shop' than you do at home. It's been nine months, and you don't want help to get clean." I was staring out at the yard, but she turned my face to hers. "Do you know, I finally went to your mom for help?"

"No way," I said, surprised.

"Yeah. Wanna know what she said? She said, 'You married him; you're on your own now.' I couldn't believe it. Everyone's giving up on you, Robby—but the worst is, you're giving up on yourself. You don't even care about getting clean."

"Baby," I said dismissively, shaking my head, "don't overreact. I'm bringing in the money, and yes, it's hard work so I have to be away a lot, especially in the summer, and then doing sales during the winter, but you work, too—you know how it is," I said, my voice a little higher and more tender as I looked into her eyes like I really meant it. "Plus, my mom never *really* gives up on me. She just says she does. Then she helps us out whenever we need her."

Tasha turned away, and this time it was me who pulled her chin so I could kiss her. "No one is giving up on anyone. I'm not giving up on you . . ." I said, as if this was all somehow her fault and not mine. "We've got this. We have to stick together. Be loyal. Believe in each other."

"Rob!" she cried, stepping back, "don't you get it? You're driving me around drunk! You're putting me in dangerous situations. You take me to a party and then leave me there to fend for myself. Not fun! I have to find my own ride home. As if that's not dangerous enough—and let me tell you, it is for a girl—then you take me to 'check in on a friend,' and I find out it's a drug drop—a drug dealer's house with guns! Even after that, you invite the shadiest people over to our home—my home, my sanctuary—and they rob us!"

Everything she was saying was true. What could I say? The same thing I always did when I was sober and looking for my next fix. "It's going to be okay, baby."

Only it wasn't.

Pain seared me like a hot iron on my flesh when Tasha told me she filed for divorce. I didn't know it was a last-ditch attempt to change me. Instead, I allowed all of my self-hatred and loathing to be projected onto her. I was enraged that the woman of my dreams would give up on me. I walked away from the conversation. I couldn't look at her—the woman I adored so much, the one I loved because she loved me for me. She was moving out of my life. She couldn't accept me anymore. That was my only focus.

When Tasha's family came to pick up her belongings on a Saturday morning not long after her filing, I was nowhere to be seen. For Tasha that was tragic. She admitted later that if I would have just *shown up*, she would have dropped the divorce and stayed with me. Instead, I focused on her abandonment and betrayal, and like a coward I shied away. Her father had already called me out, furiously letting me know he would ruin me for what I'd done to Tasha.

Deep inside, I also knew if I fought for her to stay, the cycle would continue. I didn't want to admit it to anyone, but I was a slave to substances. I couldn't go for more than a waking hour or two without them.

After the divorce, I couldn't stand all the memories in my own house—they haunted me. Tasha was everywhere, from the decorations to the gardens to the bedroom. Every room was a signal of my failure and my drug use. Dad could tell I needed a new beginning, plus I wasn't paying all my bills. Despite Big Red's income, I was relying on him to pay utilities and other things.

My father was a master at suggestive questioning. He had another bright idea—to sell the house and have me move back home so I could go into rehab. I was happy to have some easy money at my fingertips, and not having a house payment meant I'd have more money for drugs—of course, just until I was ready to turn myself in to rehab. I'd been hearing stories that rehab was actually helping some people. I didn't know if I could do it, but I needed to do something. I was losing my whole world. The thought of withdrawals had me running scared, and I felt shattered already with the loss of Tasha.

I packed up my house, getting rid of anything too filled with memories. Tasha came by with my niece to bring me something to eat as I packed. It was hard to see her, but I shared some pizza with the two girls and finally brushed off my hands. "That's it," I said brusquely. "Thanks for feeding me." I gave her a brief but warm smile, not letting my heart go back into it. "Let's go."

She nodded, and they went out to Tasha's car as I carried out the last of my belongings to my truck. Just then, I got a call from a close friend I'd known for a while. He was my dealer.

"Hey, you got any oxys?" he asked, his voice a bit high-pitched.

"No," I told him firmly as I was taking one last look at the empty house, ready to hang up. "I'm moving. I got nothing." My friend, however, didn't want to take no for an answer.

"Stay there," he said. "I'm coming by."

Only it wasn't my friend. Two unmarked cars with four police officers pulled up, in full SWAT gear, with FBI vests and rifles pointed at my chest. The guy's call was a setup. They thought I was one of Utah's big Oxycontin rings' big fishes—a local kingpin. I clearly wasn't, but I didn't give them any hassle. I'd learned that lesson long ago, and I never messed with another officer.

"Sure, you can search my stuff, no problem," I said, hands up. I may have been a little cocky because, since I was moving, I had been sure to clean up everything. I wasn't taking anything dangerous into my parents' house. They pulled me inside the house, despite the fact that I hadn't granted permission. One officer kept his gun trained on me while the others went from empty room to empty room.

"Where are the drugs?" asked the head investigator gruffly. He was clearly frustrated. "I don't see where you are keeping the oxys."

"Well, I *do* oxys," I admitted honestly, "but I don't sell."

The officers' faces fell. Here they thought they were coming into some massive bust. I didn't tell them that oxys had become far too expensive for me. Like a lot of druggies, I had turned to heroin because the same dollars went a whole lot further. Still, I knew there were no last pills, no needles, no baggies for them to nab inside the house. I was leaving it clean as a whistle to sell.

"Can I go now?" I asked. Tasha and my niece had only driven a couple of houses away and pulled over when this all went down. They were still in her car, watching everything with wide eyes. The investigator looked out the window, too, spotting my truck packed to the hilt. "Can we search your truck?"

"Sure. Do whatever."

The only problem was that as clean as I left my house, I hadn't thought of my truck. After unpacking my entire truck and searching diligently, they found one suboxone in an unmarked pill bottle. It was enough to book me. And... I had a gun. That part frustrated me beyond reason when they confronted me.

"Of course, I brought my gun! Yes, it is mine; I am obviously moving today. If you were moving, wouldn't you take your gun? You wouldn't leave it in the house for realtors or the new buyers with kids!"

It didn't matter. They had gotten enough. One pill and one gun. They had "caught" me. My niece and former spouse watched as I was cuffed and taken away from my own house and my own truck. When we drove away, I saw their faces, stricken and shocked.

The officers booked me into the Davis County Jail. Suddenly, I felt like Little Bo Peep going into Fox Supermax. It was a twenty-three-hour lockdown, and I was looking like Opie with these guys around me who were real gangbangers. I had to share a cell with a Southsider Latino. He got caught with several pounds of meth and he was currently high and bouncing off the walls of our tiny cell. Worse for me was that whole time, I was withdrawing. I was scared and pounding on the door. I had diarrhea and I started throwing up.

I kept pushing the button to alert the guards, to get help. "Look man, I need toilet paper!"

"Yeah, we'll see about that."

I didn't get any until two days later.

That weekend was the most shaming, lowest point of embarrassment for me, ever. In the meantime, I didn't dare go out into the general population. I was too big of a target, yet being a caged animal did not match my soul. I called and pleaded to my dad to get me out. In the past, before the ink was dry on my fingers, my folks always got me out of these situations. That time, I had to wait because of my gun, despite it being a first offense.

Finally on the third day of severe illness, someone said, "Man, you look like shit. Why don't you get put into medical? Beds are more comfortable there." I went, thinking I would have a nurse, some Sprite, and some crackers. It sounded soothing. Only I quickly discovered it wasn't. The medical wing meant 24/7 lockdown, where no one comes to see you. They just smile and walk by and ignore you. If it was possible, the medical unit was far, far worse.

I made another call. That time, my parents agreed to come get me from court. There I was, shackled at the wrists and ankles, the Senator's son. I hoped the judge would be easy on me for a first-time offense. I watched my parents, their embarrassment still ringing in my ears. I thought that for them, this was something they watched on TV, with the cops arresting somebody . . . only this time it was me.

I had become *that* guy.

CHAPTER 17

THE WAKEUP CALL AND THE WIPEOUT

It was far too easy to lie to myself. I kept saying rehab was around the corner, and then it was simply . . . around another corner . . . a *little* further down the road. I avoided any thought of interruption to my partying, but what I was really avoiding was pain. The thought of painful withdrawals. The thought of facing my demons. The thought of not being able to breathe. I had to push confronting those fears down further and further, although I knew I was spiraling.

In the meantime, my arrest was not enough to dissuade me from my normal routine. Once I was out, my buddies and I at Big Red's continued our schedule of working hard in the mornings throughout the valley, getting paid, sleeping the afternoons away, then getting up and getting high and staying out all night before showing up for the next job.

Dad was proud of me that I had started and was running my own business and crews. He loved to talk to me about anything that wasn't bad, where I wasn't in trouble, and he loved talking business. He had great ideas, and I listened and shared some things with him, but never, ever did I divulge how Big Red's was born!

Crazily enough, Tasha was still seeing me because I kept promising I'd go to rehab soon. Really, I would.

Only a few weeks after my arrest, some shocking news rever-
berated through our company and our crowd of friends. One of our
partying buddies who used to work with us but had moved on from
Big Red's had overdosed.

He was gone.

In the face of that news, denial and excuses could only go so far.
Now I couldn't breathe. This was real. It felt too much like Danny.
I walked off the site and wanted to hit something. I wanted to cry
but I'd never do that in front of the guys. I wanted to scream and
yell. I wanted to tear my body and its addictions apart. I wanted a
new beginning, but I had no idea how to do it.

The guys and I could hardly talk for the next day or so while
sober, but it didn't keep us from getting high. I was not prepared to
go to the funeral. I knew I had to honor this friend of mine. I kept
having flashbacks of Danny's funeral. Back then, someone had said,
"Danny's parents think it's all your fault." I never talked with them
after that day and carried that guilt inside of me like a fifty-pound
dumbbell in the pit of my stomach.

Walking into the funeral was one of the hardest things I'd ever experienced, and the reverberations of drugs and untimely death swirled
around in one big, giant mess of emotions. Seeing everyone grieving
the loss of a vibrant young man, I nearly toppled. Many of my buddies
were there, but we'd been losing too many . . . we were falling like flies.

I'd come with a safe friend, which meant a druggie friend. We'd
had to do drugs to handle the funeral for a short time. I did a little
more in the bathroom to be able to talk to people afterward. When
we left, my buddy and I had to do some more to survive the emotions overwhelming us and not fall completely apart as we finally
let go and sobbed.

Only one good thing came from all of that. A single, rational thought became locked and loaded in my brain: "Dude," I said out loud, "if we don't get help, we're going to die. I'm going to die." I couldn't shake that ominous knowing.

Finally, on the way back to Big Red's from the funeral, I started looking up rehabs. By the time we had arrived at the shop, I'd made one phone call. We got out of the car, and I looked at my friend. "That's it," I said, "I'm going into rehab, two days from today."

My friend expressed the fact that he wasn't ready. I understood. Now I had to make sure I had enough dope to last. My brain was already calculating how many times I would need to get high over the next two days before turning myself over. I went into the bathroom at the office, checked my supply, and threw a whole bunch down the toilet, flushing it and watching it go down. Then, as the addict I was, I decided to shoot up some heroin one more time before going home to my parents' house.

The last thing I remembered was walking out of the shop's bathroom. My body started to seize, and I watched my friend's eyes grow wild as I lost consciousness and reeled back. For my buddy, the nightmare had just begun. He had to witness me fall back and hit my head on the cement floor. Blood was gushing from my ears, nose, and mouth. When he checked to see if I was breathing, I wasn't. All the color had drained out of my body, and I had no pulse either. It must have been terrifying, because he ran away, scared as hell. Then he thought better of it and called 9-1-1. If he hadn't, I would have been dead.

I didn't remember the paramedics, or the stretcher or the ambulance ride. I was oblivious to the fact that I flatlined several times in the ambulance ride alone. I was clinically dead and brought back to life four times already. Suddenly, I woke up in the emergency room at Lakeview Hospital in Bountiful.

I was so groggy, although my heartbeat was erratic and there were the sounds of machines all around me. I became aware that there was a paramedic and a cop standing close by.

"Where are my parents?" I asked. Immediately from behind the curtain, my parents rushed in, holding hands.

"You're awake!" Mom cried, and bent over me, my dad at her side. "We thought we were losing you."

"Just a minute," I squeaked, and then asked the paramedics and the cops to leave. They ducked behind the curtain, but I knew they were close by and still within hearing. With all the strength I could muster, which wasn't much, I fished down under my hospital gown into my underwear briefs. My parents looked away, thinking I was adjusting myself. I had other ideas, however. I kept fishing until I could grasp it: the stash of heroin I knew I had carefully hidden in the little pocket in the front of my boxer briefs, between the flaps. It was still there. No one had found it.

Pulling it out, I quickly pressed the baggie into my father's hands, locking eyes with him in his astonishment as I demanded with my gaze that he not breathe a word. Then I passed out.

I found out later that my brain was hemorrhaging. When I over-dosed coming out of the bathroom, my head had hit the unforgiv-ing cement floor. The bleeding was too profuse; they were losing me again, and they rushed me from the Lakeview facility up to University of Utah Hospital. There they induced a coma to slow the trauma and help me heal. I was in that coma for ten full days. When I finally awoke, my mother and my sister Danielle were there.

"Please," I croaked, my voice hoarse from the tubing and the long sleep. "Call Tasha to come see me." While I waited, I remembered in horror pushing drugs into my father's hands to hide. *What the hell was I thinking?* But I knew it was because I would face felony charges if I was found in possession again. I'd been operating on blind instinct for self-preservation. I still was.

Tasha arrived quickly, and I found a lot of comfort in her presence. She told me that my friend had called her after he dialed 9-1-1, and she had made it to my office in time to see the ambulance take me away.

I was embarrassed. It was the second time the woman I loved saw me in a compromising position. I knew she still loved me, and I loved her. The biggest problem at the moment, however, was that I was still withdrawing from street drugs, and, especially since my head was still throbbing, my body craved more drugs to make it all stop.

"Please," I begged her, "go get Jeff, and bring him back with you. I need to see him."

Naively, Tasha agreed. She picked him up and brought him back.

As soon as I saw Jeff, I relaxed a little. I knew it was going to be okay. As I had requested in code on my cell phone, he brought heroin-laced nose drops in an allergy nose spray bottle. The moment he held out his hand, I grabbed the bottle, popped off the lid, and took a big sniff up my nose. Just as it hit and I knew everything was going to be okay, my eyes started to roll back in my head as BEEP! BEEP! BEEP! All of the buzzers and lights went off.

I looked up for the briefest second to see Tasha being ushered from the room as "Code Red" was called over the speaker. My "friend" Jeff had already bailed. He was gone, and I was out. That medically induced coma was also supposed to help me detox. The hospital staff had hoped, I'm sure, that I would come to my bloody senses.

When I woke up next, I felt all of the judgment and anger from hospital staff, nurses, and family. Tasha was nowhere to be seen. I knew why. I had betrayed her again and overdosed on heroin right in front of her. I had made her an accomplice to my nearly dying again. That had to be traumatic. I was such an ass. At the same time, I felt so sick. My head trauma was healing, but my withdrawals had me climbing the walls.

Still, something was needling at me even in the midst of this physical pain and turmoil. Something miraculous had happened to me while I was in that coma. It was weird, and I couldn't tell anyone about it. I was still processing it.

Seven days later, when it was time to check out, I called my friend Natalie to come take me home. On the way, she took me to my drug dealer's place. It didn't matter that I had flatlined four times. It didn't matter that I had just attended a funeral of a friend who died from this same damn stuff. It didn't matter that my business was having major struggles without me and needed me to step up. All that mattered was that needle, which I immediately stuck in my arm. I sighed. I could breathe again.

At home, it was readily apparent that I couldn't stay. I was still in withdrawal. I was still pacing up and down except for a few moments after I shot up. With the help of my parents, I checked into the rehab I had committed to before my overdose. I was ready, wasn't I? To be able to handle my jittery nerves, I took a suboxone on the way and smuggled a Xanax into rehab. Robby was still driving the bus! Unfortunately, by the second night, their meds reacted with mine.

Everything was made worse by the fact that I was now only 135 pounds—a shell of my former self, with at least thirty pounds of muscle lost in my addiction history. The moment my withdrawal symptoms of sweating, diarrhea, and vomiting showed up again, it was so bad that staff made the decision to rush me to UNI, University of Utah Neuropsychiatric Institute, for another six days to detox before I would be allowed back.

The staff at UNI lessened the pain and reassured me that I wasn't going to die from my horrific withdrawals. Even then, when I was allowed back to rehab, their demands were that I could not stop anywhere on the way—not home, not a bathroom, not a gas station, not anywhere before I arrived. They knew my number.

"Rob Eastman, knowing your past history, we will be picking you up from detox to bring you straight back here. You will not pass go, you will not collect $200, and you will not talk to anyone or bring any single thing back with you. *Do you understand?*"

I could only nod as they took me away . . . and now I was coming back.

CHAPTER 18

HOLLYWOOD'S REHAB

I didn't like how I was feeling—incredibly shaky and vulnerable—as we drove through the gates of the luxury rehab center and I walked in. This time as I prepared to actually attend the thirty-day program, I was mostly present. For the first time, I noticed my surroundings and was blown away.

This place is like a spa! A Hollywood spa, I would find out, because it was full of actors, musicians, and soap opera stars. There was a five-star chef in residence to take care of any diet, and massive, beautiful classrooms. In addition to the full-size basketball court was a music studio and a ropes course and even a helicopter to take you up into the mountains.

Their recovery model included an individualized treatment plan for me, combining AA's 12 Step Program with brain and behavioral therapy. I would also attend group therapy and even experiential therapies like working with horses and massage. That didn't sound half bad!

A guy could get used to this...

I took in the views out the back of the facility, where many bedrooms looked out on the beautiful Cascade Mountains, and realized I was the poorest kid in this facility by far. A very famous actress with red hair known for her addiction issues was in attendance at the same time I was. And, a very popular rock 'n' roll band even made a showing during my first couple of weeks.

To my shock and amazement, Three Days Grace pulled up in a massive, million-dollar bus. As I sat and listened to their private show for us, I learned some pretty cool things from the lead singer's own rehab experience—especially the principle of giving back, like they were doing at this private concert. That resonated with me.

Someday I will do that. I will give back.

But I had to first conquer a full thirty days, as pampered as I was. It was my first experience in a time-controlled environment. I wasn't locked in, but this was still rehab. I got into counseling and groups, where I started working the 12 Steps.

The First Step was easy: "We admitted we were powerless over drugs and alcohol." As I openly shared with others who were sharing with me, I couldn't help but think about the recent crap that had happened—another buddy dying, my overdose and seizure, my second stupid overdose in the hospital. "Hell yeah, I am powerless over substances," I admitted.

Even now, in this gorgeous place where I could get a massage and start working out in order to manage my raw, nervous energy, I was desperately trying to curb my anxiety, depression, and raging ADHD without substances for the first time in well over a decade. I wanted to fully commit to being there, but I was still obsessed with the idea of somehow sneaking in something so I could enjoy the rest of rehab instead of being so freaking nervous and uptight each moment. Fortunately, I hung in, "one day at a time." Except for me it was often one minute at a time.

Then I started working on Step Two: "Came to believe that a Power greater than ourselves could restore us to sanity."

Damn.

Well, I knew there was a higher Power. All I had to do was look around and see gorgeous mountains above us and the deep blue sky to know that. But I was not happy with this Power. God had been shoved down my throat since I was little, usually by people who were trying to tame me or punish me, but I felt they had lied to me. Between the Holy Ghost choosing not to partner up with me after my baptism to this god who let Danny die, I didn't know how to relate to Him or Her or It.

I felt abandoned. I felt forgotten. I hated religion. I hated God. I was so angry, I even often mocked God.

At the center there was a Native American guy with a tipi. I asked him a lot of questions. He created what he called "sacred ceremonies" and all I could say was it was vastly different from anything I had ever experienced—certainly opposite my conservative, religious upbringing. Little by little I came to realize I may not have all the answers—and religion and spirituality might not be all bad . . . maybe. The struggle was still too real.

One day I expressed all of this to the folks in my group. I saw nods, and I knew some of them were decidedly more stubborn about God even than me. Some of them had horrific stories of abuse and times their god had not been there for them. Many of them, however, had some strong feelings about the existence of God. As I looked around, I realized we were all trying to figure out how He, She, or It could restore us to sanity.

I had to start simple. For me, it started with *wanting* to trust. A little at a time, I began letting down my walls to the group, and having deeper conversations. There was something building up from inside of me that felt ready to burst. I needed to share what had happened while in my coma at the hospital, but I hesitated. I didn't even know how to bring it up.

A few days later in group when people were being particularly vulnerable, I summoned my courage. Clearing my throat, I began, "I have something to share with you that I'm still processing. As you know, I flatlined a number of times on my way to the first hospital when I OD'd. Before I woke up, something weird happened . . . but it was kinda cool, too. I don't know how to explain it."

"Go on," said a guy across from me, and the rest nodded. I looked down at the floor.

"All I know is that something happened to me in the hospital. When I was in a coma, I dreamt or saw somehow . . . I was on that hospital gurney, but my friend Danny was there. If you remember, he was my best friend from childhood who took his life eight years ago, but he was *right there.* Danny was standing there, next to me—right off to my right shoulder." I gestured so they could see how close.

Now I glanced up at the group to see fascination on everyone's faces, so I kept going.

"Well, two other people were standing behind Danny, and I could see all three of them clearly. I didn't know who the other two were. Danny looked so happy to see me! He was talking to me, trying to say something, but although he was close, he sounded so far away that I couldn't hear him. I got frustrated because I wanted to know what he was saying. When I beckoned, he came closer so I could hear him.

"Then, as he was bending near me," I continued, "Danny's head turned toward my feet. I tried to see what he was looking at. I turned my head away from him, you know, to look at my feet, and

BAM!" I smacked my hand inside my fist to show how sudden and almost violent it felt to me in the dream. "Right then my feet hit a *door* of all things—and I woke up in the ICU."

They all stared at me, stunned.

"I know," I confirmed, looking at all their wide eyes. "I don't know what to do with that."

"Did you know the other two people behind your friend?"

"Naw," I said. "Not at all. I figured they were maybe his relatives? Angels?" I shrugged. "I don't know but they were all dressed in white." I wasn't into any of that and it still puzzled me.

For the next several days, I thought long and hard about that dream. I didn't know what it meant, except that I felt strongly I was *supposed* to come back. I was supposed to live. I didn't know why. So, although I didn't trust God any more than I did when I entered the gates of rehab, I started making progress. I had structure and no drugs. For the first time in my life I could share openly. For the first time, I shared about the bullying that happened to me as a kid, the hiding from the pain, the feeling like a dumbass with the dunce cap on for all my life . . . and to my amazement at the center the therapists and staff had *solutions*! I didn't know there were any. I started paying attention.

With substances having mostly made their way out of my system, I started working out. My muscles had memory and loved the challenge. The driven athlete inside of me quickly re-emerged and remembered how much I once adored moving, breathing, pushing myself. I remembered the thrill of the soccer field and how much I had once loved my muscles growing. When I worked out, I could picture myself again on a ski slope or the basketball court. It was the first time in over a decade that I was operating on plain and simple, natural "feel good."

I started eating too. It was the first time in forever that food was important, instead of being over-prioritized by drugs. I started to speak up more. I could play this game—I'd been around leaders all my life. Within small groups, I quit being a passive observer and I started showing up, sometimes challenging others to do their best. People were flocking to me for answers. It was crazy.

What amazed me most—and what I really chose to take on—was that for the first time in my life, I was learning tools for sobriety. I wasn't learning new skills; I was learning *life* skills. Skills to live... to stay alive for.

Thirty days? No problem. This rocks! I'm converted.

I thought I had it made. Hell, I even became the ping-pong champ of the center.

Addictions, I learned, are centered on secrets. Secrets are how the sickness grows, and quickly. Recovery was all about honesty and transparency. I realized it was my lies that had always gotten me in the worst of trouble. I was finally facing those things every day.

Since it had to be an honest community for us, if I knew something and I didn't tell, it could be bad. A little over halfway through my recovery, however, my redheaded roommate from Boston snuck a girl into our room so he could sleep with her.

I ignored it, and then covered it up. A *man's got needs, right?* I wanted to keep him as a friend, and I was probably a little jealous. It made me dream of Tasha. *Maybe that could happen for me one day and he can keep it quiet.*

I kept the bro code. It was my bargaining chip.

However, my roommate got caught, and by covering for him, I was in the hot seat, too. It was horrifically uncomfortable. However, it made me realize something important: I might not have had this whole sobriety and telling the full truth thing figured out yet. Still, I brushed off the consequences and kept going, a little more humble.

Everyone at rehab quickly got to know me, from all the staff to all the residents. I loved talking to people, getting to the heart of issues. People would bitch and moan, but I would share a cool story. "Here's the tool you need," I'd say and then share. "See, maybe you are not as worthless as you thought."

I liked what I was learning, and I liked sharing what I was learning. I was ecstatic about having some tools from which to operate that didn't involve substances. It didn't really matter that I'd only worked two of the 12 Steps, right? I was thriving, if mostly at fitness and athletics again, and it was giving me the confidence to talk to people and help them.

The whole time I was in rehab, Tasha and I stayed in touch. She visited me twice a week, every week. I woke up every morning, dreaming dreams of winning her completely back over and marrying her once again, although whenever we needed to have a serious conversation, either alone or with the therapist, I was super-skilled at steering it away from anything that made me uncomfortable. We didn't really get anything worked out. She seemed happy to see me, which I loved. It made me want to sneak her into my room, but I'd learned that lesson—or so I hoped.

At rehab they made us do some things that were hard, like Family Day. That was the day where family members could come and face you and tell you anything and everything. It was hard but tender when Tasha, my parents, and my sisters came. I made friends with other residents' family members, too. I even became close friends with an older woman who was the Morgan County Sheriff's wife. Her husband came in one Family Day with sober news for me.

"There's a warrant out for your arrest," he said. It was for the investigation done at Big Red's after the ambulance hauled my sorry ass away. Charges included drug paraphernalia, possession of drugs, and more. *Sheesh, just short of them pinning a ticket on my chest as I was raced away to save my life,* I thought angrily.

As much as I was working on my accountability, emotionally and mentally, I got derailed. Here I was, making significant progress, and it felt like it didn't matter what I did—there still was a lot of crap to face. Once again, Dad started after it and began working on fixing the problem. I was still going to have to go to drug court, however. Relieved, I got back to work in the program.

Upon my thirtieth day in rehab, my parents, one of my sisters, and Tasha attended my commencement. They made a really big deal of it there, with a red carpet, music, video cameras, and more. I was proud, and for the first time in I didn't know how many years, I saw a flicker of hope on Dad's and Mom's faces. I was determined to do them proud. People lined up to tell me all these amazing things about me, and it gave me hope.

Maybe I wasn't as big a loser as I thought.

After the commencement, I wanted to go and be with Tasha but I still hadn't had the hard conversations with her. I went where it was safe. I went home to live with Mom and Dad. For the first time in as long as I could remember, I cleaned out my closet. I got rid of everything—all hidden stashes and all paraphernalia. Now I had some life skills for the first time, and some hope. *There might even be a future for myself.* I had learned how to face my demons and learned how to face living in "today." I had never done that before.

After that, all of my friends who entered rehab after me wanted me at *their* commencement—everyone I'd worked with and talked to while I was in there. That didn't bother me at all. Maybe I couldn't be the life of the party anymore, but I sure as hell wanted to continue to be "the man."

Drug court, however, was far from a celebration. It was a chilling experience. Due to my issues, even though I was a first-time offender I had to attend drug court for one full year. What that meant was no matter what I did for a living, it was mandatory to report twice a week between the hours of 8:00 a.m. and 5:00 p.m. to go in and pee for drug testing. And I had to attend three or four groups a week.

Crap! If I miss even one, I can't leave the county? It was either that or go back to jail. I watched in fascination as a woman named Kathy Morris, a teeny tiny little old lady, ran the drug court like an OG. To her, it didn't matter . . . small-time chumps like me or huge, crazy drug lords, she would tell them to sit down and mind their own business. What *she* said went—even over the judge. My charm had absolutely no effect on her.

Outside of rehab, I started sharing my recovery with the world. I was like an overzealous missionary from my former church—I was as converted as you could get, and I couldn't keep my mouth shut. I didn't even feel sorry for anyone who had to hear me. I was working out like crazy and getting back my athletic body. Dad and Mom started trusting again, started to become proud of my new life, and I was, too.

After fifteen years of feeling like a piece of crap, it felt good anytime I received an accolade or award. I still had that need to feel significant in someone else's eyes. Helping people was a real skillset of mine. I even reached out to old friends and shared my recovery experiences.

"Dude," I said one day to a guy who used to work for me at Big Red's, "you've got to face it. You're mortal. I'm mortal. We're all going to bite the dust sometime . . . but I'm telling you, life is worth doing *sober*. Naw, serious man, you think you can't now—I know it. I've been there. But I'm telling you, it's possible. It's worth it. I'm on the best high ever, and it didn't cost me a dime."

Yeah. I didn't tell him that my rehab cost my dad a very pretty penny.

One day I was sitting on the couch at Mom and Dad's house when my father asked me to share the full story of what I had seen when I was in my coma. He had caught a couple of details on Family Day but wanted to hear the whole thing. I described everything about falling into that coma, and then everything regarding my visit with Danny in dramatic detail. This didn't go along with much of Dad's church's beliefs at the time that, on the "other side," people who commit suicide are likely to go to hell. Danny didn't seem to be in hell at all.

Dad's face went very pale. "C . . . could you describe the two other people behind him for me?"

"Yeah," I nodded casually. "Sure. The guy was bald. He had glasses on and the woman had black hair. She was tiny. In my vision they were like forty or maybe a little older but not crazy old. Everybody was in white. Everyone seemed healthy and freaking happy, too. It definitely was not a sad occasion!"

Abruptly Dad, who had gone even whiter, stood. He went on the other side of the formal dining room that I'd never really went into (and with my behavior wasn't really allowed) except a couple, very infrequent times Mom and Dad were entertaining and they wanted me to meet somebody. Dad walked slowly out, gingerly holding onto a picture frame that he'd evidently pulled off the wall.

"Is this them?" he asked quietly, and then turned the frame around.

I blinked and my mouth fell open. Sure enough, the picture was an older version of the couple I'd seen standing behind Danny! First there was the balding guy with glasses. I especially recognized the kind expression in his eyes. The dark-haired woman looked almost the same, except in my vision or dream, she had not been nearly as tiny nor frail as in the picture; she had been vibrantly smiling, even glowing.

"Yeah," I nodded, astonished. "Who are they?"

Dad swallowed hard. "That's your grandfather who gave his life in his truck to save the young family on the icy bridge. And that's your grandmother . . . my mother, who took her life a year later."

I hadn't known them. I had been too young. My grandfather had been a complete and utter stranger to me, and my grandmother had only been a dark silhouette of a memory, accompanying the smell of coffee and cigarettes.

Holy shit.

Despite what I wished, I wasn't a 2nd Step hero. Even when I left the center after my thirty days, I hadn't been able to move beyond that step. Yet that experience with Danny and my grandparents was so clear and undeniable . . . I tried to clear my head. As we looked at the photo, my body was shaking almost as much as Dad's was. I couldn't imagine what was going on in his mind as he zoned out in deep thought.

God or the Universe knows I'm not much of a faith guy. Yet He, She, or It sure gave me enough of *something* so tangible from this experience that I couldn't deny it.

CHAPTER 19

FROM SACRED TO SACRILEGIOUS

Upon my exit from rehab, whenever I started anything, I was *all in*. Shortly after moving back in with Mom and Dad, I started going to the gym. Just like in rehab, I didn't go for a twenty-minute run a couple of times a week. Oh, hell no. I was there pumping weights and cross-training almost every day of the week for hours, feeling great and pushing myself even harder.

Unfortunately, I wasn't as committed about putting the work in on things and relationships that I had already screwed up. I still let Mom and Dad and my siblings down. Worse was my failure with Tasha. My former wife had started dating other people again. She was playing hardball with me. It wouldn't be so easy to woo back the girl of my dreams. Yet this was a place where I still didn't take full accountability for how badly I'd hurt her. Deep inside I knew it, and I wanted to make it up to her if she'd get back with me, but I wasn't facing my own responsibility in the breakup or how long it might take to repair.

When I found out about Tasha dating through a mutual friend, it crushed me.

"Hey, get rid of this Mike guy," I told Tasha, "and we'll work it out." Only Tasha was now smart and savvy enough that she wanted me to prove myself. She gave me time to do that while she dated others . . . but my ego couldn't handle it.

She didn't pick me. So, I didn't even try. In my mind, I would have remarried her in a heartbeat! I couldn't yet see my own accountability playing any sort of role in how badly I had hurt her, or in her decision to date someone else.

Two can play that game was what I thought instead. For the first time in years, since before dating Tasha, I peeled my eyes wide open . . . in case some good-looking chick stepped into my life.

I had started playing soccer in a competitive league again—the premier men's league in Park City—and I began feeling on top of the world. I started training for triathlons with my sister Maegen, especially once I had regained some strength. As I gained confidence and control, I became less and less shy about myself. I trained a lot, and I was on fire!

One day I was finishing up another brutal workout at a local gym in Bountiful, a commercial gym, loving every minute of it. As I wiped the sweat from my brow with a towel and took a long haul off my water bottle, I glanced over to the padded stretching area outside the locker room, where something had caught my eye. Actually, it was a *someone.* Tiny and petite, this girl was beautiful and, I could tell, extremely athletic.

Suddenly, I figured I might need to do some stretching, too. I sort of "stretched" in her direction and casually introduced myself. "Hey," I began, "I can show you a better way to stretch that hamstring."

When she looked at me with her beautiful brown eyes, I knew my life would never be the same. She was really, really cute, with brown hair and a cheerleader body. She was spunky, strong, confident—and LDS. That's what my parents always wanted for me, so

I knew that getting hooked up with her would be a win-win-win situation.

We kept flirting, and soon we started dating. Instead of the old "Let's go to a party" dates I was used to, Angie and I experienced dates that included workouts, hiking, and even movies . . . you know, things that "normal" people who are not using drugs do. On one of our first dates, I took her to an alumni deal at the Hollywood rehab.

"Angie," I said, "you need to see that recovery is who I am." I was living, breathing, and speaking recovery *everywhere*. And she was wide-eyed because I was a fire-breathing preacher about the importance of my sobriety. That brought us closer together really fast. It felt so good to have something positive to say and to build after what felt like an entire life of negativity.

Every day I woke up feeling stoked. I was telling the truth—this was my new life, my new passion, and fortunately for me, Angie fell in love with it all, too. To keep my recovery, I went to the 12 Step Back Street Club in Davis County three to four times a week. Yes, it was court ordered, but now I loved going. I also returned to Orem once or twice a week for recovery aftercare. The support there was amazing, and I rocked it.

The only problem was, I was still seeing Tasha on the side from time to time. We had never stopped caring about each other, and I couldn't seem to let her go. But I wasn't up to the challenge of doing the deeper work to really keep Tasha and claim her the right way. Angie and I were falling hard for each other without effort, and it felt good.

I didn't tell Angie about Tasha. And I didn't tell Tasha about Angie. I was hedging my bets.

As Angie and I were dating, it was a turn-on that she was as into me as I was into her. She had strong beliefs, which was also hot. She was more collected than most girls I knew. It didn't matter that she was really small, because Angie was feistier than shit. I called her a honey badger. Her father had passed away when she was really young, and since both of us were no stranger to trauma, we found we could have these deep conversations that weren't easy to have with just anyone.

During one of these deep convos, Angie said, "Rob, I think you ought to see the missionaries. There's so much that got screwed up in your mind from your trauma as a kid that you never got to see the Mormon church for what it is. If I'm here beside you, would you give it a try? At least you wouldn't have to hate the thing that your parents and I both love."

I blinked and thought hard for a moment. I mean, this was the place where I had felt so betrayed, the culture that seemed to hate me, especially when I got deep into drugs and alcohol. Now that I was in recovery, however, I was starting to see things differently—more clearly and completely.

I looked into Angie's beautiful, searching eyes . . . and melted. She got me back into the church, although not in a preachy way. My awesome girlfriend made *me* do the homework and let each discussion be on my own terms.

As I sat on the bench beside her in the chapel, the chair beside her in the classroom, or the couch beside her during missionary lessons, she just let me be me. The woman loved me deeply, and I loved her in a more mature way than I ever had loved before. If only it had been enough.

I'd been brought up in children's Primary and tween and teen Sunday School, when I couldn't have cared less about the nuts and bolts of it all. But suddenly with Angie, after all the personal growth I'd made, all the new life skills I was putting into use, I wanted my old sins washed away. I wanted to start again, clean and new.

I rejoined the church at thirty-one and became more active, in the ways a man soon to be married did in our church. Taking on more spiritual responsibilities felt good to me, especially to have people proud of me. In my mind it was the best thing I could do for Angie and me, as I wanted the Spirit to be with us.

"Look, your life is finally where we hoped to see you," said Mom.

Wow, I checked all the boxes:

Once again an active member. Check!

Working steadily so I can support a family. Check!

Marrying a good member of the church. Check!

Great truck and building a house to support my new family. Check!

It was great that Angie saw my good and my bad. I believed her when she said there wasn't anything we couldn't work out. We continued dating, soon getting very serious, and my parents loved her. She saw past most of my manipulations and called me on them, rightly so. But that didn't mean I still didn't play the games I was so damn good at!

These manipulations put me in awkward positions at times. Deep into our courtship, I thought I was being sneaky and thought Angie and I wouldn't marry in the temple. *We can do that later,* I thought, still feeling completely unworthy. But Angie wanted a temple wedding. In the eyes of our culture and my reestablished religion, those vows meant an eternal family, beginning with me and Angie.

That level of forever was promised with marriage in the LDS temple; it demanded the highest level of commitment. You can get married outside the temple or you can get married in, but then you'd make a very sacred commitment, a vow to your loved one for eternity. Angie had enough guts to call my bluff; I was going to have enough guts to meet her. We were to be married that year, in late summer of 2007.

My ego said I was all new, and I was freshly in love. It felt too damn good to be wanted by two incredible women. But Tasha and I *had* hooked up before and during the time I was dating Angie. That wasn't temple or covenant preparedness. I was not being my word. But neither of them knew the truth, right? I could totally pull this off.

The day before we were to get married, Angie was getting her hair done. Unbeknownst to either of us, Tasha was friends with Angie's hairdresser. That's when shit hit the fan.

The doorbell rang at 2:00 a.m. at my parents' house, only a couple hours into my official wedding day. I answered the door to find Angie. Her face was red and blotchy, her eyes swollen from betrayal.

"What happened with you and Tasha?" she demanded. "I want to know all of it."

I stepped back. "What are you talking about?" I asked. Lately, I hadn't even talked to Tasha. It had to have been at least a few weeks, but what really threw me for a loop was hearing my fiancée say my ex's name out loud. *Uh oh . . .*

"Imagine my joy, Rob," she said bitterly, "when I'm getting my hair done for our beautiful morning wedding, and my own hairdresser tells me that you and your ex-wife had not only remained friends, but that you had never really broken everything off!"

Her eyes flashed dangerously and her voice became loud, almost hysterical. I flinched as she continued: "She said you two have been 'more than a little friendly' since you got out of rehab . . . even after meeting and dating me! Is that true?"

I stood there, astounded. Our sacred wedding at the temple was on for 10:00 a.m. Everything had been going my way, with no consequences for my actions . . . until now. If I blew this up, with so many people counting on me, I didn't think I could handle the fallout. My guilty button worked really well; it was extra-special. Plus, I still had to be "the man."

So, I did what came naturally. I lied.

I reassured Angie that what she'd been told never happened. She kept looking at me with those broken-hearted eyes, questioning everything we had built between us, even as we went ahead and a few hours later got married in the temple.

How could I tell her Tasha and I had an undeniable connection? How could I tell her that my ego justified that I wasn't hurting anyone? I didn't open my mouth to anything truthful until we got to the temple. When I said my vows, I meant every word.

I didn't know at that time that an addict's need for instant gratification doesn't go away overnight. I wanted to feel loved, and needed to, more than anything else in the world, and that led me to lie. Still, no one except Tasha and the hairdresser—well, and then Angie—knew about it, so I felt safe.

My new wife and I lived with my parents for a month or so while I continued to get everything in order in my life and work. Mom still hovered over me like she had all of my life, and I didn't mind. Angie and I even got in a fight once over that fact. Rising early every morning for work, I asked Angie if she would start to make my lunches for me. But here's the thing . . . she was also working.

"No, Rob," Angie said firmly. "You can make your lunch, like I make mine."

Logical, right? Only I didn't do it. I was furious that Angie wouldn't get up at 5:00 a.m. to make me my lunch. Mom heard us arguing and quickly jumped in.

"I'll do it," Mom announced. And just like that, Mom made them for me every day until we moved out. God bless Mom. I could always revert to a little boy in her presence, and she'd have my back.

Angie and I had a house built in new, upscale Foxboro, west of Woods Cross in North Salt Lake, and we moved in before Halloween. I stayed super busy in recovery, with work, and playing indoor soccer and hockey. I was such a different person than my old self. Angie called me Mr. Rogers. I was friendly in our neighborhood, outgoing at church, and I was so busy, so happy that we had built this awesome, beautiful new house for me to pay for and of course a big new truck to boot. I had to start adulting.

This became even more apparent because Angie and I were purposely trying to get pregnant. When things didn't work out right away, I couldn't joke about it. It was a sore spot for Angie and I didn't want to hurt her. I just kept loving her.

In recovery, I was now committed more than ever. I was making great money. I continued making my amends to people, and these were heartfelt amends. I wrote them out, then visited each individual in private, and asked forgiveness. I meant it. I felt it inside.

I had been working on my relationships with God, my parents, my wife, and others. But what I didn't do was identify my relationship with pain. I coasted on the pink cloud of happiness, until I encountered something bigger than me again, and my ego thought I could handle it all . . .

One morning several months into my marriage, I was playing indoor soccer with my team. Confidently, on the rubber beebee playing surface, I went in to score a goal. I felt in the prime of my life—more fit than ever before and loving every second of my physical prowess. I set to plant and shoot the ball like any other of the ten million times I'd done it before.

No one even touched me. I only felt the rubbery turf slip and a huge, sudden POP like a gunshot to my knee. Completely debilitated, I crumbled onto the field, my ACL torn off.

As I screamed, my buddies came over to help me. Even before they were getting me up and off the field, before I thought to call my wife of less than a year, before it hit me that I had been clean and sober for nine months, I told myself, *I gotta call someone.*

I didn't know that I needed to understand pain. *Captain Obvious.* Pain had taught me lessons so many damn times. You think that life is going to stop teaching you the layup. But pain was the common denominator of all my challenges. Only instead of welcoming it to the table to have a conversation, to rise to meet it, to face the challenge of it, to come to know it once and for all . . . I caved.

I made that stupid call.

Then I had to have surgery. *Okay, I got this.*

Angie stayed home with me. But in the middle of the night she called a neighbor for a priesthood blessing because I was in excruciating pain. It felt like my leg had been cut off! I was writhing, as bad as what I felt on the soccer field—perhaps worse because there was no adrenaline. People from our church came over and gave me a blessing, but all I could think about was how to get rid of the pain.

They left and Angie had to go to work. Within an hour of all of them leaving, I had a needle and drugs in my system. The pain went away, but the shame and fear came back. I had just married someone in the temple but now it was all screwed up.

I'm the recovery guy ... but I'm not.

So I kept lying . . . to everyone. *How in the world could I uncheck the boxes?* Angie was still trying to get pregnant, and the more she focused on trying to have that baby, the less her eyes were focused on me.

After a few weeks it didn't matter. I spiraled too quickly. There was no such thing as "control." I didn't understand that recovery comes sometimes brutally slow, but relapse is a freakin' fast spiral. Nearly overnight, I became a lying, cheating, completely manipulating, full-fledged druggie again. Angie couldn't trust a single thing I said. I blew apart employment and personal relationships nearly as fast as I blew out my knee.

Even then, suboxone, which was supposed to be my medical hero, my protagonist to keep me from addiction, became my antagonist. It made me feel like I had sobriety, but it wasn't true. Even if I wanted to get high, the receptor had already taken the load. To get relief, instead of taking two suboxones, I took five.

I was only able to hide it for a few months. Then one day Angie walked in on me in the bathroom, when I'd forgotten to lock the door. For a normal human like Angie who had never seen someone shooting up, it was frightening. I saw all the blood drain from her face and she looked at me in horror.

"What the heck are you doing?" she cried.

"Look," I begged. "I've only done this a little bit. I'm going to stop," I promised.

But I didn't.

On top of that, I was not fulfilling my duties at work—even while Angie worked. I lost my employment. She, on the other hand, was good at keeping a job and it was a good job. It was so good it gave me the time to hustle and get dope. The spiral continued, this time faster and faster.

Finally, Angie called me out on all my dirtbag behavior.

"So, you're going to keep seeing Tasha and you're not going to bother going to work?" she asked.

"So what? What are *you* going to do about it?" I sneered back.

By that time, she didn't even want me to touch her. She'd come home from work, and the sight of me there, high as a kite, made her mouth squelch up in ugly anger. She said that nowadays I made her sick.

"Look at this house, Rob. Look at your truck, my car, our eternal marriage. Someone has to work. Someone has to work *at it!*"

It wouldn't be me. The adulting I should have been doing took on a whole new level one day when I was withdrawing. I couldn't last more than twenty-four hours without a high. But Angie had been having some symptoms and needed to take a pregnancy test. She wanted me to go to the store with her and come back and see the results. Only my phone rang.

"Stay with me, Rob," she begged. "I need you here with me."

I was bouncing off the walls. My entire body was back to needing drugs like air. I tried for another few hours and finally I gathered my keys. How could I stick around to see the results of the test if I couldn't even think straight? I had to go out and grab a quick fix.

"I've got to go talk to somebody real quick," I panted, heading to the door.

"If you walk out this door, don't bother coming back!" she cried in pain and disbelief.

I walked out. After I got high and settled down for a brief moment before the drugs' irrationality won out, I knew I needed to go home. When I walked in the house, Angie was sitting in the kitchen, sobbing. My wife looked at me, her face worn and wet. Her eyes filled with terror.

Oh my God, this is it, I thought. *I'm going to be a dad.*

After many months of trying to conceive, here Angie was pregnant—in the midst of my addiction. The day that should have been so joyous I had made all about me—again. Suddenly I felt in a time warp and my whole world flashed before my eyes. This was serious stuff. This was being a dad. This was what my own father had tried to prepare me for my whole life. With every fiber of my being, I knew I wasn't worthy.

As the days followed, I kept trying to pretend that I was making this whole marriage thing work, but we were in danger of losing our house. Worse was how I continued treating Angie. When it came time for the baby to be born, I wasn't there for my wife emotionally, physically, or mentally. Sure, I was "around," but I was simply not present when Angie went through one of the hardest, most terrifying experiences of her life.

Labor was tough. Even though I had snuck off to the hospital bathroom to take something to relieve the edge, I could still feel her pain through her cries. The baby was stuck in the birth canal and I thought her cries of pain would kill me. The doctor said Angie was going to have to have an emergency episiotomy to give the baby more room to come out.

Then Angie's anguish turned into one of the most joyful experiences of her life as she brought our little baby girl into it. It was January 30, 2009, and this was a day that would change my life forever . . . just not *yet*.

Sophie's newborn skin was purple! She wasn't breathing or crying. There was so much anxiety and fear in that delivery room. Then her skin turned to gray, and she started breathing. It was such a relief. From being in the birth canal for so long, she looked like a reptile or an alien. She had a fluid sack on the back of her head, and her tiny head was misshapen, as many newborns' are from birth—but I didn't know. I'd never had a kid before! Her eyes were gigantic, and her tongue was black! I was so embarrassed I pulled the little baby beanie over her head quickly to cover up the weirdness before I took her out to greet my whole family sitting in the waiting room. My sisters saw my embarrassment and laughed at me. Having kids of their own, they knew better and still took pictures.

After all the "oohing" and "ahhing" over the alien creature, I took the baby back to Angie and told her I needed to go home and get a shower. Another lie. I went straight to my dealer's house. I couldn't handle all that stress and Angie's pain. I needed to be numb. It was all too real and my daughter was here. It was in this numb state that I gave my daughter her first bath. I felt awkward, and I felt completely unworthy, in a million different ways.

CHAPTER 20

"IS THIS LOUD ENOUGH?"

Within a few days, much to my relief, Sophie's head regained its natural shape. My little alien child became the most beautiful baby girl I had ever seen, with huge, Disney princess eyes. Something about looking into them touched me to my soul.

As soon as Angie brought the baby home, I found I was always hovering over her. When she was sleeping, Sophie was so quiet, I kept checking on her every few minutes to make sure she was breathing. Still, I was scared to hold her, like I might break her, even as I marveled at her tiny fingers, toes, and perfect nose.

One thing I knew, I wasn't worthy of her. I couldn't stay clean. Angie was just as nervous about being a new parent herself. As the days ensued, my wife became fierce. She became the real protector . . . the one I should have been. One day I got so high, I was completely out of my mind. I wanted to jump into my truck to drive somewhere. Angie tried to stop me, and my aggression became much more than verbal.

She was little and feisty. I was bigger and plain mean, since nothing could keep me away from my drugs or my truck. When I got back later, I overheard Angie on the phone talking to her mom, sobbing and nearly hysterical. "He's like Jekyll and Hyde, Mom! One minute he's stoned and so, so cruel to me. The next morning, he wakes up beside me, and he's my best friend again—not even remembering what an ass he was the night before. He'll be so kind and tender, and I want to love him and trust him—until he does it again, like tonight. It's so hard! It's too hard!"

We were in deep trouble, and hadn't even been married for two years when Angie went with me to see my drug counselor, Dave. He was a 260-pound dude who didn't bullshit, yet the same one I was completely lying to as well now. He saw right through it.

They were talking about all the things Angie was doing to try to keep me sober, from trying to stop me from using to keeping me off the road when I was using—even when her life was at stake.

The counselor stared at her. Right in front of me he asked her, "Why are you still here? You have a brand-new baby, Angie! Who is taking care of you?"

"No one," she breathed, and another tear coursed down her cheek.

The counselor looked at me, not one ounce of sympathy in his eyes. "Then that's a problem. Rob, if you do X, or Y, or Z again, then Angie—you *leave*."

I'd mistreated every woman in my life, using each one as a way to power me up, like gas in my tank—and when that ran out, I went to another gas station. I was supposed to be a protector, especially for my new daughter. But the moment I had made that call after my soccer accident, the moment I relapsed, I was behaving in every way like the man I was raised *not* to be.

One night, shortly after that counseling session, even though we'd had a really good day, everyone could tell I had used or was wanting to again.

It was both.

God, I don't know what to do anymore. I can't go to work unless I'm high. But if I'm high, I can't go to work.

Work didn't "work" anymore. It was now my job to stay home and take care of the baby while Angie supported us. Someone had to pay for that house I was supposed to be providing. One day I fed and diapered the baby, but there wasn't enough formula in the house. Sophie and I loaded up in the truck, heading to the store for formula for my hungry baby girl . . . but somehow ended up at my drug dealer's house. I spent the money meant for baby supplies on drugs. I barely made it home before I got the baby and me in the door, then shot up . . . and fell unconscious.

I didn't awaken until after Angie arrived home to find me passed out on the floor. I was more ashamed than I had ever been in my entire life. It was worse than when I hurt Tasha. That was Angie's wake-up call: it was clear that I was a harm to myself and others. She had tried to give me every chance she could for me to change. Finally, Angie came to a conclusion one mild Sunday in June of 2009—at least, mild in every way except for the drugs I was doing and the havoc I was causing.

"You're so mean," my wife said bluntly. "Too mean. I'm not putting up with it anymore, Rob!" Then she took the baby and moved out to live with her mom. It was Father's Day.

Over the next couple of months, I couldn't afford to keep shoes on my own feet, much less keep the house that Angie and I had built. With a heavy heart, I put it on the market to sell. Now over thirty years old, I felt humiliated to have to move back in with my parents. I had lost everything inside of six months—my house, my wife, my daughter.

Dad's health had been struggling, and it was rough. He'd had to have a kidney transplant that my sister Maegen donated for his survival, but he wasn't managing well.

Summer passed, and at night after I used, I imagined being with my daughter, Sophie, and being a good father to her. But what I saw in the mirror wasn't anything like that daydream. It was all too much. *And I am not enough.*

Proof of this was the fact that through my parents or my sister was the only way that I could see my own little baby girl. As Sophie grew more beautiful each day, I grew more haggard and worn. My parents were worried all over again. My siblings were, too, although I could tell as I overheard them on the phone that they were sick of the fact that every conversation revolved around me and not them, not their grandkids or spouses.

Sitting on my parents' couch one night toward the end of August, I was beyond depressed. My body drooped and my head was bowed, too heavy to pick back up. *I can't keep a job. My mom is making me breakfast, lunch, and dinner.* With my sullen eyes on the floor, I glanced from side to side. *All these people deserve better.* Then I had a seed of a thought that took root and wouldn't let go. *If I'm out of the picture, it will fix everything . . . it will fix it all.*

Within a few hours, as dusk kissed the evening sky that I didn't notice, I bought some heroin and took it home. In the privacy of my bedroom that I'd occupied off and on since childhood, I put enough heroin in the spoon to kill a large African elephant. In fact, I knew it was enough to finish off an entire room of people. *God, this is the last thing I can do for everyone,* I thought as I slipped away.

But instead, the worst possible thing happened: I woke up.

When I realized I was alive, surrounded by my own vomit in my childhood bedroom, waves of tears streamed down my face. *God forgot about me!* I screamed inside. *I can't even kill myself properly.* I felt like the biggest waste of space on the planet. My hell was like the movie *Groundhog Day*, and I was certain I'd have to live the same day over and over again.

Later that morning, Dad came down to my room and handed me a piece of paper. He had the saddest look on his face that I had ever seen—and I'd created plenty of sad scenes before this one. This time was different; it was deeper, more wounded.

Then, as Dad silently shook his head at me, I knew what had changed: for the very first time in my entire life, my father, my hero, had given up on me. Apparently he had visited me in the early hours of this morning and thought I was dead. It wasn't until he heard noises in my room, me snuffling and crying at my unending hell, that he came down to check on me.

I wasn't the only one with a wet face and a wild, lonely isolation in my eyes. I looked at the paper he handed me, wet from his own tears. It was my obituary.

As if my shame hadn't been deep before, I physically cringed at the thought of him having to creep down those steps every day, wondering if this was the day he would find me dead—having to write the last words about me that would ever be written and per-haps spoken.

I stared at him, then at the paper. There was a moment of choice.

Rather than asking for his help, which I desperately needed and felt most unworthy of, I ran. I hopped in my truck and sped away. I didn't come back. *I can't do this to my dad. All the pain he's suffered, all the important parental figures who took their own lives . . . and now I'm doing it, too.*

That hot August summer day, I became homeless by choice. I drove around and sat in my truck. In fact, I didn't bother doing anything at all for three days, except to feel all the pain and shame of my miserable life. Over and over in my mind, I thought of my daughter Sophie. All I could think was that if she ever, truly, got to know me as a little girl and a young woman, she would be so embarrassed. Just like Mom. Just like Dad. Just like Angie. Just like my siblings.

I can't do that to her—not to Sophie.

All the voices in my head screamed that Sophie was better off with almost anyone *but* me. Sweating in the hot sun, I gazed at the temperature gauge: 96 degrees. I kept watching until it went to 95, then 94, then 92. Finally, at 82 degrees as the sun was going down, the suffocatingly hot evening turned into night.

It was August 31.

I drove slowly to my parents' house, knowing Sophie had been dropped by for a visit. As the wind cooled my heated skin to some degree, I realized yesterday had been her eight-month birthday—something to be celebrated. I hadn't been there. *They* were taking care of her. They were celebrating her because I wouldn't . . . couldn't.

Dragging myself out of the truck's cab, I went inside to say goodbye. I could hardly look into my little girl's large, loving eyes or acknowledge her toothless grin as she babbled at me happily. Sophie loved my folks so much, and my sister. I could hardly bear to see her adoring eyes on me. *Not worth it.*

Hoisting her out of Mom's loving grasp, I clutched her to me, one last time. I kissed her, stifling my sobs. Then I placed her carefully back in my mom's arms, kissing her before I hugged my dad. Taking care not to lose my nerve, I made the excuse of using the restroom.

In reality, I had nothing to relieve from my bladder. The punishing heat had taken it all. Instead, I crept into the other room and stole a pistol from Dad's gun cabinet. Shoving it down my pants so it wouldn't be seen, I yelled "bye" to everyone on my way out. No eye contact. Why bother?

Wearily climbing back into my truck, I slowly drove up Lakeview Drive, toward Bountiful Boulevard. After several minutes of driving, I parked in the parking lot for Sessions Trail. It would take several minutes for me to hike up to hit the top of Sessions, up behind the LDS temple behind my parents' house, the gun now on the seat beside me.

Finally, I climbed out of the truck with the gun in my front right pocket, a small cooler of booze in my right hand as the liquid courage I would need to pull the trigger. I took the steep hike up the trail to the overlook. The rocky path led high above the city, but I didn't really see it: I was blubbering and blinded by tears. They were the kind of tears that hurt so bad that I couldn't see.

My life is coming to an end. I won't be around to hurt my parents, hurt my siblings, hurt my friends, hurt my girlfriends or my wives anymore. I realized in that moment I didn't really want to die, I was just tired of hurting everyone around me. *This is it. This is the end.*

I sat on the permanent wooden bench at the top, pretty much eye to eye with the statue of Moroni perched on top of the temple. My constant bawling went on. It was a good thing I was the only person on that trail, because I cried harder than I ever had in my life. That was the last thing I would see—the origin of my childhood, the city I'd lived for most of my adult life . . . and where I'd lost everything.

The argument that had been raging in my head for days—that felt like all my life—kept going.

Are you really going to do this? one part of me asked.

Everyone will be better off, said another. *I won't be an embarrassment to the family name; I won't take anymore from my family. I won't hurt any more women—won't break their hearts.*

I made a list in my head, like I'd been taught in the Hollywood treatment center, drawing out the "Pros and Cons" regarding a problem—in this case, for killing myself. The Pros seemed to far outweigh the Cons. I cried and cried, until my shoulders stopped shaking. I cried until there were no more tears. And I sat there as another feeling arose.

I wasn't sad anymore—I was pissed! Pissed at the god who wouldn't let me die from my recent overdose or any of my overdoses, pissed at the god who hadn't taken my life before this, pissed at the god who had gotten me into all this mess. I didn't believe in a god, but I was so pissed at *my mother's God* that I suddenly intended a most dreadful retribution.

I had been taught all my life to revere this God, to listen to the still small voice that would somehow "guide my way." *Bullshit.* He had never shown up for me. I fell on my knees in the dirt and put my finger around the trigger. Then my head betrayed me. I had a vision of my daughter and my mom.

As far as Sophie is concerned, any man could come into her life and do a better job—a better job than me.

I looked at the glowing Bountiful Temple, its light stark against the dark night sky.

Man, my mom—the woman who is so sure of her faith, so sure about it all that she loves her god, a god who has never once answered one single damned prayer for me. I'm going to pray to her god, so when she meets her Maker she can say, "You failed me."

Cocking the pistol and pointing it toward my mouth, my voice dripped with bitter, tearful rage as I proclaimed down the mountain, "I don't know anything about a 'still small voice.' I'm going to need something louder than that! If I don't get a sign by the time I open my eyes, I'm pulling the trigger."

Nothing.

Yeah. Just like I thought.

As I was opening my eyes and my pointer finger began to press down on the trigger, the barrel inside my mouth, it happened.

BAM! BAM! BAM! BAM! BAM! BAM! BAM! BAM!

My finger dislodged and I nearly dropped the still-loaded gun at the intensity of brightness before me. I saw flashes of color and radiating booms lighting up the darkness, brighter than day. *What the hell . . .?*

The Bountiful night sky was filled with fireworks, as if it were the 4th of July, not August 31st.

What the hell? I thought again, incredulous. *No one shoots off fireworks this time of year.*

Regardless, undeniably vibrant colors shot across the sky and more loud booms erupted into the night, shaking my bones and feeling like thunder beneath my feet.

I dropped to my knees in the dirt, my mouth still wide open in shock at the fiery display that went on for several minutes. When the last firework finally guttered out, silence fell once more upon the mountain.

Then a voice behind me asked, "Is THAT *loud enough?*"

CHAPTER 21

FORGET HOLLYWOOD. IT'S TIME TO GET REAL

Sobbing again, I dove face first into the dirt on that mountain, scared to death of whomever or whatever had spoken behind me. I didn't dare look. I was deathly afraid of God, but to my core, I could not deny what had just happened.

"Is THAT loud enough?"

My heart had leapt from my chest into my throat. When my trembling subsided enough that I could control my limbs, I still didn't dare glance back. Instead, I bolted to my truck, my hands fumbling with the keys as I started the engine. Then I raced away, down the mountain.

With as much certainty as a few minutes ago when I knew I was going to hell, this time as I drove, I knew exactly where I was heading. Still shaking, my adrenaline on hyper-drive, I popped into Mom's and Dad's living room where they were on the couch, watching TV.

"I need help," I begged, and I walked over and handed the gun to my dad. Taking only enough time to explain what almost happened, I said, "I know I've cried wolf before, but I am in serious trouble. I'm headed to the LDS hospital." I rushed back out to the driveway. I didn't tell them about the voice. I didn't want anyone, especially my parents, to know I'd made some sort of connection to some magical being—much less God.

I drove straight to the LDS Hospital in Salt Lake City. I couldn't stop anywhere. I was so broken, and still so scared. After I pulled into the parking lot, I tried to check myself into detox. I had to go to rehab. I had to or I would die. However, after my last experience, I knew rehab wouldn't take me yet.

What had I taken that day, they asked? *Alcohol and cocaine.*

The stocky registration nurse at the hospital looked at my intake form, filled in with shaking fingers. He shook his head. "We only work with opiates."

"Wait, no, you have to take me. I *have* to detox for rehab."

"Sorry, dude, it's policy," he replied.

I stared at the registration nurse and dug my fingers into the chair. My moment on the mountain wouldn't let go. "I have to stay," I insisted, my voice low but stubborn. "If I leave here, I'm not going to make it."

"Seriously?" the nurse asked, his eyebrows raised with concern.

"Yes," I nodded firmly, my knuckles white. I gestured with my head behind me. "If I walk out those doors, I'm a dead man."

He stared back at me. "Dude," he said again, but this time he added, "Hold on."

I sat there, shaking in that chair, refusing to move, to release my palms in my desperation. In the meantime, my heart was still beating wildly, and my thoughts were racing as fast as I had raced down the mountainside.

What was that voice? What happened on that mountain?

Sitting there with my thoughts felt like hours, but within twenty to thirty minutes, they got me into a bed.

September 1, 2009, was my first day of sobriety. After a few days in the hospital's detox, I volunteered to go to rehab. Well, that was all fine and well, but Dad was not a fan, and certainly not pleased at all the money he had spent at the Hollywood rehab.

"Dad, I have a plan," I said, looking at his grim face. "There's a place. It's called The Ranch—a rehab down south."

He grimaced at the sound of it. I couldn't blame his reluctance. I had promised too many times, up and down, that I'd be cured by the next big thing, and I'd always failed. I didn't want to lie to him, but going this time really *did* feel different, maybe because it was coming from somewhere deeper inside me.

Five days ago, I would never have gone anywhere near something like this, but after my experience on the mountain . . .

"It's supposed to be different," I continued to explain to him. "Better, longer, cleaner. Brass tacks. Less fuss, no mussin' around. This is real rehab."

"How is this The Ranch supposed to be any better? Son, how will this be any different?"

"I only know they have a good reputation," I admitted.

A few of the guys I had been hanging out with before my relapse, the serious ones, had come from there. An older soccer buddy from my high school comp team had attended The Ranch, and Jason gave it glowing praise. He was now the recovery guy—but he had stuck with it.

"Plus," I added, "they are spiritually based. It's for sixty days instead of thirty, and Dad, they are way less expensive. It's also all male residents. No females."

He looked at me. If I was going to forego females for sixty days, it might mean something. Since losing Angie, I hadn't been without a girl by my side since junior high.

Much to Dad's relief, we found out the program was not only sixty days inpatient, it was eight months outpatient, too. And if for some reason a touch-up was needed, a patient could have thirty more days without extra cost, guaranteed. In other words, as long as I fully completed the program, I could come back for free if I faced trouble again.

The cost was $20k. Even though it was not as pricey as my prior rehab, that was still a big chunk of change. Their return policy turned out to be my insurance policy. It was probably all that saved me.

Finally, when Dad nodded, I felt like I could breathe. I knew when I came down off that mountain this was my last chance. I put the shovel down; from my perspective, this was it, too. My willingness to keep fighting was gone. I had to face this addiction.

It was different than giving up. I was giving in.

I didn't care about the spa, massages, or the ropes course where I could kick ass, although I was grateful there was a gym. I knew I needed *real* help and I hoped this program somehow would be it. It was the most comprehensive rehabilitation program—everything I had been searching for.

The Ranch was located in Bluffdale, Utah, south of Salt Lake City in a more rural area. As we drove up, I saw a sprawling, two-story brick building with immaculate front grounds and terraced porches. As large as it was, it wasn't overly fancy. There was only a small gym, a sauna, a horse no one would ride, and an alpaca. I still got nervous about enclosed spaces and liked the warm, open feel of it.

We climbed the steps to the front door. Walking in, there was an entryway with two large, circular staircases that led up to the second floor where I figured the residents lived. Even though it was an all-male facility, nothing was dumpy or trashy. Actually, there was a certain understated elegance to it but it felt like a place I might be able to let my hair down.

I noticed a few of the residents during check-in, and immediately I saw that some guys appeared to be a little cliquey, while other guys were genuinely smiling at seeing a new face, and looking me in the eye—even if I couldn't hold their gazes yet.

The only problem? Robby was still driving the bus. I went in so fried. I was assigned a room and a roommate, but I couldn't stay awake during the day and I couldn't sleep at night, either. The residents more than the counselors got on me real quick. Within a day or two they made me start joining groups, doing my fair share of chores, getting on a schedule, and working the Steps.

Here I go again.

"Step One: Admitted that we were powerless over our addiction." *Just like last time.*

Only this time flashes of every checkbox that had come unchecked appeared before me, and my eyes swam with tears. After I quit crying, I looked at the long sheets of paper and the writing there that was difficult to understand.

I found I could make it through the first step easily. Sure, I already had entered the grounds (mostly) humble and out of desperation, but not very deep into my questions. For the first several days, I was still feeling sick after detox. It didn't help that I was down forty or fifty pounds from where I should be—all lost in the last few months of my spiral where drugs were air and more expensive and more vital than food.

The Ranch supported male bonding during rehab and healing. I went into what I would call the work room, where group therapy took place and other events. On the wood-paneled walls were pictures of all kinds of residents and past residents. I was surprised to see that our counselors were former residents—former addicts. Above that were large letters: "Band of Brothers."

At first that felt cheesy to me, although I let myself acknowledge that I hadn't felt that since my soccer team, and long before that in high school sports. I guess I had matured enough to know I was a dick most of the time to the younger guys. A part of me really longed for the camaraderie of a team working toward the same goal, but it felt too fresh, too vulnerable. Everyone here was a stranger.

As I was feeling better, I noticed we all had more in common than I thought. I tried to fit in and work the system with my charms to get out of chores, groups, or deeper Step work, but the 60-day guys could see right through my magical skills. There was even a guy from the prison who was a member of the Silent Aryan Warriors (SAW), a white supremacist gang, who called me on my shit and was transparent to me. No one let my games rule the day. It was time to get down to business.

The program was big on calling an addict out on his accountability. All my survival mechanisms wouldn't work here—any broken rules equaled points against me. Once a resident hit fifteen points, phone privileges were gone. Eighteen points meant no family visits. Yeah, accountability sucked.

My brothers gave me a metaphor to represent my ego in physical form. It was a brick. I wasn't allowed to physically put it down until I put my ego down in my mind. Come to find out, I wasn't the first guy to come in with a big head and old habits trying to find a way around my accountability and pain. Others were given bricks, too.

But most guys were given a simple house brick. Me? Oh, no. Mine was a freaking *cinder block*! I had to haul that pain-in-the-ass thing around wherever I was—chores in the kitchen, working out in the gym, and especially to group. I felt a little ganged up on.

One resident was friendlier to me. He was more of a cowboy than a city slicker with his Wranglers and deep voice. "Bro," he said warningly, after noticing me stare at my papers and then out the window for twenty minutes. "You need to do your homework, or you'll *never* get out of here—or get rid of that brick."

I looked at him and cleared my throat. Everything on the pages was too much for my brain to handle. When the letters jumbled up in my eyes, I cringed. "Uh . . . um, can you read this to me?"

"Are you kidding?" he said with disbelief.

"No," I said quietly, feeling my face turn as scarlet as my hair, and I glanced at the ground.

He looked me over once more, from head to toe. Then he sighed and strode over to me at my little table. Like my mom, without making me feel any more embarrassed or small, he read me the assignments so I could complete them and the rules so I knew not to break them.

He's the reason I stayed.

In group treatment a week later, I was sitting in one of the hard wooden chairs around the circle, complaining about my wife—how she left our home with our baby girl. I played the starring role in my pity party. Suddenly, the same tough, red-haired SAW dude started in on me. Inside I started to quake a little because I could tell he was tougher than me. He looked like a biker. In fact, he looked horrifically scary and I had been avoiding him the whole time I was there.

"When did this start?" he asked.

"Two months ago," I affirmed, my victim-voice scratching out air.

"No." He looked at me pointedly. "When did you start hating yourself?"

I paused, my eyes wide, and the whole room grew silent. "Wh—when I was a little kid," I finally admitted, my voice small.

"It's time to apologize to him."

"Who?"

"Your little dude. Your little Robby."

No one had dumbed me down like that—to have to go all the way back through my hell of adulthood was enough of a mess. But *to apologize to that little kid inside of me for hating him all of these years?* I'd never dug that deep . . . and I wasn't sure I wanted to. I didn't know if I could, but the freaky biker guy opened the door.

One evening down in the work room, I started writing things out about childhood. Remembering Drew falling, remembering Mrs. Rose in kindergarten, remembering getting hounded, haunted, shot at with pins, and beaten up by bullies daily, I began to feel such intense emotion that I wept.

And suddenly I *knew* there was an evil presence in the room. To me, the lights actually dimmed. The temperature got bitingly cold, even as tears were coursing down my cheeks. The evil was so omnipresent that the guy working his Steps beside me cried out, "What just happened?"

I had to get up and rush out of the room.

Fortunately, I had grown vulnerable enough that I sought help. I was given a spiritual blessing, and someone sat with me while it was being done. Just like I had denied the existence of God for so long, I'd denied evil in the form of a devil. The Adversary seemed to know that if I succeeded with this program, he would lose me.

During that blessing I came to realize that I had been one of evil's best dark-side soldiers during my years of addiction. Even as I had fled the work room, I was flat-out determined *not* to serve the dark side any longer. Peace filled me, and I was advised to get straight back to work, so I did.

I couldn't say enough good about the fact that it was an all male rehab. I had been learning that women filled a hole in me, like street drugs. I needed to wean myself off that addiction, too, if I ever wanted to be healthy and repair my relationship with my wife. In the program, however, I also had to work through how to be vulnerable with men; that had never been on *any* radar.

As I worked, I realized that the Hollywood rehab had represented a half-inch depth for me. I was grateful for everything I'd learned there, but it was pretty much a day spa. Sure, I'd recovered and addressed some of my triggers, but I only did the first step.

I never managed to fully accept the second step of the program—putting my faith in a power greater than myself—much less moving on to all the other steps. Being vulnerable and receiving a blessing was all new to me. Without the drugs, I could feel energy. I could feel love being offered.

Despite the 12 Step groups I had participated in for over two years as the recovery guy, I'd never made it to the fourth step—except to skip over a couple in making amends. Here at The Ranch, there was no playing small; it was twelve for twelve.

Thirteen pages in, I looked down at the words that told all about my growing up for the first time. I was pretty proud that I had laid it all out. I had never written this many pages in my entire life! I kept going for a bit and turned it in.

"What is this? How many years did you write up?" my sponsor asked.

"Eighteen."

"Eighteen?" He flipped the papers back to me. "Get this shit out of here."

I looked at him, infuriated. So, I went back to my writing space and wrote this big resentment about him. That bled into forty-three pages, and finally, I got down into some of the core wounds. Bringing it back to him, I was surprised when he giggled.

He'd played me. He'd played the part of the tough guy!

"This looks better," he said, and I could tell he meant it.

My sponsor acted like my bishop or ecclesiastical leader. He let me share all my wounds, all my mistakes, and all my deepest sins. Then I grabbed my entire book of misery, took it outside in the cooling of the September sky, and I lit that book on fire. It felt so good!

There was one thing that I kept out of that book, that I couldn't bring myself to write, but despite that, 99.9% of exposing one's broken spirit was pretty freaking clean! I felt better than being rebaptized. I felt immersed in the fire before me; cleansed. Then, like a phoenix, I began to rise.

As I progressed and received my 30-day chip, I grew to understand there was a *huge* difference between thirty days sober and sixty days sober. At thirty, there was a push back on my ego and now, I was finally getting the message—acknowledging pain almost daily, but there was no suboxone to quiet cravings; we couldn't even smoke or chew.

After that, from the child me to the adult me, looking at *all* of my life, all of my pain, all that I had run away from, things started making sense. I put down the cinder block, literally and figuratively. I surrendered my ego.

Under this pressure, I started to *see* and recognize so many of my behaviors. One by one, I began to own them. I got reacquainted with "the God of my [very limited] understanding" one step at a time . . . the God who had found me on the mountainside and had made himself or herself known to me.

At first, after the mountainside experience, I questioned myself. I *had* felt a presence. Was there someone there, even though I hadn't seen anyone? What I came to realize was that He was there. And God had always given me just enough to know that there was something out there better for me than the hell I'd been living in. And, what I learned from that experience is not that God hadn't answered my earlier prayers. That was a lie I told myself. I hadn't had the balls to go to work and do what he was asking me to do, so I didn't get what I was asking for.

I started to get to work—real work.

It began with family group therapy. As my mother, my father, Angie, my siblings, and other relationships that were precious to me piled into the room, I realized from my writing that I'd never acted as if they were precious. In those transparent and honest conversations, I started to understand the part they played, and what my behaviors had done to strangle my relationships. Still, those family days were not about shame. There was tenderness, acknowledgement of steps taken, and reserved celebration. After all, except for Angie, they had all been through this with me before.

Mom and Dad, who were also working their own steps, took a huge one. They let me know, "We're done." That meant that all of my actions were my own and they weren't taking over-accountability for them any longer. I nodded in agreement. It was time for me to pull my big-boy pants up. I didn't know what that would entail.

As I made it to forty-five days, I started to find my leadership skills again. I could easily confront the newbie egos that walked in the door and encourage new residents to put down their own bricks and become brothers. Once closer to completing sixty days, I worked really hard. I needed to finish the steps. I needed to fully awaken *me*.

It felt so good to be drug-free again and earn my 30-day chip and, upon graduation, my 60-day chip from inside rehab. When I left, however, that's when the "real" chips started coming. These were chips I earned facing the day-to-day shit.

I went to ninety meetings in ninety days. Then I went five days a week and would continue for two years—and not because I was court-ordered. It was because I needed to. This time, the impetus was from the inside.

Good thing, too, because Angie dropped a bomb.

"We're over, Rob," she said firmly, but with tears in her eyes. "We're divorced." Then that feisty honey badger of a woman I loved so much, the mother of my baby girl Sophie, walked away.

I was really upset. I had grown and matured so much, but that didn't matter one damn. We were through. Upset didn't even begin to describe how brokenhearted I was. She had been coming to visit me regularly in rehab during family days. *Why couldn't she tell me then, while I was there? While I had that huge support system?*

Now I was back to living with my parents. Although I had just made a huge inner transformation, I had no confidence. Angie's announcement solidified my failure. I was scared, fragile, and weak. Right in that moment of weakness happened to be when my brother Drew called. "Hey Robby, let's go to Jackson Hole together!"

I knew what was behind it. In my early days at the Ranch, when I'd had zero confidence in my ability to fully get sober, I had shared with Drew and a roommate that if my life ever got to a place again where I needed drugs, I would end my life because at least I would die sober. I had to go to extremes with everything, and back then, relapse was a slow death. Drew knew this, and he felt I was at that moment of choice and needed a pick-me-up.

"Wow," I said, in spite of my misery, "that's actually a great idea!"

That will get my mind off Angie . . . for a little bit. The thought of some time with my brother, being able to talk man-to-man, felt both nerve-wracking and more than a little wonderful. I envisioned us walking along the riverbanks and trails, talking and seeing the awe-inspiring Tetons, maybe Jenny Lake. It was one of my favorite places to go. I figured sober, Jackson Hole would probably be overwhelming in its beauty. I started packing.

A few minutes after we got on the road, however, my friend Trent called me. "Robby, what happened to your truck? I saw it on a flatbed truck on Fifth South!"

What? No truck? I hung up and quickly started making some calls. It was gone. My big, fancy truck had been repossessed—for good reason, but I hadn't even known.

I walked back in, in a daze. It was clear that when my dad said he was done, *he was really done.* Natural consequences for my behavior now existed. This was what my counselors in treatment would have said was the very best learning stick. The bank came and took the truck and whatever else my parents had been loaning me money for that I'd been too mentally sick and addicted to pay for.

That's what my first few weeks out of rehab looked like: my wife announcing we were officially divorced and the bank taking everything I owned. It was hard for me not to hold sheer resentment against Angie, but especially my folks. After all, they'd been my magic carpet, my soft-landing place, my forever safety net! It would take me a few more months of sobriety to realize that they hadn't pulled that out from under me; *I had.*

Very soon, because there was no safety net and I was sleeping on Dad's couch, I had to get a job and do the adulting thing . . . at age thirty-one. It kept bugging me to realize that the whole time I had been an addict, and even as that old recovery guy, I'd masked myself with the persona of a high-rolling dude. As long as I had material things that I could hide behind, I had felt somewhat empowered. Now everything was gone. All the masks had been taken away.

I thought I was in full surrender during rehab, but my 90-day chip really meant something. I was raw, but I was real. I hated being this vulnerable, but every day, one day at a time, I kept waking up to what my next breath looked like, my next step.

It was time to trust in myself for the first time since I stepped foot into Mrs. Rose's kindergarten class. My higher power that I said that I believed in had removed the dunce cap and let me know that I was loved and worth living . . . but that it was up to me now to save myself.

CHAPTER 22

A FISH CLIMBING A TREE

Nothing says success at age thirty-one like being the guy living out of your parents' basement. Everything was a new beginning. I was starting over: job, relationships, money . . . but it also meant a *blank slate*. I had learned during rehab that many beliefs I'd had about myself since I was a little kid were not true—they were something I'd come to believe deep down during traumatic moments, and I'd carried *those* beliefs forward. Maybe they weren't all true.

I could barely consider it, but my experiences made me think a little differently about going back to school. Just the thought of it gave me PTSD. I had such nasty memories of school, most of them stemming from feeling stupid and from bullying.

My counselor at The Ranch let me know that there was such a thing as an evaluation for college that would help you understand your very own brain, and how it's wired for learning. *Wow. You mean you can understand how your brain works—strengths and weaknesses—so you can figure out how to actually learn at school instead of struggling and failing?*

My difficulty focusing, directing my wild energy, and maintaining information was real. That was a part of my life from as early as I could remember, but my counselor told me that this particular psych evaluation could help with modifications to the school system and testing so I could learn and grow . . . on *my* terms. Something about that sounded rad, sounded cool, sounded *freeing*.

He said, "Rob, I'm talking about vocational therapy. Yeah, you've got to do certain things to get your life in order. Get a job, get a bus pass, get on food stamps, and housing assistance can give you the best opportunity to succeed while you're building your life. But vocational therapy can help you determine your greatest skill sets so you go into a field in college and a career that suits you, your personality, and your brain the best."

"I don't know, man," I hesitated. "I've been told in junior high and high school that I had ADHD. It sucks to study—and oftentimes I struggle to read."

"Did you know there are special privileges for those who have ADHD nowadays?" he asked. I shook my head, remembering only that when my tutor helped me, I was able to pass.

"So," he continued, "you can get tested for primary vocations, get a note-taker, and get extra time on tests. You'll thrive. Rob, you're such a go-getter in other areas of your life—you can do this!"

But what would I do? What could I possibly be good at?

A sweet friend of mine and I were involved in a conversation about likes and dislikes when she told me about the field of psychology—that it involved the study of the brain and motivation of behaviors. When she said it calculated mental characteristics and emotional factors that determined how people acted inside of themselves and their relationships, I was absolutely fascinated. Secretly, I hoped I might be able to take (and pass) some courses.

I didn't know if I could. I couldn't ask someone else to read all the material to me like I had throughout school and even rehab.

This could be another dead end. Still, my counselor was right. I was a go-getter. When I wanted something, I found a way to make it happen, even if it didn't look like everyone else's strategy.

I decided to sign up at Salt Lake Community College and talked to the counselor there. "Let's do a test to see where you'll place." My scores revealed that in English and math, I'd be required to take a full year of uncredited courses to catch up. That kind of sucked.

The test also clearly indicated that I had ADHD. I told the counselor about my strong desire to pursue psychology, and he suggested the psychology assessment. It wasn't an evaluation of my mental fitness—this was a vocational test to see my vocational fitness with psychology in mind.

I walked into the office, as skittish as a cat in an elevator. I was happy to note that it was set up like a therapeutic office, not an exam room, or I might have high-tailed it out the door. The walls and furniture were white and soothing, including a wood desk, some tools of psychology, and a flip sheet. One woman administered the entire test, and fortunately for me, she was very kind. The test would take three or four hours per day over two days.

Within minutes of starting, I discovered how flat-out grueling it was to work my brain like that—and that my nightmares remained real. First I read written material, and she'd ask me what the story was about. I struggled like crazy. *Damn, I'm failing miserably. I know it!*

I tried not to let my rising emotion come up, even though it stung my eyes at times, especially as the end of the first day of testing drew near. Even though she was a professional and let very little slip and show on her face, I felt her sadness and frustration alongside mine. People had bullied me my entire life over having to take special ed courses. *No wonder I had to have tutors all my life!*

I was so dejected when I left. I sobbed on the way home. Then I almost didn't make it back for the second day. *What's the use?*

But I wasn't one who left things undone. I dragged my ass back into that office. *Maybe I can find what I suck less at*, I reasoned. At The Ranch I had learned to face my pain, lean into it, find out what was really behind it. Still, it took everything I had to get there.

This time, on the second day, the test facilitator showed me little blocks. They were half black and half white. Then she showed me a paper design and instructed me to put that together to match the blocks. I did five or six of them. Then I remade the first one without even having to look at her paper again.

Today, the very professional woman couldn't hold her poker face—she peered at my blocks and then shifted through all her sheets. With an astonished glance into my eyes and back down at the sheets she said, "I have never seen anybody do that."

"Really?" I asked, doing the second one from memory. "Well, yeah, if I get to touch something, if I get to do it, get my hands on it, then I do it!" Then I put the third one together from memory.

This time the woman set all the papers down. A great big grin crossed her face. "Rob, I'm serious. I've *never* had anyone complete this part of the test so quickly, and then recreate them lickety-split like that!"

I smiled. At least something was a little more second-nature to me. I put them together backwards and forwards just for kicks.

At the end of the day, the facilitator let me know it would be weeks before I got the results. She let me know how they scored the tests so I would be prepared.

A score of 70 = mentally challenged.

A score of 80 = fluent in reading comprehension and basic skills.

A score of 110 = genius level.

Yeah, good luck with that, Robby, I chided myself, knowing how brutally I'd failed the first day.

Finally, weeks later as promised, a full twenty-page report arrived. For the first day, it showed I had some distortions in thinking, some major errors, and yes, that I had definitely struggled with learning the way the material was presented the first day.

But the second day?

I stared at the sheet and put it down for a moment in disbelief. Then I picked it back up. Were they serious?

Spatial memorization and problem-solving? **I was at 120.**

Holy shit! From what the facilitator said, that's beyond *genius level!*

I sat there and let that information all sink in, as horrific memory after memory after memory flashed through my brain . . . until the real truth of it all sifted through a new strainer.

Mrs. Rose, I am not mentally challenged, I'm not an idiot, and I never deserved that fucking dunce cap! I was a fish trying to climb a tree. I'd never been taught how to learn in the way my brain worked.

The test showed the college what they needed to know about me to enter and how I needed to learn. Speaking of psychology, I was fascinated with the way I'd discovered I learned best. *If I can do this kind of learning, I can do other kinds of learning!* It was a brand new day.

I came back and told the counselor, "I want to take psychology. I don't want a degree—I want to learn."

Through a Pell Grant, I was able to sign up for psychology courses at Salt Lake Community College, or SLCC, in the coming semester, taking a three-hour block once a week. The classes were twelve credit hours of class time and that meant twenty-four hours of study time per week.

On my first day I was jumpy. As I walked across campus, it appeared to me like everyone was either twelve years younger than me, or a professor. Add to that the fact that as I walked the sidewalks, I was completely terrified and my anxiety ratcheted up to all-time high levels. *I don't do school like everybody else—like anybody else.* And I realized, as a young adult or close to being an adult, I had never done school without substances. Not one day.

Entering the classroom, I sat down and opened the huge textbook. Flashes of more memories filled my brain. My body began to shake uncontrollably. I felt my skin go red. My heart was pounding and I felt like I was going to have a heart attack.

I bolted out of my seat and ran out of the building. I started sobbing, and bawled all the way to my dinky little piece-of-crap car. All the way as I ran, I had this argument in my head.

Voice one: *Start the car and get the hell out of here!*

Voice two: *If you run now, Rob, you will never get over this. You will never get better.*

I sat in the car for a few minutes, sobbing. Then I just sat. Finally, I scrubbed my face with my hands, climbed out of the car, and went back to sit down in the big classroom again. I stayed until class was over. I didn't hear a word.

I couldn't remember my first three psychology classes because of so much anxiety and fear. I thought for sure I was going to get called out on how stupid I was, and the whole class would know it.

By the fourth class, I was able to start paying some attention, and to my fascination, I learned about a psychology theory called "The Spotlight Effect." Essentially, when you are suffering from deep anxiety, especially in social situations or crowds, you're worried about what others will think about you, your appearance or behaviors. Your anxiety feels like you have a bright shining light on you—a spotlight in which everything fades around you and people can't help but see you in all your faults.

Yet, as the professor explained, in the studies, they realized that almost everyone is so busy attending to their own lives, thinking about what's for lunch and mentally preparing for their 4:00 p.m. meeting and even being nervous about their own appearance, that there is a very slim chance that they're even noticing you.

As casually as I could, for the next few minutes I put out my feelers around me. I began to notice other people fidgeting in their seats, pulling down the hems of their skirts, fixing their cuffs, pushing back their hair, glancing around and hoping no one would notice they dropped their pen and made a loud noise.

BOOM!—I got it. *No one was really looking at me!* I could apply that theory to my own life and my own anxiety. I knew I would ace the quiz and *that* test question, no-brainer.

After class I went up to my instructor and told him of my experience. He stared at me and a smile crossed his face as he nodded. "Tell me about you, man."

As I did, his eyes grew wider and then wider. Finally, he said, "Rob, I want you to go home and write down your story. Then I invite you to take each principle that we are teaching for the rest of the course and apply the research in this book to *your* story."

I did exactly what my professor suggested. Using that method, I discovered that at least with psychology, I could apply it to myself and retain 100%! Knowing my strengths and weaknesses, I began studying—not by reading but instead by listening to books. All the textbooks were on audio, and I found I could listen and then apply the teachings. And because I was learning, I didn't care so much about the grade as about retaining what was important to me.

By the end of the first semester, I glanced at my 3.95 GPA. I hadn't needed a tutor, a note-taker's help, or even extra time. I did it myself!

As I continued to study psychology and bring it home, not only did I apply this in my own life, I observed my nieces, nephews, and my friends. Just like with my innovative learning processes, I realized, "I'm not defective! I have my own thinking processes."

Quickly I discovered that all levels of psychology were self-therapy. I moved along with the course material, continually fascinated. I saw so much of myself and other people I cared about in these paragraphs. It never went too deep until I got into abnormal psychology. This wasn't funny like Mel Brooks' *Young Frankenstein*. Even then, I got equally excited to discover what I was *not*.

Passion and purpose and fire began to light up my life, without drugs. I started applying what I was learning to my life, *my* life, including getting up in the morning, and it was time to apply it in my life skills and relationships.

This wasn't school . . . it was an *education*.

CHAPTER 23

SACRED DECISIONS

They say in rehab you can't get and stay sober for a person, but I *had* to. I had once lost Sophie, and now that I had my head on straighter, she was becoming my world. Early in my recovery, my brain desperately wanted to pick up where I had left off in the *heyday* of my everything—and was frustrated when I couldn't.

No big bad truck.

No beautiful Angie.

No custom-designed house.

No prolific business.

No sweet baby Sophie.

Fortunately, in my sobriety I did start earning back privileges to spend time with my baby girl, and that was magical for me. I didn't take her for granted, and I picked her up every chance I got. My time with her was precious. It quickly dawned on me—I needed to step up and be the provider.

Still, the fact that I hadn't been stable enough to run a business was lost on me. I had gotten used to having the prestige and power of owning a business. My ego made me think there was no way I could work for $10 an hour.

I was still looking for something better. I was taking way too long.

One day about six months into sobriety when I returned to Mom's and Dad's house from visiting a friend, I came home to discover my mother had burnt a roast. Not just burnt it—she'd been playing the Marvel superhero Human Torch, because that poor puppy was completely disintegrated.

The house? It was filled with thick, horrific black smoke. Apparently, my mom had put the roast in the oven, then forgotten about it as she took more time at a meeting after church than she'd intended. Fortunately, she and Dad did not arrive home to an inferno—only to enough smoke damage to ruin their day, and the curtains.

Mom aired out the house as best she could and we were all freezing, but it was quickly apparent that it wouldn't be enough. The smoke was in danger of ruining everything from carpeting, flooring, photos and furniture.

Dad got me a job at a disaster cleaning company called ServPro, at ten bucks an hour. On my first day, I talked myself up. I was selling air again. I was a lousy employee. Old habits of doing just what it took to get by died hard and I covered it up with all my talk. I was also back to being a little more humble.

On the days when I had the privilege to be with Sophie, she was rambunctious. As a toddler, she could now climb out of her playpen, so next I encircled her playpen with the couches to keep all that energy contained as I hung out with her. Soon, however, she was climbing over me and climbing over the couches! I would get worn out in half a day of having her, and then I found I would get cranky.

One winter day after I found myself frustrated with her natural exuberance and energy, I checked myself: *Am I gonna be that guy, that father that gets pissed at my kid because I have no energy and can't keep up with her?*

I remembered that my most precious days of childhood were all about the fun, physical activities with my dad and mom: skiing, snowboarding, water skiing, sports . . . I even remembered Dad jumping on the trampoline with us and flinging himself into the great pine trees around our yard! I knew I could never be my dad, but I wanted to be *that* kind of dad with Sophie—one who would encourage her in all her energy instead of being upset by it.

I went down and met Neil Anderson at GPP Fitness in Bountiful and told him of my dilemma. I was still smoking cigarettes and chewing. I talked to Neil and started coming to the gym a few times a week. Sometimes I'd up and leave without doing much at all, but eventually, I started coming more frequently.

Dad quietly observed my efforts in the new, mellow way that had come over him post-treatment, and especially since his kidney surgery the prior year before I went into treatment. He wasn't well, and I knew it. We began to have long and deep conversations about life.

One late winter day he watched me as I played with Sophie, chasing her around under a row of chairs we put together.

"Son," said my father, "who do you want hanging out with Sophie as she gets older?"

Another huge grin stole over my face as I thought about this beautiful, innocent little girl with her big princess eyes and infectious giggle. "I only want the world for her, Dad. Good people in her life, like you and Mom and the family. Good friends as she grows up. Good guys when she begins dating—although I don't even want to think about that right now." I could feel my blood pressure rising at the thought. *I might be that crazy shotgun dad,* I realized.

"Hmm . . ." he said, scratching his chin. "And so you don't want her hanging out with questionable people, I take it?"

"No way. I want her hanging out with someone who is going to treat her right and decent. Someone with self-respect and respect for her. A real man, who can protect her and take care of her and watch over her—someone who will always want my baby girl to shine, to be her best, to do her best. Someone to support the world-changer she's going to be."

He simply nodded. Then before I could say anything more he asked, "Rob, how is she going to know who that person is? How is she going to know all those qualities in a person? A girl learns the level of respect that should be given to her from her daddy, precisely, from how he treats her, along with the friends he chooses to be around and allow to influence her. Think of the people you're hanging out with. Would you trust these men or women to babysit Sophie alone?"

I was about to pounce on Sophie with the pillow, which would have sent her into another uncontrollable fit of giggles, when I stopped, the pillow hanging out as if in midair.

Hell no. I got it. In that moment, nothing became as clear to me as the man I should be for my daughter. The rest of the day followed in a blur because my mind was moving a million miles an hour. I had already been committed to care for and take care of Sophie, but that realization began to profoundly mark the decisions I made from that point forward.

In psychology, I was wrestling with some new theories of human behavior. I wanted to challenge the ideas I was reading about. I wanted to see how the body responded in fight or flight. I found I could apply all the theories of psychology in the gym, and instead of being a dog on the treadmill that had to be told to go or stay, lie down or walk, I became a tiger. With psychology, I could be tired, but I kept going, even in a cage fight—and with a good attitude! I learned to budget my time and my energy as I learned to pace myself. I kept reminding myself of the quote by Phillip McGraw: "Life is a marathon, not a sprint."

A marathon . . . I should begin training for one. I can do that, too.

I started running with my sister Maegan to train. The Ragnar Relay Series was a series of long-distance relay races. Teams from six to twelve runners would train to run approximately 200 miles over two days and one night, not stopping for anything, not even darkness. Now that sounded like a challenge.

It was scheduled for June 17 and would start in Cache Valley. I kept training like crazy, and when I didn't want to show up for a training or a run, I used my own psychology against my ego . . . and won.

One Saturday after I got home from one of my runs, Dad was in the living room, lounging in his easy chair—something he was doing more and more these days. Maegan's gift, that of one of her kidneys, had certainly extended Dad's life, but it didn't look like it would save it—not in the long run.

The good news was that he and I were getting along so well now. I wasn't fighting on every corner in my ego. I was becoming the man I knew my father wanted me to be, and as a sober guy, that felt really good. I hadn't forgotten our last talk about Sophie. In fact, I would never forget that talk. Still, in the midst of my psychology studies, there was something I wanted to know.

I crouched down near his easy chair and cleared my throat. "Hey Dad, you know how last night I gave you my nine-month chip?" Since I left rehab, I had been presenting and giving my parents each monthly chip I'd earned.

"Yes," he nodded, and the corner of his mouth lifted as he patted me heartily on the shoulder—although I noticed it was not as strong as it would have once been.

"Can I ask you an honest question?"

"Sure son, what is it?" He looked at me curiously. "And I hope all of your questions are honest. Maybe I'll even give you an honest answer."

There's my dad. I chuckled, then got serious again.

"Why . . . why didn't you ever let me fail?"

Dad paused for a long moment but his gaze was locked on mine. Finally he spoke. "I saw your failure as my own."

I blinked. *Ah. Okay. That's worthy, I guess.* It wasn't right, because I'd never experienced natural consequences of any of my stupid behavior with people, relationships and money, but of all people, I could understand it. If I failed, he failed, and that was something that Dad and I had in common: neither of us liked to fail.

Still, as I stared at him, I realized he'd let me be a huge financial burden for thirteen years, and I'd never stopped him either. I let him help me anytime he or Mom would. He'd cleaned up my other messes at school, in London and Israel, with Tasha. It had felt vital for me to have the adventures, the houses, the trucks, the girls, the lifestyles . . . but until a few months ago, *he* was the man to pay for them—instead of the one who should have.

I kissed the top of his head before I ran down to shower. *You're a good dude. I will be lucky to be half the man you are in my lifetime.*

A day later, Dad asked me to write down ten goals for my life. I putzed around a little and finally put down some things that, to me, felt *huge*. I found myself shaking, even as I wrote them.

When I was satisfied, I brought them back to Dad. In his loving way, he looked them over, nodded, and then took my shoulders and made me face him. "You are dreaming too small, son. You are dreaming too small compared to what you've shown me and others you are capable of. Go back and do it again—only this time, don't hold back!"

With my recovery so fresh, and having messed up so greatly in life before, I was afraid to dream too big. In fact, I was petrified. Still, I trusted this man. I looked around the house and what he had built from such humble beginnings, after losing his father and his mother: a beautiful family and amazingly successful businesses.

A week or so later, on June 8, 2010, the man, the senator, the father and grandfather attended an appointment with his diabetes specialist. He was fine when he was in their clinic, but something happened on the way home.

Mom and I were home when a call came in for Dad. She went to find him knowing he should be back, but he wasn't. Me and my sister hopped in her car. Desperately we searched roads we thought he would most likely take, trying to find him.

Then Mom called us.

"Dad called me. He sounded panicked but I couldn't make out what he was saying. I heard people in the background asking him if he was okay; then he suddenly hung up!"

We were all baffled. On our way back to Mom's each of us started making calls to the police, to the fire department, and finally hospitals. The EMTs told my mother, "Oh yes, we found him in Salt Lake pulled off the side of the road. We dropped him off at IMC Hospital."

Immediately, we drove there and began asking questions at the desk. "Can we please see our dad?" my brother and I both demanded.

A nurse walked up and stopped next to us. "Who are you guys looking for?"

Mom replied, "My husband, Dan Eastman."

"Oh, he passed away." The woman suddenly caught herself, but it was too late.

What? No!

Everybody started sobbing. I'm sitting there thinking, *Wait a minute, God. I did everything you asked of me, and you took everything away I care about.*

It seemed Dad's blood sugar plummeted while he was on the freeway headed to the pharmacy. He'd pulled over to the side and was waving for help, but by the time anyone understood what was happening, he was gone.

The first call I made was to Angie, since she was still my best friend and my dad really liked her.

The family was wanting to see my dad but we couldn't go in yet. We were standing out in the large waiting room, pissed at the whole thing. One of the doctors brought us back behind the doors and said, "I'm sorry you heard about his passing this way."

I stared at him. "At this point, we don't care. We just want to see our dad!"

After they had cleaned Dad up, they let us in to see him finally. Dad looked normal, like he was asleep. He was even still warm and soft. As we were holding his hands, it felt almost as if he was holding ours as well. It was tender and emotional. We all sat with him until his body went cold.

He was only sixty-four.

I didn't sleep for the next couple of days. I was so broken. We were all so broken. Those next few days were super intense. My mom was so grief-stricken; she and Dad were such a part of each other's lives. He had always been larger than life. Instead, the family all sat and lay in Dad's room, sleeping next to Mom or hanging out on the floor or in Dad's special chair.

There wasn't much time to think. We had to jump right into planning things, talking about who would do what at Dad's funeral. We decided each of his kids would speak, and we all named our talks "My Dad." None of us thought of him as "our dad"—it was always "my dad" because that's how he treated us. I was grateful he got to see me clean and sober for nine months, and I vowed to myself to live every day moving forward as if he were there.

Our whole family was crushed. In fact, our entire community was crushed. The whole time I was dressing for the day, I was in denial. *This can't be happening!* Only when I pulled up into the neighborhood of the area church, the Bountiful Stake Center, did I realize that not only was the entire church full, but the surrounding neighborhoods were full of cars, too. Dad had affected a lot of people and their lives in our small community, as well as the bigger community of the state, with all of his service.

In my eyes, this was proven by the number of people who came to pay respects, and the three different kinds of people who showed up at my dad's funeral. In the church, five or six hundred seats were filled, plus standing room only in the aisles and foyers of the church.

As far as those three groups of people, first there were the big-wigs I'd been surrounded with all my life because of Dad. Governor Herbert, Dad's friend, showed up and spoke, saying what an honor it was to pay tribute "to a man who's left a very large footprint," adding that "Utah is a better state—it's a better place—because Dan Eastman has trod this land and has served his fellow man." Lt. Governor Greg Bell sang "Danny Boy" during the service, and I lost it. So did Uncle Russ and other dignitaries from church and the state government.

Next there were the loads of community folks—our friends, neighbors, people who had served with Dad from the school board to the senate, people who met him in the grocery store and at church, people who had bought vehicles from him through the years and loved his customer service, and people who loved the man who lay in the casket before them.

Finally, there was the last kind of folks in the crowd that defined my father. There were five young men who came up to us, each individually throughout the services and said, "You don't know who I am, but your father gave me my first job and put me through school," or "Your father saved my life and helped me fulfill my dream." Each one of these young men would share stories of how he found them down and out and gave them a job, gave them a chance, gave them someone to believe in them.

Mom and the girls and Drew and I all looked at each other, shocked. Of course, we knew Dad was an upstanding, Christlike kind of guy . . . but we had never met these young men, nor known of our father's unconditional generosity towards so many others. We realized he had never intended us to know—he was that selflessly giving.

Dad was more Christlike than any person I'd ever met. *How much damn time I've wasted and how many opportunities? These other people jumped on those chances and now I don't even have the opportunity to apologize or say I love you.*

I knew that day I would never forget my Uncle Russ's words as he presided over the funeral. Instead of the resistance I faced in the past to his messages as a bigwig in the church when I didn't believe in God, or didn't believe that I believed in the same God as him, I felt the truth of his words. He looked down at Sophie and all her cousins on the front row.

"You little grandchildren need to know that your grandpa has passed through the veil from this world to the next. I would guess there was quite a fuss made when he arrived, just like when you came here . . ." He wiped a tear from the corner of his eye. "And so now we say goodbye for a season, for he will be busy. He won't be selling Jeeps. What will he be doing? He'll be teaching the gospel."

As we made our way out of the church and put the casket in the hearse, we had a police escort. (They weren't doing police escorts anymore, but they made an exception for my dad, and it was the Utah Highway Patrol who accompanied him.) Then, every lane on every street we drove down on the way to the cemetery was blocked by the fire department all the way there.

When we arrived at the cemetery, the National Guard and military men did the military salute. Good friends sang a song and bagpipes played. I was moved and humbled as I saw everybody else there was just as impacted.

As we were leaving, Governor Leavitt pulled me and my brother aside and said, "I want to step in as your surrogate father. I know if this happened to me, your dad would do the same for my sons." After the day we'd experienced, I knew he was right.

On the way home, still overcome by how dedicated so many people were to my father, his example was no longer like a shadow I tried to live up to. Instead, I came away from his funeral with the desire to be as *honorable* as my dad.

Uncle Russ was right, too. Dad wouldn't be selling Jeeps but that was minor compared to all the good in the world. I felt in my heart that moment that if heaven was a place where more people were served, more good was happening, and more opportunities to *do* good were presented or made, Dad would be at the heart of it, in the very thick of it . . . because that's exactly who he was.

CHAPTER 24

RUNNING FOR MY LIFE

One week after Dad died, I ran the Ragnar.

I didn't want to do it. Sure, Angie and I had been training for it, but I missed Dad with a deep, searing, physical ache. He'd become my best friend, my confidant, my north star in so many ways. In fact, I couldn't help but think about Dad in heaven. *He's probably running the show now. I might as well pray to Dad today for strength . . . and whenever I need help and guidance.*

I started praying more and having conversations with my dad, who was now someplace else. I didn't want to tell anyone, but it felt like another place I wasn't worthy to go to. But oh, I wanted to see him badly. Then I started looking around at me, at my life, and trying to see my situations the way my dad would. I'd imagine what he used to tell me in our talks about raising Sophie, and what he might say in his protection of what had become most precious to me.

"Think of the people you're hanging out with. Would you trust these men or women to babysit Sophie alone?"

The answer had been a "hell no," and I had changed my friends because of it. I started hanging out with people with bigger dreams, and greater desires to impact the world for good. If I even felt tempted to slip back into more comfortable friendships with those who didn't expect much from me because I was feeling so lonely,

I imagined Dad saying, *"What kind of conversations would you be having if Sophie was there? If you can't do it around your daughter, you shouldn't have that conversation."*

Losing my dad was like earning 90-day, six-month, and nine-month chips—it was that hard! I remembered how I used to come home and give those chips I'd outright earned this time to him and to Mom. They deserved them as much as I did, because they never fully gave up hope in me. They quit being that soft landing place that didn't serve me, but they never gave up on their son Robby.

After Dad passed, I knew I would continue to bring him my chips, only this time I would put them on his tombstone, even though I never felt his presence there. God knows I ached for it.

In the meantime, my entire family kept pressuring me to finish my commitment and run the Ragnar with Angie. There was no way I wanted to be out in the dark, alone, and the weather forecast looked awful: cold and rainy, like how I felt inside. After hearing "You know Dad would want you to do it" for like the fiftieth time from my family, I decided to fulfill my commitment.

I was right. The weather was crappy, and although I snoozed a bit in the van of runners, I was too keyed up to rest. Finally, when it was my time in the wee hours of the morning, they let me out on the highway, on the side of Echo Reservoir, north of Coalville, Utah, which sounds about as exciting as it was. Barren, dark and very steep, it was muggy in the slashing rain. I couldn't see; my headlamp gave off little light since it was so foggy; and I could hardly see where to step. I wanted to prove myself to my entire team in the van behind me, including Angie, but from the first step, I wanted to bawl my eyes out and quit.

This sucks. Shoulders heavy, huffing and puffing, all I could focus on, grueling step after step around the lake, was the fact that I'd lost Angie even though she was with me tonight on our team, and then I'd lost Dad. Was God really that cruel? Another series of steps and the answer came. *No.* Even in the hardest times, someone was there for me—on this side or the other. I flashed to one of my last conversations with Dad on his living room couch, when I finally shared my experience on Sessions Trail on the mountainside when I heard the voice, "Is that loud enough for you?"

Dad had become unmistakably quiet and misty-eyed. He'd already been amazed that his parents were part of the gang of my guardian angels. As I finished my story of racing down the mountain to him and Mom, needing to get checked in to detox and rehab, Dad and I both agreed—it *was* loud enough! My angels had been doing their job!

The memory filled me with a little bit of peace that at least I had shared that part of my soul journey with Dad—but it wasn't enough. Gasping, I was trying like hell to sustain deeper breathing, my muscles screaming on the ten miles of rolling hills, while my brain and my ego fought with me, telling me it was time to give up.

Suddenly I felt a strong presence right beside me in the dwindling light. Someone was running beside me! Out of the corner of my eye I could see *him*, matching me, stride for stride.

Oh my God, it's Dad! I had to fight back the sting of tears as a beautiful feeling came over me. He was right there, almost tangible in the ghostly mist beside me. He was so real, I wondered if anyone else might see him. It wasn't frightening at all—I could feel his presence encouraging me. I felt my father's joy, his overwhelming love, his "Attaboy!" even as my body and mind and spirit started working together instead of against each other. I started running faster, the beat pounding out in my mind and heart. In fact, I made it all the way up that last incline and burst around the lake with a speed I'd never accomplished—less than an eight-minute mile.

I carried Dad's presence with me for the remainder of the race, the remainder of the week, the remainder of my life. It changed me. The only thing was that experience was like a drug to me; I craved that magical, heartfelt and close connection to him. It made me chase him up and down hills across Utah and the country.

Things really started to shift that summer when I woke each morning thinking about Sophie, pretending Dad was watching everything I did. Now I had two fierce driving forces to stay clean. I realized I had so much more in common with my dad than I thought. For one thing, I *was now* humble enough to work a $10-an-hour job. I was now humble enough to be grateful for it. And . . . something deep within me knew I wasn't put on this earth to wake up and go to a job I hated, reeling with anxiety on Sundays because of that intensity of dislike. It was time to chase my dreams.

ServPro had been a Godsend, allowing me to work as their marketing manager for two full years, but it was time to be my own boss.

I began working with Neil at the gym, and I started training people. Along with my humble pie, I had been eating up all these new psychological realizations, and Neil had also been teaching me additional philosophies of mind and body. In my own workouts and what I designed for others, I kept pushing the limits—and my clients loved me. I did that for two years for free, then finally started to charge.

A beautiful byproduct of this passion and their focus on something super-positive was that my clients' recovery was stronger, and suicidal ideation went out the window. I discovered when there is a goal, a bigger purpose, and an adventure, it can take a much higher priority than death—and it can be a hell of a lot of fun! When I wasn't working, these guys and a few brave gals worked out alongside me. I even determined we were all going to train like Navy SEALs!

Along came Mick, a raging alcoholic. He was athletic, competitive, and a *great* guy, but due to his addiction he had suffered a continuous loss of relationships, loss of his integrity, and the loss of jobs to the point his new boss paid for him to go through my program. After Mick's girlfriend dumped him because he wasn't taking care of himself, he lived with me for a short time.

Mick and I talked psychology. We began using behavior modifications, where it was vital for him to work through what every human has to face: why he felt he was not good enough. Why he was using alcohol to self-medicate. And then, we had to test his mettle.

"What do you do when you want to quit?" I asked Mick. "You keep going—and harder. You stop running away from the pain and you push through the pain." I bought these resistance bands that were like ten-foot bungee cords that we tied to each other as we went up into the mountains to train and run. Since we both had a competitive streak, we were determined to push each other. People thought we were crazy.

Mick was a bit taller and faster, so I had to run faster to keep up with him. I was stronger than him from all my training and so *he* had to pull more weight to balance this push-me-pull-you up and down the mountain. I told him, "If I fall, you keep going anyway!"

A couple of times I bounced and had to scramble to get back up—otherwise I'd have been dragged on the trails. Since we always had the desire to "one-up" the other, we kicked each other's tails up and down the mountains and we both got quicker and stronger in a hurry.

"How many times do you feel like you want to quit?" I yelled one day near a summit as he started to drag. "On the mountains, we don't quit. So why do you let real life kick your ass?" I felt him move faster, then summit like a warrior.

That winter when the snow fell, we threw on shoes and shorts and nothing else. It was colder than a *mothah*, and we sure as heck were not going to stop and freeze! Mick learned a deeper will to push through the pain and push past it. The metaphor was applicable to sports but then he started applying it to everyday life. By the time he was in his fourth, fifth, sixth month of training, he stopped letting life kick his ass. He grew to marry that girl who once had left him, become a committed dad, and a smart and effective businessman.

During that time, I pushed myself harder than I ever had as well. Mick and I were definitely more elite athletes by challenging each other. We often went beyond Navy SEAL stuff and I challenged my clients to the craziest stuff. We became phenomenal performers.

I learned so much from those adventures; they shaped who and what I would become. This was way beyond physical prowess. Leaning into pain and fear to find out what I could discover about myself broke the limits on me. The idea of what I *should* be? Busted. The idea of what a working father *should* look like? Shattered. The idea of what kind of a coach I *should* be? Annihilated. So, as I grew and surpassed my fears, I wanted to change the game.

I loved how I could work with even the hardest egos, the sharpest minds, and the stupidest mindsets—like I used to have. In the basement of my mom's house, I was training housewives who hadn't moved for years to run half marathons and love their bodies for the first time in decades—maybe ever. I was also training people straight out of recovery and even straight out of prison. It was thrilling to see their results! I got up every day, and the pace and changeup were enough to keep up with my high-energy ADHD. *I am damn good at this!*

Only one day, I walked into my mom's house with two former prisoners by my side. My sweet, sweet mother, now a widow, was busy in the kitchen with my sister. At that moment, I had a strong realization. *Dear God, I am putting my mother at risk.* I had been using her basement as my safety net—yes, again—and it was time for *me* to be the protector for her with my dad being gone. When it came to my dreams, I had done so much talking through the years. It was time to step up and start acting.

That day, I pulled the trigger on a dream I'd been mulling about in my head since the day I'd written my goals with my dad. I opened Eastman Fitness and Wellness in Bountiful. I wanted to honor the name of my father and family, and where I came from.

I had been training people in parks and elementary schools, in lakes and up mountainsides. There and in the gym, I continued to be all about psychology, recovery, and fitness. I started training for cage fighting, of all things! While I prepared for my first two fights, my clients and I got ready to run obstacle races, too.

That first year, I not only ranked in world obstacle racing, but right on the heels of Hurricane Sandy I placed #142 out of 1,097 in my first World's Toughest Mudder competition at Raceway Park in New Jersey. It was so cold, hundreds of people were hospitalized for hypothermia. I was thrilled not to be one of them. I had trained too hard, too long.

I was filled with pride and joy. I'd been training outside all year, and learning to push through my pain. I was so determined a competitor, I even beat the Navy SEALs team and a man who was a triathlon Olympic medalist. It was the hardest physical thing I'd ever experienced to that point, and I felt like it was a huge win for myself, my family, and my recovery.

I was finally walking my talk. *And I am no longer a fish climbing a tree. I am a freaking monkey, making that tree mine and loving every swing of it!*

I'm pretty sure I got more people to cage fight and run ultra-marathons than anyone else on the planet, even as I was teaching psychology, recovery, and fitness. I taught them to discover their truths and realizations. My clients bought into the adventure and my passion *for* the adventure, and continued to excel as long as they didn't quit.

Deep in my heart, I hoped Dad would be proud of me. It was never lost on me that because of my own behavior and his death, he would not see my greatest accomplishments in my life. Still, I liked to think he could witness them somehow, like he did on that misty mountain race. I continued to miss him with a desperate ache.

When I hiked into the mountains, however, it was different. I felt Dad's presence. He was there somehow. I was learning spirituality by talking to my dad and quieting my mind. One of my first lessons from him was that if I didn't learn to love myself, no one else was going to.

A couple of years after Dad's passing, I felt I now had a pretty good idea of who I was. I still stumbled through relationships, especially when there was no potential. But my sobriety was everything to me. It was the only thing I had that I could genuinely be proud of—facing those demons. I was obsessed with my accountability; I had to be.

No matter what, sobriety came first. I had to keep it through all my personal journeys and the loss of friends. I knew I couldn't do anything for anyone if I wasn't sober, and this time around, I didn't want to be "the sobriety guy." I wanted to lead by example. But one major thing was getting in the way.

I needed a sign from God. I was seriously pissed off at Him. He threw three of the biggest relapsers at me: relationships, money, and death. He took my wife, took my stuff, and took my dad. I was mad at the whole idea of God.

On a cold winter day, I made a decision: *I don't want to be part of the Latter-day Saints Church. I'm going to pull my record.* Besides, one of my sisters called me out: "There's no way you're going to be in the Celestial Kingdom, the highest degree of glory in our church." That was where Dad was, I knew. She meant I wouldn't get to be with him.

To hell with all of it! If I go and tell the local leader everything I've done and repent of my sins, they'll for sure kick me out. No one has treated me well in the church leadership anyway.

So, I bypassed the bishop and went straight to my stake president—a higher ecclesiastical leader in our area. He was someone I'd never met before because of the few times I'd attended as an adult, I had always gone to Mom's stake in her area, where Dad's funeral had been held. I didn't dare pull my name from the records of the church because Mom would kill me. This was my easy out.

I was ready to purge everything toward this purpose, but before I could start, the man looked at me with infinite kindness. He said, "I want to let you know what this repentance meeting is all about.

Everything you have been through is like a heavy sack of rocks. Even little things add weight. If it's a little thing, it's a little rock. If it's a big thing, it's a big rock, but they all add up to a *terrible weight* that we carry around with us. However, Rob, if you are honest and dig deep, you can leave this whole sack in the corner and walk out a much lighter and freer man."

Well, I wasn't ready for that level of inspiration or kindness. I did my part of the repentance process and told him *everything* about my past; so much so that I hoped it truly shocked him.

After all, I was cleansing myself of the church, too.

Instead, the next words out of the stake president's mouth were, "Do you feel better?"

I shrugged, a little taken aback by him. "Kinda." I was still gearing up for the fight. After all, I'd already done the "expose the soul" thing in writing my "book" of offenses during treatment at The Ranch, so this wasn't a big deal. That heavy bag of rocks? It was the anchor on my heart of not being good enough for God.

"Do you want to meet again in a few weeks?"

"Yeah. That would be good," I heard myself saying. Those words were the most shocking thing for me to have said all night.

"Is there anything else?"

I shook my head.

Then I paused. This man didn't judge me. He didn't look at me funny—even after all my repeated indiscretions and sins. In the past, for much smaller things, church leadership had gone as far as ridiculing me and telling others details of my life they had no business knowing. This was the first time someone treated me the way I'd been taught that Christ would have.

I had a sudden realization. Before I walked into that room, Christ already knew what I was going to say. Even though I said it and repented, *it was still the action I needed to take*, the thing I had to work through. That action was why I didn't have to carry that stupid, heavy sack of rocks regarding the church anymore . . .

But there *was* one last thing . . . it was sucking at my soul. It was something I hadn't dared to share during rehab's Fifth Step—that last 1% I'd held onto with all the rage, the guilt, the shame and self-loathing I'd carried for so long.

A tear slipped down my face in the silence of that room. I kept trying to open my mouth. I'd never told anyone on the planet what I'd considered my darkest, most humiliating secret.

Taking a long, shuddering breath, I told this man now, about how I, a badass with women, was shocked to have been sexually taken advantage of by a man. I described waking up after passing out at a party and realizing a man was on top of me, completely against my will. I let the truth come out—what that act had done to me on the inside, and how it had only added to my library of self-loathing.

The room remained quiet, but something had changed. In this man's eyes, there was only kindness and compassion, along with the mist of tears that matched mine. It rocked me. Except for my dad, I'd never really experienced that kind of shared compassion before.

Finally, he cleared his throat and spoke. "I'm proud of you, Rob. Now, go leave that one in the corner, too. Own who you are and *be your own very best person.*" I felt like I walked out of there a free man.

That man kept his promises and stayed in touch. While I didn't go on a religious journey, his friendship set the stage for my spiritual quest to find more truth, choosing not to be ashamed or afraid of it.

In fact, later that same stake president asked me to talk to a boy who had come into the state from Haiti. His behaviors presented as gay, although he thought he was hiding it from guilt and shame, worry and anxiety. He was suicidal, and his hiding in plain sight was the same behavior as mine.

"Are you a good person?" I asked him after we talked for quite a while. "Do you help others?"

"Yeah, all the time."

"I thought so, from what you've been saying. So if you do things right in your life and go up to meet your Maker, do you think he'd say, 'Oh, yeah, you were amazing, but you can't come in because you're gay.' I mean, seriously, would you want to be with that kind of God anyway?"

"No," he breathed.

"Me neither! But I will tell you this: Living behind a mask is dangerous and harmful. Just be you. Be a good person. Can you do that for me? Can you do that for yourself?"

That kid gave up a lot of his guilt and his masks. Without that weight, he became a successful student and would report to me from time to time what he was up to, his new friends, and all the service he was doing in the community and on campus.

I thought, *Wow, there is huge power in learning who you truly are, what is in your DNA, what is in your soul—and what is not.*

Like this kid, I started not caring what other people thought of me anymore—but about being honorable in my actions like I promised myself and my dad I would on the day of his funeral. This alone started changing many of my relationships. I found that higher path of honor was unbreakably linked to my spirituality and my growth.

Fortunately, this began to crack the wall between Angie and me. I would never be the love of her life again and we both knew that. But because I started treating Sophie differently—as completely precious and in my care as her protector and supporter in life— Angie started seeing me a little differently. My high energy meant I still pushed things a lot, but not with my relationships. Well, at least, not as much anymore.

I had become very grateful to Angie. She never wanted to take Sophie away from me; she wanted her safety and what was best for her, too. That made us partners in raising Sophie. I appreciated that it was always important to Angie that I had a strong relationship with our little girl.

CHAPTER 25

PROMISES, PROMISES

As much as I worked on being "the man," accountability was still something I struggled with. Angie and I were getting along so much better, but there were times I couldn't pay child support and she knew exactly what to say to set me off. On my accountable days, I was so insecure I felt about ten years old under her scrutiny. On my nonaccountable days . . . well, things were worse. Then Angie got remarried, and as much as I was happy for her and Sophie, my resistance to another man in Sophie's life was nearly debilitating.

The first time Levi asked to meet me, Angie said he wanted to go out to dinner, on neutral ground. As I drove over, I "postured up" the whole way there, raising my shoulders and puffing out my chest. "I'm going to tell this dude just who the hell I am!" I shouted out loud. "How he's going to raise my daughter, and his job is to *stand down*. I'm in charge here!"

I was so worked up by the time I got to the restaurant parking lot that I acted like I was ten feet tall—and my ego was certainly taller than this guy, whom Angie described as definitely taller than me.

But before I could climb out of my truck, a strong feeling overcame me. "*Do you really want to be enemies with this guy?*" a voice said inside my head. I crumbled. I got out of the truck a different man the one who had driven in.

Within minutes of being in his presence, I realized that Levi was a gentle, salt-of-the-earth kind of guy. I also knew that he was exactly what Sophie needed.

One day Angie was after me for child support again, and I finally turned to Levi. "Dude, I don't want to be mean to your wife, and I really like you, but I have no money. I don't know where you want me to get it."

Levi didn't even flinch. "Just be the best father you can be. Do what you need to do for your recovery. Be good to Sophie and Angie. I got you." He didn't say another word for years—he really did have my back and the girls'. It felt beyond good when later I would cut him a check for several grand. Because of the amazing man he was, I was able to look him right in the eyes and mean it when I said, "Thank you."

I didn't date for two years after Dad died. After one of my last conversations with him—and the many conversations I continued to have with him in my head—I still was striving to be the kind of man I would want Sophie to date and marry. At the same time, I was a thirty-five-year-old male, and I wasn't blind.

One day, my buddy was teasing me when a smoking-hot girl walked by Cafe Rio, a local Mexican restaurant. Just seeing her interrupted my peaceful inhalation of my burrito. I couldn't help but stare as she walked by, wearing a hoodie that only fighters understood that said "Tapout", and an athletic cut to her body that could not be denied.

After more of my buddy's pressure, I hastily gobbled the rest of my food, then flagged the woman down before she left the parking lot. I couldn't believe it, but I asked her out. She said she was single. It was October 20 of 2013. The next few days we were so head-over-heels in love, we got engaged on the first day of November on Pier 49 in San Francisco!

So blissfully smitten, I thought I had found heaven on earth. Julie easily became an ultramarathoner. Boxing? She did it. Rock climbing? She was game. Tough and beautiful, she was a cheerleader for me pushing past my fears and opening my facility. Her children ended up being some of the greatest blessings of my and Sophie's lives! Julie's daughter Bailey became Sophie's very best friend, and her son Trey became my reason to coach a new sport. It would change my whole world forever.

After we married and moved to Mueller Park in Bountiful, it was she and her kids who helped me move Eastman Fitness into my first retail facility by that December. I was training for my third MMA cage fight. It all felt unreal to me and so beautiful.

It was uncanny that every single one of the professional and personal goals I'd set with Dad was coming true. I was now even more scared. I could manifest great things if I wrote them down and focused on them. It was all a matter of priority. And now I had an angel watching over me, too. I didn't take it for granted.

Julie's son Trey wanted to wrestle at Mueller Park Junior High. I was four years sober by then, and in the prime of my life. I told him, "Let's do it! I'll volunteer."

I went to the school and talked to Coach Mangum—the same guy whose team I wrestled against in junior high. "Hey," I said, "I'd like to volunteer."

"Uh, can't do that," he replied. "At least not yet. Every coach has to do a background check and get fingerprinted."

"Okay," I said, my heart falling. "I promised my son. Where do I gotta go?"

He told me, and I shot over to the office, filed for a thorough background check, and got fingerprinted. They mentioned it could take up to two weeks, so I prepared to wait for the results, but the next day I got an email.

"DENIED."

Immediately, I retracted into that scared, always-in-trouble little boy, completely insecure. My whole body went limp, filled with shame. As I sat there reading the email again, I thought about my first cage fight. At 155 pounds, I was in the best shape of my life. In my mind, I had always been able to wrestle or fight anyone. I was this kickass ultramarathoner and nobody my own size could touch me.

So, when I saw a post on Facebook from "Steelfist Fighting" mentioning that they were needing a short-notice fighter, I knew it was a sign. Getting up, I went into my mom's bathroom and stood on her scale to see if I fit the requirements. Then I typed out a response on my phone: "I WANT TO FIGHT." I trained for a couple weeks, feeling pretty pumped. When fight night came, however, within thirty seconds, my opponent took me down. He took full mount, straddled my chest, and began pummeling my face.

The most extreme fear and anxiety overcame me. My ears were buzzing, my teeth were buzzing. *Damn, I've invited a whole bunch of people here. This is on TV!* It wasn't like being in a bar fight where after a few punches people stopped. It wasn't like a playground fight, either. *I'm locked in a cage, for hell's sake!*

After that first round, in my corner I could barely breathe, and I certainly couldn't hear. Looking at my opponent, he was bouncing like a hungry lion, and I was already smoked. I felt like a little kid again the moment the coaches left.

As soon as the bell rang, it was the same deal—I kicked him, and he got me down and kept pounding my face. Finally, he choked me out at the end of the round. I got up and the crowd was cheering, but not for me. The darkness of self-doubt and self-hatred won. I had embarrassed myself and my family. I shook my opponent's hand and took the walk of shame, where the loser goes out to see the doctor—and I discovered I had to walk right through the crowd.

"Dude, that was awesome!" declared one guy, high-fiving me. "You did so good!"

Wait, WHAT?

"Man, you're so brave!" said another.

"Yeah, that was awesome!"

Every table was congratulating me. The only person talking trash on me was *me*.

After that fight, I realized I had done all this spiritual work to make amends to all my family, friends, and neighbors . . . yet I had never made amends to me.

I went on and took a few more fights. It was important to train with a number of different styles. I even trained in Taekwondo under one of my favorite coaches, Master Will Pace. Everything had to do with learning, not winning. Honor, camaraderie, discipline, self-love, and finding new limits were my focus.

I had a new mantra: "Win or learn. There is no lose."

I won my next two fights. I rediscovered the reason I started fighting. I wasn't angry anymore—not at me or at Dad or at God. I didn't need to prove myself.

So now, was I going to let a simple thing like "DENIED" get in my way of volunteering to coach?

I thought about it. *If I were the guy having to decide if someone was worthy to coach my kid, I wouldn't let someone with a record like mine anywhere near my kid—unless he talked to me.*

I went to the official's office and sat with the guy who denied me. "Where would you like to start?" I asked him. "I'm not that guy anymore." I told him my story, including my recovery. By the end, the man had tears in his eyes. He took my application and stamped it "ACCEPTED". That was the first of a series of amazing miracles.

For one thing, Trey and I got to spend time learning together. I certainly wasn't salt of the earth like Levi was to Sophie, but I found that I could relate to Trey at that age. I understood his insecurities and fears, and I also saw his incredible strengths and talents. In fact, I was able to see these strengths and talents in all of the members of Trey's team.

Within days of our first practice, they became *my* team. I took an unbelievable pride in these young men and discovered I could just be myself, and they listened to me along with their coach. Further, I found that when I listened, we related. Like the hardened guys I'd been working with, these young men, in their efforts to please us and meet their own inner challenges, rose to the occasion.

They were not the only ones. Parents who initially looked at me with fear and trepidation—the redhead with the fiery temper and the mouth who genuinely loved their kids—they started to love *all* these kids as well. We were a community, living and loving *out loud*. Wrestling went from a few sets of parents and solid wrestling moms in the stands to a gym full of cheering fans. The kids were adored, and rightly so.

I fell in love with the ability to teach these young men to face their fears, their depression, their grades, and the importance of doing hard things. By the end of the season, we were 8 and 2. A year later, I was approached by a mom named Suni Mason. Her son was wrestling at Millcreek Junior High, a rival. "Hey, do you have any interest in head coaching?" Her son was a 7th-grader.

I stared at her. *No way you're getting into real coaching without a good ol' boys club.* Then I caught myself. I'd said the same thing a year ago about volunteering, and look what I had proven, if only to myself!

I went over and applied, but first I was going to make a point with the principal. I had recently gotten a half-sleeve tattoo and was proud of it. He was Mr. Right, all coat and button-up with a tie. He was doing normal stuff, sitting at his desk doing paperwork, when I came in.

"Here's what I can bring to the team," I said, without hesitation. "I love these kids. I care about these kids. I'm also willing to lose my job over the way I coach."

He raised a brow.

"There's a lot of coaches who allow parents to pressure them and play politics. I won't do that. The first thing on any of my teams is mental health. The sport comes second or third. If they can look me in the face and tell me they gave 100%, it's good enough. But to do this, I need support from you."

He ended up putting in a good word for me.

And so I started as head coach at Millcreek Junior High, with zero background in wrestling except this last year as a volunteer and my wannabe weekend warrior degrees. I did the work and got certified for $1,200 and forty hours of training, but my passion burned so deep in my soul! I was all in.

And here was the cool thing—wrestling became cool at that school, too. Kids wanted to be around me—and be part of a cool team. *I realized we're all looking for something greater than ourselves to be a part of, and something to show the greatest parts of ourselves to.*

Still, I needed extra hours and income to keep my gym going. I applied for a job and became a tracker of the high-risk youth at the school—the kids who were struggling just to stay in class.

My new job was to take these rebellious, lazy, smart-mouth kids during the last hour of their day and make sure they were getting homework done and meeting goals. No small task.

I wanted to have real talks with these kids. It was obvious their home lives sucked. I was supposed to help with math, English, and science. Yeah, those kids were way smarter than me, but they lacked confidence, life skills, and passion. As I listened to their stories, I realized they came to school to rest and to eat. School was their survival—but survival only because at home they were often tending younger kids and, too often, facing neglect or abuse.

It didn't matter. The other kids at school looked at my after-school bunch like they were . . . nothing, worthless, invisible. Worse was the way that other teachers looked at them. I remembered that feeling all too well, and I realized that at home and at school, these kids were in a cage fight every day—a fight for their very lives.

I had my work cut out for me. I had some new promises to fulfill. And maybe I was one of the only ones who could.

CHAPTER 26

SHATTERING STEREOTYPES, INSIDE-OUT

"What?" my mom screeched. "A tattoo?"

I could still remember the terror in her voice that day when I'd been wrestling with my cousins before a holiday meal. My shirt had traveled up to reveal a forbidden tat on my back and my cousins immediately tattled. The joy of the get-together was shattered, if only temporarily.

My upbringing had taught that tattooing the body was darn near sacrilegious. Our bodies were temples, and to scar it permanently with ink should be unthinkable. So, for years, despite the rebel I often felt inside, and despite how I respected and admired the artistry, I had never inked my body until earlier that year. It took attending a Utah Jazz basketball game where I watched as the opposing team came onto the court. Suddenly one of the players came onto the court fully sleeved, his extremities covered in badass-looking tatts. I was not the only one who watched in amazement as the whole arena went silent. Yeah, he was a magnificent athletic machine, but it was more than that. His tats were mesmerizing.

For some reason, right then and there I experienced an instant connection between symbology, badassery, and also something I was really loving to do: blasting open stereotypes. As I was working with some of the high-risk youth at school, my half-sleeve was causing murmurs amongst the parents of my new head coaching position. All I could think of was how valuable it was for us as humans to have opportunities to look past the *outside* of a being and see what was true on the *inside*. With these kids, I found I was having to do the same thing.

Every day the level of trust from these kids was growing, but I was hearing more and more stories of the hell they were facing at home. If I wanted to have an ounce of positive influence on them, I had this little sliver of enforced time in my classroom each day. How would I use it?

One of the patterns I noticed was language that was disrespectful towards women—whether it was a girl talking or boys. I decided that was where I would start. I may have taken my own mother for granted for decades, but I certainly wasn't any longer. What if we started with something that honored mothers? The only thing was, it couldn't have anything to do with being cheesy or writing a poem.

The artistry of poetry stuck out to me, but for it to work, it had to be something that would speak to the kids. As I was driving to school one day, I hit the palm of my hand against my forehead. *Of course! RAP!*

Starting that day, the kids had an assignment to write a rap song, describing only the positive qualities of their mothers. At first, they were not going to do it, thinking it was stupid, but then some of the kid "rappers" started getting into it. Pretty soon the whole classroom was erupting with positive stanzas about their moms.

I would never forget the looks I started getting from some of the teachers who shared the same hallway and could hear some of the beats coming from our classroom. One teacher in particular always looked at me with the evil eye, as if I wasn't doing what I was supposed to be doing in the homeroom. The principal stopped by one day, prompted, I was sure, and his eyebrows raised when the kids were delighted to break out into the raps—about their moms!

A few of the kids told me stories of equally dumbfounded parents when they went home to share their kind thoughts about the women who brought them into the world and were doing their best to raise them.

As my wrestling team was starting to take off, the junior high principal became a fan of my off-the-cuff approach to caring for kids whom most of the rest of the school had forgotten.

We weren't getting a lot of homework done in class, but I was doing my best. I noticed a daily pattern of chaos. Like me as a youth, they reacted to the tides of stimulation, rules, peer pressure, assignments, school and home politics, and so much more. Moment to moment, they weren't directing their own lives, just surviving whatever came their way. I had another idea, and went and checked in with the librarian at the school to find that we had a number of chess sets. Dutifully, I checked them out and brought them into my classroom.

You would have thought it was the lamest thing in the world when I introduced to the kids what we were going to do next. But as I was able to use the metaphor about the boards of life, about the battles, the bullies, maneuvering, taking risks and chances, being bold but being wise . . . and the kids started to listen.

Then the busybody teacher, who reminded me a lot of the tattletale across the street from my house when I was growing up, peeked into the window of the classroom and a look of fury came over her face. When the bell rang, she marched up to me.

"Who do you think you are—being lazy and letting the kids play games? You're supposed to be the leader, getting them to do their homework! They are failing their grades, and you and your 'coaching' and 'inspiration' are doing nothing but putting their stakes in their graves that much sooner."

I could tell she cared about the kids, but I also knew she wouldn't hear a single thing of what I was trying to tell her. I was right, and she huffed off.

It *will only be a matter of time* . . . I thought.

Sure enough, the principal came to visit my homeroom the next day as the kids were seated at their desks across from each other, jostling and joking as they played their newly learned chess game.

"Rob, can I talk to you out here?" he asked.

"Sure," I said, to the "ooohs!" from the kids who could tell I might be in trouble.

"What's up?" I asked, as if I didn't know what was happening.

"Can you tell me what's going on here?" he asked, his eyes wide. "I didn't believe it when I heard you were playing games in the classroom. Can you tell me the logic behind this?"

"Principal," I said respectfully, "have you noticed it's not just 'games' but a specific game?"

He looked in the window a little more closely.

"Yeah," I affirmed, nodding.

"Okay," he said. "A game with a little more finesse for certain but . . .?"

I pushed a little further. "Tell me, what's the problem you have with all of these kids? What is the one major issue that they all have in common that you would like to have influence on?"

He stared at me, then cocked his head as he thought deeply. "What I've noticed is they're prone to knee-jerk reactions. Instead of taking a breath, they're the first ones to act out in class, the first ones to say something inflammatory, the first ones to throw a punch. Their biggest struggle is not realizing they can stop and make different choices."

"Exactly," I said, nodding with a wide grin. "And what are you forced to do when you learn how to play chess?" I prodded.

The principal looked into the window. "Take a breath and think. Think of a forward move—even a couple forward moves—or you're dead meat, in checkmate."

"You got it!" I said, beaming.

He looked back at me, his eyes equally wide but with a different expression this time. "Keep on doing what you are doing," he replied, shook my hand, and walked back down the hall.

When I came back into the room, the kids couldn't believe I wasn't in trouble. Neither could the busybody teacher, but the kids were learning some very new, very vital life skills, especially the moment between cause and effect; the difference between reaction and *response*.

Still, as another month passed, I realized that the kids really did need to pass their classes. They were starting to make wiser decisions, but that had to translate into passing life *and* tests to survive school and life. I did a lot of research on the internet, checked out what other teachers were doing with high-risk students—not just in the US but in classrooms around the world. I learned some interesting things.

One afternoon I looked out at the class after some announcements.

"What if you didn't have to take home any homework?" I asked seriously.

"What?" demanded several quick students at the same time. "No homework? No way!"

"What if *you* made *me* a promise that you would concentrate on your schoolwork while you are here at school—in this classroom and in all of your other classes. That you would do your best, every single day, and I could promise that you wouldn't have to take home any homework?"

I was met with looks of sheer skepticism.

"No school does that, man," said one student slowly. "You're crazy. As much as the principal is a fan, he's not going for this one."

"We'll see," I countered. "Would I have your word?"

"Hell yeah!" "Yes!" "Totally!" came all the answers.

After class I went to see the principal. I laid out all of my research and asked him to come in and see the kids and talk to them about "our" idea. He kept shaking his head. "Rob, this is the opposite of what you've been asked to do."

"I understand that, but research is showing that homework is counterintuitive to a student's well-being. If they can be asked to concentrate during their hours here, to give their word, and they can be free to go home to the survival zone that they're in, but not add stress and trauma to what they're already facing, studies show they'll be more effective *in class.*"

"I don't know . . ." he said. I could tell he was thinking of Mrs. Busybody and the other teachers. How would he explain this, of all things?

"Let's just try it," I urged, sincerity pouring out of my voice. "You let me know they're already failing. They're already in danger of not passing this year's curriculum. What can it hurt if we try something that might work?"

He needed time to line it out and talk to a few of the teachers. Within a few days, however, the principal came into our classroom. I noticed his tie was loose, his top button was undone, and, as he sat on the front edge of my desk in front of the kids, he was trying to be cool. He looked awkward and I absolutely loved him for it.

Silence permeated the classroom.

"Your teacher, Mr. Eastman, said that your class has a proposal."

Big grins started to spread on all the faces in the classroom as they all nodded.

"Will you give me your word you'll work your guts out, do what your teachers ask . . . everything you can do in the time you are at school? Every day?"

Vigorous nods greeted him. "Yessir!" they nearly shouted.

"Okay," he said, looking each of them in the eye. "We'll try this. If your grades slip further, we'll have to stop the experiment, but we're willing to try it and see."

No one was more surprised or pleased—except maybe the principal—when it came time for the end of the term and I discovered that everyone passed nearly every class. Some were even getting Cs, Bs and one or two As in certain classes!

The principal and I saw each other from across the cafeteria one day as I was headed to gym, and we grinned at each other. Our smiles were not nearly as big as the ones plastered on our kids! It was incredibly satisfying to experience.

That spring, I taught Sophie how to ride a bike. Just like when she was a toddler starting to walk, then run, that girl was a speed demon and fast becoming a neighborhood terror. *Good thing I'm back to being Mr. Rogers.* Then I laughed. *Mr. Rogers with an attitude.* I noticed how people started treating me differently now that I had a half-sleeved arm in tats: Some good, and some immediately judgmental.

That month I coached both my girls' soccer team again. As I became more known in the area for my teaching and coaching, people started talking to me about my story. Upon request, I was given my very first speech at KSL, a local news station—and I bombed it! I blanked out on stage, where no words would come, and my forty-minute stint petered out to twenty. I promised myself that would never happen again.

Fortunately, I survived, but life was busy. I ran a 50k race on May 30th. This was not an Eastman "fun run." Oh now, it was 33 miles in the mountains with a 7,000 foot elevation gain! The kids I was coaching couldn't believe it—their coach worked out way harder than they did at times.

In June I started to transition more guys out of prison, and I met Jeremy and Randy. I had a rule: anyone who asked me to be their coach had to spar with me first. When Jeremy darkened the door of my gym, I almost rethought this rule! He was covered from head to toe in gang tattoos. Still, I reminded myself to practice what I was preaching and embodying—that it was what was on the inside that mattered—and how any person could be trained and train themselves to act differently on the outside.

Soon enough we discovered that Jeremy, who was called "Boulder" because he could hit like one, was a teddy bear on the inside. My girls even called him Uncle Jeremy. He respected me, and in my presence and that of my family always put away his persona. His twelve-year-old self came out and he treated me like a respected elder or dad.

I began coaching MMA and training with these two guys. It was to be Randy's first fight and my second fight. By the end of June, I won my first jiu jitsu competition and ran my sixth Spartan race, both on a broken foot. I was so dialed in on physical pain at this point I used it to teach me only valuable lessons.

Still, there were needs in the community not being met. Adults and kids deserved physical training and a reason to live. I hosted my very first Eastman Family Recovery Foundation Fun Run for Mental Health at the end of that summer. I didn't make people run 50k; I dialed it back to a tenth of that. It was fun to see so many gym participants with their families, and school kids and their families as well. In my small town, the message of mental health was getting out. To have powerful and open conversations in a place where that had been relatively taboo felt so good.

Julie and I moved to Woods Cross, into a duplex. I was hoping the change of scenery would do us good as there seemed to be a lot of drama at home. By the first of the following year, we had grown out of our current Eastman Fitness location, and we moved our gym to Centerville. Rock climbing had become a new fitness obsession for me, and I started incorporating it into my training.

That spring I had my own boxing match, and I was actively training boxers three or four days a week. I coached Randy to our first MMA title in mid-May. Shortly thereafter I started my IOPC Program 1-on-1 Addiction Coaching certification. Like my father said I could, everything I put my mind to, I was achieving.

As the weather melted into hot summer, we attended my twenty-year class reunion. It was the first time I had ever attended in two decades. I loved seeing everyone and being clean and sober. People couldn't believe it was me. It was a great summer in nearly every way.

I was starting to build my fitness summer youth camps and they were growing—fast. I was coaching a lot of MMA, and Randy won our second belt in August.

We also held our foundation's second Fun Run for Mental Health. We called it "Light the Night," a metaphor for the power that is possible when we choose to bring light into the darkness. It was stunning to see a sea of moving glowlight necklaces, and to feel the camaraderie of so many extended friends and family in the community running together, laughing, supporting and cheering each other on. That night, Mike Leavitt and Governor Bell showed up in support, and my heart warmed at the presence of these two great men who not only loved my father so much, they had maintained contact with me and my family through the years.

Light the Night was not only successful from a public standpoint, I personally experienced something so deeply healing it surprised me. I had humbly asked Cathy Low to be our main keynote speaker—my late best friend's sister. As her inspiring speech about Danny and her experiences poured out on the crowd, I felt the power of Danny's sister at the podium, her words affecting people. There were tears of great hope upon their faces.

When Cathy and I had reunited in private months before, it was also joyful and healing, but, awkwardly, I asked her point-blank about the rumors I'd heard after Danny's funeral—that her family blamed me for Danny's death.

Cathy had stared at me, her eyes wide open. "You and Danny were like brothers!" she cried out in astonishment. "Of course we never held any ill will! I promise you, Robby, my parents would attest to that, too." I felt her sincere words wash over my whole body. I had held onto that deep-set guilt and shame for too many years, never taking it to the source and instead listening to rumors. It taught me a great lesson. Because of that I had also shied away from Danny's parents all this time.

I met Cathy and Danny's parents for the first time since Danny's funeral at a wrestling match. My eyes stinging, I went straight up to them and threw my arms around them. They hugged me equally as hard. There in the stands, they told me the truth, that they'd never blamed me for Danny's death. We sobbed right there in the stands, holding onto each other, and shared a moment of grief and deep release. I felt another tremendous shift inside of me. I was growing emotionally by leaps and bounds in so many ways.

Still, there was drama at home, and it was breaking my heart. Julie and I couldn't seem to break free of an unhealthy cycle where we were both participants. I looked for opportunities to change our marriage and to work out my deepest issues on the inside. Two came almost immediately.

The first was when a buddy of mine called me and asked me to be an active participant in a humanitarian effort that included a mountain climbing trip to Nepal to the base camp of Everest! *This was something Dad always wanted to do!* It took on new meaning when three of my siblings decided to go, too. The opportunity reminded me a little of all the personal growth I'd experienced during Outward Bound—plus as one of the leaders, I would be able to put to use the extreme fitness skills I'd been engaging in for years now. It was another bold adventure that would change lives!

Not long after accepting the trip and preparing to go, a "For Sale" sign caught my eye. After checking it out, Julie and I decided to buy a farm in our local area. I felt it could teach our three kiddos at home how to work hard, and how to care for something other than themselves. It could be a lesson for *all of us* in nurturing—how things could continuously grow, if we let them—and supporting them. As we moved out and started the farm life in addition to everything else we had going on, it felt like this farm would offer the opportunity, like nature, to make us or break us.

CHAPTER 27

EVEREST OR BUST

I looked at the team roster for our grand adventure with unbelievable pride and satisfaction. That my siblings and I had gotten this wild idea—to do good in the world and honor our father together the way we'd actively been taught as a family—was so compelling and joyful to me, it seemed unreal.

Holy shit! We're headed to Base Camp . . . at Mount Everest!

And we'll carry Dad with us.

In fact, when I discussed the climbing adventure with Danielle, Maegen, and Drew, they each got most excited to find out it was for a purpose bigger than any of us. My buddy, an oncologist for Gamma West, asked me to get involved with their nonprofit effort called Radiating Hope. We would be going with a group of cancer survivors and their doctors, inspiring them and supporting them, which meant the climb would carry an even deeper meaning for our family.

I was also stoked to share with my siblings everything I'd been learning since recovery. There were so many things I'd come to study and see firsthand about mental fitness and my psychology studies. I knew these things would play out before our eyes, as there were intense psychological and physical ramifications from visualizing success and health, creating adventure, and giving back to others. They would benefit as much as the participants.

We all paid a bunch of money and also got sponsors to be able to go. After all my mud runs and wilderness adventures and triathlons, I was excited to find out that we were being accompanied by some very famous summiteers. One was Brandon Fisher, a man who was known for summiting the world's tallest seven summits. There was also a famous Sherpa named Lhakpa Gelu Sherpa. Lhakpa was born in Nepal, learned English as a guide, and had summited Everest more than fifteen times! In 2003 he made the fastest summit of the legendary mountain *ever*, in under eleven hours—a feat that took most climbers weeks. I couldn't wait to meet him.

I continued training the way I had since starting my recovery—balls to the wall. Drew was in great physical shape, and Maegen had been training off and on the past few years. Danielle was the least trained and prepared, but she and I trusted that we would all make it.

The adventure began long before the climb. First was collecting the very specific gear necessary for our survival. It was surprising to learn that we would only be packing 25 to 30 pounds of the gear ourselves on the trail, as our Sherpa guides and porters would be carrying the rest of what was needed. It seemed crazy to me, but they said the higher we climbed, the more we would need every extra ounce of energy just to take a step.

I didn't quite believe them.

Our entire group arrived in Kathmandu in mid-April. Situated in a bowl-shaped valley in central Nepal, it was a nasty, polluted place, but full of rich and beautiful culture. It was the first time my siblings and I tasted adventure like this since we were little. It made us all feel a little nostalgic for Dad. He'd been the one who introduced the world to us. I hoped to do the same with Sophie.

The humanitarian portion of our trip came to light here in Kathmandu, and we were educated on the fact that in Nepal, cancer was a leading cause of death. They needed over a hundred radiation machines to serve the high prevalence of cancer, but the entire country had only six working ones. We had joined RadHope and Gamma West in donating and shipping four more machines to the hospital. It felt great that our efforts were a small part of that.

From there my siblings and I climbed into an insanely tiny plane. On our way, our nerves were shaken when we were told that Lukla Airport was considered the most dangerous in the world. The runway was only 1,800 feet. In other words, if you didn't land at the very beginning of that runway, you hit a mountain.

I gritted my teeth during the whole landing as the mountain reared up in front of us. *Whew!* Even as an adrenaline junkie used to tall mountains, that was enough for me.

Lukla was the village where our trek to Everest Base Camp began. With no more vehicles or roads, we would traverse a network of villages connected by footpaths as we made our way up. We met our Sherpa team so we could start trekking along the Dudh Kosi River. Most of us were geared out to the max, and I laughed as our Sherpas came up in their flip-flops, leather fighter jackets, and skinny jeans inspired by America. *Oh boy, this is going to be good,* I thought.

After the first morning of trekking, everyone was given orders to get settled in and get some rest. However, Drew, Jacom, another crazy adventurer, and I were too antsy. Since my time in Outward Bound, everywhere I went, I always took deflated soccer balls and a pump because that sport happened to be the international language. I brought enough balls so that in every village we could give out at least a soccer ball or two and a pump. So now, we pumped up a ball and found a leveled-out soccer field made of dirt with some wood goalposts.

Children peered out of the mountain village doorways, looking at us curiously. One kid had enough courage to come straight up to me. "My best four . . ." he motioned, "against your best four . . . for that ball," he said in broken English and sign language.

"Little stud," I laughed, "you can have the ball just for coming over here!"

And we let the games begin. A few more from our group joined, and the whole village came alive with spectators with joyful smiles. Eventually, we were playing eleven on eleven! It was one of the most breathtaking afternoons of my life.

Watching the looks on everyone's faces as we interacted, laughed, and didn't need to know the language struck a chord in me of connection. I was filled with so much gratitude that day, it felt deeply spiritual.

During my hiking, I had time to think. As a coach, I also observed as some of my fellow adventurers started facing challenges. Some leaned right into those challenges . . . some ran away—just like I had done for most of my life. As I watched them, I realized how much I had learned on my journey. *I'm on a mission to change mental health. It's beyond fun runs and physical exertions . . .* I thought, feeling it in my bones. *It's like I have a life calling.*

As we continued interacting with the villagers, I started thinking about how these two cultures—the Nepalese and American—differed so significantly. I watched kids who were the same age as my kids on my wrestling and volleyball teams, but with grins as big as the Grand Canyon. Their faces were filled with joy, whether anyone was watching or not. As I watched, I realized they all knew each other. None were on their phones. They loved each other and their community. They interacted, held hands, smiled at one another, and supported each other up the mountain trails. *We could learn a lot from them.*

As the air got thinner with the passing days, our group didn't take rest for granted any longer. For each elevation gain, our muscles needed oxygen and robust nutrition. Where we were headed, there was a lot less air and not nearly enough nutrition, especially when the locals were surviving off one carrot sandwich and ginger tea. Food was medicine for our group, especially Coca-Cola Classic and Snickers bars. I learned that the cola ate bacteria in the stomach and the Snickers gave much-needed carbs, sugar, and protein. *Sign me up for twelve each!*

Despite having traveled extensively as a young adult—from London and Scotland to Costa Rica, Israel, Egypt, and other parts of Europe—back then I hadn't *lived* yet to understand or process fully everything I experienced. Back in those days, I was running headlong from pain. Now, I was able to sit still, even when breathing heavily. Between the cultures, the colorful monks, the curious villagers, and the spiritual blessings placed on the hikers approaching the formidable mountains, I saw how different life could be. How simple. Not blurred by materialistic things. I began deeply appreciating stillness and simplicity.

Dear God, I thought, *I'm becoming a minimalist.* Beyond my self-teasing, however, something was sticking fast inside me. I was having deep, spiritual connections with every interaction, with every step, appreciating the slightest touch, a curve of a lip, the meeting of eyes that went far beyond language, even with members of our group, and the stunning connection to nature had my heart beating even faster.

As we climbed from village to village, tea house to lodge, our Sherpas kept reinforcing "slow and steady." That would get us there, they promised. Even so, tempers began to flare, and more physical issues began to manifest within the group. My fellow lead got sick and decided to stay back. Suddenly I was the one whom most everyone was going to besides the sherpas for support and to solve problems. We kept climbing the paths, one step at a time.

Then my brother Drew, our consistent warrior who no one had worried about for a second, suddenly got extremely sick. *It must've been something we ate*, I figured, as suddenly I started feeling really crappy, too. *This is not fun.* When he and I both got the "Khumbu cough," a deep, bronchial cough that wouldn't go away, I started getting nervous. I was also starting to get a headache from hell. Even in my state, I realized, *It can't just be the food.*

Drew and I were experiencing altitude sickness, and not getting enough oxygen. The human body simply does not function well at high altitudes above 8,000 feet, to the point there was even a name for these severe symptoms: acute mountain sickness (AMS). At this village, our available oxygen was *half* that compared to sea level. Even us high-altitude residents from Utah needed to rest and let our bodies adjust.

Drew, ever the positive warrior, kept insisting to me that he was fine.

The next day, I was assigned to take the group of folks who could physically manage the climb to Gorak Shep: "the base camp before base camp." I barely stumbled up there myself, and I was feeling beyond exhausted. I could have lain in the middle of the trail. I hadn't even had time to acclimatize or rest when one of the Sherpas came up and said, "Your brother is sick."

"I know," I said. *He's feeling like me.*

"No, he's really sick. He's at only 40% oxygen, Rob. Do you know that at 80%, people are hospitalized? He must go down, now!" My heart sputtered but I felt a surge of adrenaline and went looking.

When I came upon him, I stopped short. Drew had an oxygen mask on. I was about to give him shit when I saw his eyes. They were open, but he was *not there.* That scared me. Drew really was in bad trouble.

We laid him down, but it was clear his blood oxygen for his 200-pound, six-foot frame was not going to keep him alive. Any moment he was off oxygen, he passed out. We called Nepal's version of Life Flight, and we waited . . . and waited. At that point, it felt like the movie *The Neverending Story* from when I was a kid, and equally as frightening. Nearly every afternoon in the villages anywhere near the base of Everest, the "Nothing" comes: blankets of clouds push up stormy moisture, and it gets dark and impossible to see. That day, like most, the helicopter couldn't get to us. It was frightening because Drew now had pulmonary edema. His brain was swelling in addition to the fluid impinging on his lungs.

One of the Sherpas got ready to take him down 3,000 feet. *Oh my God,* I thought in fear, *that path that we barely made it up?* In my mind, there was a 0% chance that my brother was going to make it out alive. My blood ran cold and I was determined to leave the group and go with him.

The Sherpa, who seemed half Drew's size, helped him onto a pony. Frantically I was looking around at how I could grab my stuff and follow. The girls were in the same mindset, but Drew would not let us leave with him. In a rare lucid moment, with raspy breath, he demanded, "Finish what you started! For me, for Dad . . . for yourselves." He made us promise, then he was gone, following the Sherpa down the mountain as the girls and I breathed our own prayers for his safety.

Drew had been my climbing buddy and my roommate. Now I was alone, and I wasn't thinking clearly. The bad headache was back. After dinner, I had to figure out just how to get to my room. It was only thirty steps, but each one felt like eternity, like it was literally killing me.

Suddenly in my body, I received a strong warning: *"If you lie down, you will never get back up again."* Instead, I sat at the edge of my bed; it was my turn to be in trouble. If I screamed for help like I wanted to do, I'd pass out and possibly never wake up. From sundown to sunup, I sat there, thinking I was going to die and worried about my brother.

How am I going to tell Drew's wife if he doesn't make it?

Somehow, I survived, and that morning, I looked into the equally haunted eyes of my two sisters. Danielle and Maegen were as terrified for Drew as I was, and we had not received word yet. Most of our buddies were having a hard time, too—even the ones we all thought would not really struggle. I realized there was a reason why Everest itself was such a feat, when getting to Base Camp was often one of the most grueling adventures anyone experiences in their entire lives.

Surprisingly, after some food, I felt like I had enough energy to guide the members of our group who were still functioning. To my utter joy and relief, my sisters came with me. Now we had two men to honor on the journey: our dad and our brother—though we were still unaware if Drew had made it down to safer altitudes and medical attention. The only thing keeping us on our path was the promise we made him not to stop.

We felt Drew with us too now as we pushed forward.

It was a little over two miles from here to Base Camp. My feet felt heavier than missile silos. Each step was excruciating. Every five steps, we had to stop to take a breath. It was ridiculous. Finally, we were down to just one mile. Then a half. Then a quarter mile. Ultimately, we dragged our asses into Base Camp.

That's when we got a radio call with news from the Sherpa who took Drew down the mountain. He had dropped Drew off at La Preche, a few villages down . . . but no one could confirm if his condition had improved or worsened.

I looked at my sisters. At that point, we couldn't wait until we could also descend and learn more about Drew. We decided if possible, we would take the helicopter down to check on our brother. I even designated another team lead, but it was hard to leave everyone we'd grown so close to and loved. We all started to bawl. It was tender for everyone, and we sent most of the team back down the mountain to a somewhat safer elevation. That moment felt like the end of the season with my teams at home.

My sisters and I waited for the helicopter for fifteen minutes— then thirty minutes. No helicopter.

"Sorry, guys, you've got to hike down. The helicopter is not coming."

So Danielle, Maegen, and I took off. When we got all the way back down to Gorak Shep, the whole world had fallen apart there. Forget *The Neverending Story* . . . this was *Game of Thrones*. All the psychological and physical effects I had warned my family would be afoot amongst us as humans were happening before our very eyes, creating an "us vs. them" mentality. I even had to remind myself of it in the middle of the drama.

As I stalked around reminding people we were a *team*, I suddenly couldn't find my beautiful sister, Danielle. In the midst of that chaos came one of the most hilarious situations of the whole trek. She was ill, experiencing altitude sickness of her own. I found her in one building with oxygen on . . . and no less than twelve guys eagerly checking her pulse. *You gotta be kidding.*

I glared at all of them. "You sure as shit are not doctors!"

Somehow, we all made it through that night. We headed out the next day to this little place where our brother was supposed to be, but he wasn't there! Feeling a little disheartened and very afraid, we were determined to reunite with our brother. My sisters and I hiked down almost halfway back to Lukla. Fortunately, a helicopter was able to find us at one point, and within minutes, we arrived in Namche Bazar to find that Drew was not only alive, but feeling so much better!

The relief that the girls and I shared was palpable. I couldn't help it. I sobbed quietly, liberated from one of my worst fears—to lose another man I so deeply loved and so greatly respected.

With Drew feeling better, we had a little informal celebration a few days later, the four of us, sharing about our experiences, laughing and sometimes tearful at profound moments as we sat out on the balcony of our little rental, looking out over the smoky but colorful skyline of Kathmandu.

Our conversation was so real and tender, in fact, that I somehow thought it was okay to turn the tide of conversation to one of my sisters, calling her out and telling her she deserved better than how she was being treated in her marriage. While we all felt that compassion for her and truly worried for her well-being, I was the only one talking. In reality, I was preaching at her—and that took it too far, especially because I had my own issues at home.

Drew intervened and suddenly things got heated as he stepped in front of me. He and I started piping off at each other. There on the balcony overlooking Kathmandu, I got up in his face and he got into mine.

"Fuck you!" he cried.

"No, fuck you!" I returned.

"No, fuck you!" I grabbed him and he grabbed me, and we were grappling over the balcony rail. The girls started screaming at us to stop. They were terrified—and rightly so—that we might throw each other off. It looked like a scene from a stupid movie, where someone might land miraculously, or someone might really die.

"Dude," I yelled, "just tell me what's really bugging you! Just let it out!" I knew his anger was so much more than me calling out my sister. All the walls were down, and there was an unmistakably deep, intense rage and hostility towards me in his eyes.

"You really want to know?" Drew demanded.

"Yeah, I really want to know!"

"I hate you," he snarled. "I hate you! From the time you were in elementary and junior high and always taking your shit out on me, to the time you were in high school and always in trouble, to the time you were sick, and then when you were in rehab—twice, mind you—you always had Mom and Dad. We didn't get them!" He gestured to our sisters and himself as he screamed, "You're *still* all that Mom ever talks about!" Our sisters, still wide-eyed, nodded sullenly in agreement.

"It sucked!" Drew went on. "Once I grew up, even though I didn't need them anymore, it still sucked. Every time any of us called, it was always, 'Robby this' and 'Robby that' . . . and now Dad's gone, and I will never get that time back! Don't you understand? I will never get that time with him. It's lost. It's gone. I hate you!"

That was the biggest dagger—the one that killed the old me and the old relationship between Drew and myself. That old me would have clung onto excuses and stories. The other me that had been growing, maturing, experiencing gratitude . . . that part of me knew that everything Drew was spewing out absolutely needed to be said. It was true. It was his experience. Plus, I *needed* him to say it exactly how he was saying it. I listened to every word as he continued to vent. I had no idea how long it went on and I let the words carry over me and through me. Truth was truth.

Only when he was out of adrenaline and close to tears, I replied softly, "It was never my intention to take Dad and Mom away." I hung my head, but kept going, my voice raw and cracking with huge, huge emotion as I admitted, "You're right; I was very sick for decades. I never wished for my mental health to be an issue—but it was, and you missed out because of me and my choices and my disease."

I crumbled. "I'm sorry, Bro. I can't fix it or take it back. No amount of amends makes up for this. You have every right to feel the way you feel." I didn't speak anymore for a bit, listening as he continued to tell me what he needed to tell me—what he'd needed to share for so many years.

Our sisters' wide eyes mellowed. After a time, they loosened their white-knuckled grips on their chairs.

Then began one of the deepest, most beautiful conversations I'd ever experienced with my siblings. We let down all the walls between us. They were themselves and talked about when and why and how my illness had ripped them apart. They also got to share how healing it was for them to have me there with them. As much as I felt deep regret, I couldn't do one single thing about the past. However, I could start that minute, and continue to be an honorable man now, as I had promised my father—if they'd let me.

They let me.

All of our relationships with each other got stronger because of Nepal. We'd experienced an amazing opportunity to be real siblings that built each other up and supported one another. We lived lifetimes during that trip in the Himalayas, and we learned that we needed most to be real and honest. Everything changed for all of us.

I was not the only one who had been running from pain. People avoid conflict and absorb pain. What we discovered is that when you release it and share it with the people who love you most, you can receive something so powerful and healing if everyone is on the same page, seeking the same thing. My relationship with my siblings definitely wasn't perfect—but we were much better than we had been for so long! And the other three who had forged bonds in misery because of me were now able to forge deeper bonds in abiding love together.

I wish I could say that Drew and I never experienced another intense spat again. However, we learned that resentment doesn't go away in one cussing match. The good news was that Drew and I now knew what game we were playing. Plus, Dad's voice resided in our heads: "*You're the last males in the family. You have to take care of each other.*"

For Drew to get mountain sickness opened a lot of eyes—in Nepal and at home. I learned that whenever someone gets sick, just like with Dad, it strips away all that is not important and reveals that which is. As a family, our excursion and even this near-tragedy helped us get back to fundamental priorities.

Nepal brought within me unbelievable transformation. Here I'd been on all these excursions: the ultramarathons, the rock climbing, the sky diving. I could have paid millions of dollars to do all those things and not have learned as much. Mother Nature challenging my deepest fears about myself and death solidified the fact that I needed to continue to attack my anxieties—look them straight in the face. It was to be one of my greatest practices and teachers.

Months after returning home, the lessons were still unfolding. I realized I could write an entire book on those experiences and each of those amazing people in Nepal. In the end, the biggest "zen" result for me was truly learning to be present in my relationships and who I was coaching or teaching. I realized, observing my team members and my clients, that we were all making our way to and from a "Base Camp" in seeking to survive our everyday lives and to create some beautiful, pinnacle moments that would bring meaning and energy to life itself.

I also experienced spiritual highs and breakthroughs that were hard to explain. I learned meditation not taught in church. Growing up, I was told that connection with nature was for hippies, but in Nepal, surrounded by the breathtaking mountains of creation, I felt the Spirit so much stronger than I'd ever felt. A profound, unfathomable connection happened to me that had never taken place inside of a building. I would never look at God, people, or nature the same way again.

CHAPTER 28

WARRIOR IN THE GARDEN

If you look to nature, everything you need to understand life itself will unfold before you.

The farm turned out to be a great thing for Sophie. I had realized that if a person could have compassion and care for animals while young, that love and dedication would have a lifelong effect. Having responsibility to take care of animals really served my daughter's natural instincts. Without me having to be her alarm, she would get up at five in the morning and feed and water the animals. Same thing every evening.

One cold winter night, it was blowing sideways and freezing cold, but I still sent her and her friend out into the cold to do the chores. They needed to bust up the ice and go into the barn to feed the animals. I felt a little guilty being *that* dad, yet at the same time it felt important that Sophie do what she said she was going to do, because I never did that at her age.

Ten minutes passed and I'd expected them back already. Fifteen minutes passed and her friend was back inside where it was warm. After twenty minutes, I got up to go check on her and threw on my coat, shivering in the extreme cold. The barn door was closed but I could hear Sophie chattering away.

What the hell . . .?

I slowly slid open the door to peek in. There she was, talking with the horses who surrounded her, braiding their hair, and brushing them out like they were lifelong buds. I stood there staring, open-mouthed.

My daughter's found joy in the work. She's found peace in the pain. She's a warrior.

As she grew, Sophie's love, care and compassion for animals was also translating into her love and care for my downfalls. We began to have open and honest conversations about being human, what happens when we mess up and fall down—and how vital it is to get back up. We talked about *how* to get back up. We also talked about being prepared.

I remembered when the goat at her mom's was pregnant, my little Sophie used Google to look up what to watch for, studying up on deliveries, including breech babies. She had a whole emergency kit set up and was awaiting the arrival of the little one.

When the mama goat was giving birth, a bunch of us adults were sitting around, not knowing what to do as time passed and the goat was clearly in excruciating pain, bleating and crying to the point it was breaking my heart. The baby, however, wasn't coming out.

While we all gaped, completely helpless and then dumbfounded, my little girl threw on her farm gloves, reached inside the goat, turned the breech baby, and pulled it out. She saved both the mama and the baby! She was prepared—every day—for what she was facing. Since that night, she had successfully delivered eight more goats. Sophie was teaching me.

It was difficult on both Sophie and me when we had to say goodbye to Julie and her kids. As difficult as it was for us both, I watched as Sophie's mental preparation for things served her here, too. She had conversations with her mom and with me. She kept in touch with the people she loved. She put all the lessons into what she was learning at school and in her friendships and relationships. She kept teaching me.

Funny enough, these were the kind of preparation and fortitude lessons I was trying to teach my wrestlers and volleyball players at school. Fortunately, my new principal, Brock Jackman, backed my endeavors like my last principal. He attended as many wrestling functions as he could. I loved that he would hug the kids and give his congratulations. Pretty soon, the fans were insane after every match. I would make everyone from the stands come in and congratulate the team—no matter how they showed up on the scorecard.

It was part of what we were establishing as "the village effect." My team and I continued to care more about the mental health and wholeness of each kid than we did about winning, and interestingly enough, the boys truly began to respond.

As a result, refs loved us, parents loved us, even parents from other teams loved us when they saw the result of the community we were building.

"I wish others would coach like you and your team," parents from other teams told us. That made me look around to see what they meant. I believed in showing high respect for other coaches, but it made me uptight, too, even angry, when I witnessed too many of them on their cell phones—even when one or more of their students was in the middle of a match! That felt disrespectful. Even worse was when they screamed at the teens, degraded them, and even abused them or threatened them like some ridiculous parents I saw in sports.

My coaching team and I made a pact: we would never show that kind of behavior—and while each kid was accountable for showing up, we would not call him or her out in front of others. As long as a kid honestly felt like he or she showed up and gave their very best that day, *that was that.* On the flip side, if we felt a kid was giving up on himself or herself for whatever reason, we would take them away from the group and quietly ask what was happening. These kids were facing some pretty intense things, but knowing that they had one or more adults that truly believed in them was pure gold. It was only a matter of time. They would get back up. They would show back up, becoming warriors for themselves first.

So, just like I did when I was teaching the high-risk kids at school, I made mental health number one. Making sure each of our kids was mentally thriving on any given day was far more important than the win/loss column.

And what did that turn into? An undefeated season!

A parent came up to me after a major competition—but he wasn't one of my kids' parents. He was from the other team. "Dude," he said, "you've pissed a lot of people off!"

"Oh yeah?" I asked, my eyebrow raised.

"Yeah. Early on, people were saying you had no right being a wrestling coach. You had no background—you haven't risen in the ranks; you're teaching these kids things they've never done." Then he lowered his voice and looked around conspiratorially and grinned at me. "Dude, you brought Bountiful back out of obscurity and Millcreek into prominence, and these kids are on fire! I'm not supposed to root for you, but secretly I do. Way to go! You've gone from being the villain to being secretly loved."

My face turned red. I didn't know what to say, but he clapped me on the back and walked away.

Some of the boys I coached in junior high joined us when they hit high school. I would never forget Brendan, who didn't care who or what was around us. Whenever he saw me, inside of school or outside, Brendan would run and leap into my arms. The little dude made me laugh—and as he got older, bigger, and was becoming a badass wrestler, it was harder and harder to catch him and not drop him!

Brendan cracked me up. Raised by a single mom, he'd had few male role models but shined in wrestling. His senior year, he followed my coaching to wrestle at his natural weight of 170. It scared him, but I cheered my guts out as he went all "assassin" on his opponent and ended up dominating him in the first round. The second round they were evenly matched, then Brendan pinned him in the third round. The auditorium was in shock. *Brendan just obliterated the national champ in the first round of the bracket tournament!*

Most important to him personally that year, he was preparing to serve an LDS mission. "Coach, from the time we first started wrestling, I knew you cared more about me than any title. I know all of the lessons you've taught me will serve on my mission for God." I knew that to be true, and hoped they would serve for his whole, entire mission in life as well.

I never dreamed when I was young that I'd ever be working with kids—and certainly not in a school, of all places! But even thinking I would ever have a positive impact on anybody . . . it was humbling. In my addiction, having felt for two decades that I wanted to leave the planet, it was so satisfying to be able to love and show up for and inspire these kids. I didn't take a minute of it for granted.

I also didn't take for granted that my skillsets had been developed directly from my fails. They could learn from that, too.

Once, my goals and dreams had been so small. It was Dad who taught me the power I had to visualize and manifest as well as direct my journey in the direction I chose and with those I loved. The power was beautiful and terrifying. However, the moment I started including what I wanted for others to experience—health clients, kids, educators, full classrooms—I found that even when going up against political systems, my teams and I were meeting and exceeding our goals together.

And, I thought, *I finally get to be me.*

That winter I was on a date with a woman I had begun to like, but she didn't know a lot about me yet. We were in Walmart when two Hispanic kids came up to us. "I remember you!" one exclaimed, shaking my hand. "You were a speaker at our school. You changed my life!"

The other guy grinned at me. He nodded and quietly added, "You saved my life."

This woman looked at me, her eyes wide. I didn't know what to say. As much as I wanted to boast that I was dealing with people's traumas and helping them come out on the other side, I wasn't winning every battle. There were people around me in recovery and in the schools that slipped through the cracks. In our area, the need was great and called for greater resources than I had alone. We all needed the village effect. I couldn't brag. I remembered the kids I wasn't able to reach in time. Their faces haunted me.

Still, my dad seemed to remind me, it was all in the Creator's hands. I just had to continue to do my part.

One day my friend Chuck took me out to lunch. He had noticed I completely changed from the guy he knew from high school. We talked about families, and he admitted he was having a rough time being a parent.

"My kids don't want anything to do with me," he complained, "yet they're miserable! They keep making lousy choices." He paused. "Sophie sure seems different. Tell me about her."

I thought about it for a long moment before replying. "Well, she's everything I'm not," I admitted frankly, "in the sense that she's adventurous and confident in that adventure. She's well-spoken and understands boundaries. We get comments from teachers and parents all the time who are dumbfounded by her level of compassion and kindness. 'You don't know us but your daughter found our daughter in the halls of the school . . . and we want to thank you.' She can show up for a single kid in the hall, and she knows how to rally thousands of students in the gym. She's incredible. I give her all the credit."

Chuck stared at me. "So why do you think Sophie is the way she is?"

"Well, to be clear, Sophie is a rare breed of her own." I went on to explain that my daughter had been practically born into Alcoholics Anonymous. "I didn't have a sitter when I was in recovery and she was the cute puppy in the room."

He laughed but said, "AA? Isn't that where . . . people bare their secrets? What happens when they fail, and such?"

"Yeah. Against all arguments that I was stealing her innocence, I brought her with me. Things are happening to all kids at much younger ages—more than what happened to you and me. Now, you know, most people look at her and think, 'Oh what a cute girl!' because she is stinkin' cute. What those people don't know is that little Miss Innocent one day came home in junior high and informed me: 'I'm wrestling. You're not my coach, but I need you in the stands.' She'd been watching me for years—and she recognized when and how she needed my support and would tell me. I gotta make damn sure I am there for her."

"She is wrestling?" His face showed shock and surprise.

"Yep. And she's come a long way," I explained to Chuck. "Over the last few years, Sophie came out of her shell. She got involved with friends and student body activities. When she didn't win the student body officer election she fought hard for, she didn't run away with her tail between her legs like I would have. Nope, the next year she went for SBO all over again—and won! She has more confidence at thirteen than I ever had at thirty-three! She'll even say, 'Dad, I don't need you to fix this—I need you to listen to what's going on.' Then she'll fix it."

"How did she get so special?" he asked, finally pushing his plate away.

"Well, all I can tell you is that Angie and I and Levi did the hard stuff early. We parented 100%. And whereas I always had false bottoms that my parents would save me from, I learned how to sit in the pain with her. I never took it from her. I wouldn't dare. We've developed a relationship where my daughter can come to me and she trusts me."

"That's interesting . . . and impressive." He admitted, "I'm always trying to save my kids, you know, from the hard stuff, from harm—"

"—Yeah," I interjected, and looked at him squarely, "but, Chuck, is it doing them any good? I mean, are they able to face their pain, or are you always taking it from them? Saving them? My parents loved me and they showed it by softening every blow. I never learned to face my own pain."

"Me, too," he murmured quietly, and I could see it in his face.

"You know, dude, when you think about it, pain is inevitable for any human to face at some point in their lives. I would rather

Sophie face the hard stuff first and early, while I'm there to walk beside her. She's going to be off on her own soon enough."

I paused, hoping what I was about to say would sink in. "I would rather Sophie be a *warrior in a garden than a gardener in a war.*"

My friend's mouth popped open in surprise. "Wait, 'a warrior in a garden rather than a gardener in a war' . . . isn't that a Bruce Lee quote?"

"Yeah, an old Chinese proverb he used. But think about it. If I walk beside Sophie as she faces life's pain, but she learns how to lean into it, learn from it, grow stronger from it now, she'll be equipped for life.

"I always thought I wanted to be *that* father—you know, the one that scares the shit out of every boy that comes to pick up his daughter—and I could be, but I realized that for the most part, I would only be able to be there to help her pick up the pieces in the aftermath. In order to *prevent* something happening to Sophie when I wasn't around, she had to learn how to stand on her own. And that girl . . . she's learning how to do it."

Chuck sat there dumbfounded. But I knew everything I'd spilled on the table between us was truly sinking in.

I wanted it to sink into all the parents I was working with, too. So many of them I witnessed couldn't even function in their own lives, face their own pain, but they would swoop in and save their kids from pain in a heartbeat, fight for their kids' limitations rather than let them figure out how to work through them to become their strengths.

Sophie, on the other hand, called me the other day. She was crying.

"I just got called to the principal's office. I'm waiting to go in."

"Yes! Finally!" I cheered.

"No, Dad, I got into trouble."

"I know, and now I am pumped. Tell me about it."

After Sophie groaned into the phone, she told me the story. Apparently, she and two friends were standing in the school hallway. Another kid came up, being a dork, trying to flirt with her friend, but when he didn't get the response he wanted, he punched her friend and then their guy friend.

Sophie was next but she stepped in and decked him. Then he ran and told the principal what she had done. I was a little floored at first, because Sophie was so much like my dad—she could handle her way politically around almost every situation, but this time she'd stepped up to the kid and punched him back.

"Okay, honey," I began calmly. "You know we don't condone violence, but it sounds like you had a lesson to teach this kid about boundaries. Talk to your principal. Before you say a word, ask him to check the videotapes and then call me."

The principal did, indeed, check the videotapes. Sophie *and* the boy were disciplined, although each a little differently. One thing I knew, that kid wouldn't pull that again near my daughter.

Two weeks later over dinner, Sophie told me that despite her recent challenges, she made high honor roll. I looked at her, her thick beautiful wavy long hair and pretty blue eyes.

"We need a drug test," I joked.

"Dad!" she rolled her eyes. But as dinner progressed and we were talking she said, "I've got the best plan. You know how 8th grade doesn't matter, but 9th grade really does? I need to budget my time better for studying so I continue to make this year really count."

Who budgets study time? "Forget the drug test," I crowed, "we need a DNA test! Whose child are you?"

Now a groan.

For one of our daddy/daughter dates, Sophie asked, "Dad will you go on a suicide prevention walk with me?"

That's my girl, I thought. *What kid wants to raise awareness for a heavy subject like that on their time off?*

As Sophie and I continued forward in life, I loved the fact that she wanted to introduce me to all of her friends. That was cool, but at a choir concert that I attended to support Sophie, no one was more surprised than me when they stopped singing and Sophie stood up to the mic. She pulled out a letter she had written, and began to read:

Dear Dad,

In choir, Mr. Saunders asked us to think about who our heroes were, and I have so many amazing heroes like my mom, my grandma Shanna, or my stepdad, but you are definitely my biggest hero. Most kids' heroes wear a cape and a mask, but my hero is covered in tattoos and has a red beard. You have always fought for me. You turned your whole life around just so you could be my dad and be a part of my life. You always push me to try new things and be brave, strong, selfless and fear-less and have always believed in me even when I didn't believe in myself. You have taught me that I am capable of anything I set my mind to. You have made my life so much better and I am who I am today because of you. And you always inspire me to do good and make the world a better place.

I love you so much, Dad. You are truly my hero.

Love, Sophie

My new life had come full circle, and in my own eyes finally, no longer filled with self-hatred but deep acceptance. I felt I had become a man that my father would be proud of—perhaps not the precise one he'd envisioned, but uniquely myself, able to commit to and keep promises, one who watched over my daughter . . . and did not save her from the world but equipped her for it.

A warrior in the garden.

CHAPTER 29

UNEXPECTED WARRIOR

My entire world revolved around Sophie and my work as a coach and a trainer. Still, there was another female who often washed in and out of my thoughts. This one had known me all my life, usually didn't understand me, but loved me unconditionally. I respected the hell out of her for it. Most of the time.

It was my mom.

She had always been her own woman, but since Dad's passing, she had more fully come into her own. Mom stayed close to each of us as her kids as well as her grandkids, and she stayed constantly busy doing her community and church service. To my knowledge, she never burned a roast again, but that woman served on more councils, business boards, and committees than anyone I'd ever met. It made her formidably well-rounded in education, business, and many things in life, but the one thing that still seemed to baffle her was me.

I woke up one morning and realized I had made a huge mistake. As much as I had once deeply resented her for saving me from my pain one too many times, when I looked back through the lens of truth, I realized that it was actually *Dad* who created most of the soft-landing places of my life.

He had lived with too much pain. He'd lost two parents who had taken their lives, though for different reasons. To save me from my own bad choices, he denied me my natural consequences. Trouble with teachers? He'd led the school board. Trouble with coaches? He'd hire new ones, better ones. Trouble with the law? He'd work to free me. Trouble with money? He had given me job after job, vehicle after vehicle. I had blamed Mom for living a super-codependent role, but it wasn't fair.

Where Dad was at, he could handle my resentment, but it was like Dad and I had already done that work together—before he died and in his presence after. I now felt only overwhelmed with gratitude for everything he had done. It was Mom with whom I realized I needed to do my deeper inner work. *Wow, I've been mad at God and Mom—two other presences in my life who have shown me so much unconditional love.*

I took a deeper look at my past. This time I allowed my accountable eyes to see: Mom had been the one who was always looking for solutions, not soft-landing places. It was Mom whom I limped home to when I got hurt; she was the one who tried to get me on Ritalin so I wouldn't be kicked out of school; she was the one who made me do my homework until she couldn't the way I needed—then she immediately hired tutors to help me. She was there a thousand times after that, and she was the one who let me fail when I needed to fail (even when Dad hadn't) and yet she praised me every single time I got back up.

I had taken her for granted. The realization washed over me in an enormous wave. *I have so much to be grateful for and make up for.*

The moment I moved from resentment to deep respect, my world changed. I stopped trying to fix my mom, and I didn't get as upset when she tried to brainstorm solutions with me when I brought her problems I was trying to sort out. She wasn't into politics or big displays of power, but her tongue could wield truth like a sword when it needed to. She was making a difference all across our region, but very quietly.

I realized that when Mom left this planet, we would likely have a lot of people come up to us as we had dad, strangers whom she had meant the world to. Only this time, I didn't want to wait that long. I looked around at who she was, what her life was all about, and suddenly it wasn't only Dad whom I wanted to emulate more; it was Mom.

As the months unfolded, I took this new energy out into everything I was doing and it flourished even more. That was good because I was working in intense spaces with kids and adults, their emotions, their motivations, their trauma, their secret dreams.

In the meantime, I was also called to be a teacher at intimate retreats with millionaire and billionaire CEOs. We quickly discovered they were facing many of the same issues as high school kids, just on a different level—and many of them were using the same coping skills from back then. Our inspirational retreat turned to the subject of sobriety and preparedness.

Even as the teacher, I was humbled enough to see this. *Holy shit, my parents gave me so many badass experiences to learn life skills and face things. It wasn't anyone's fault that I didn't choose to water those seeds. I chose to hide.*

As some of these CEOs were talking about stuff from their childhood, I remarked, "The saying 'time heals all wounds' is a lie. Taking action instead of running away; facing your pain; and working on your own life is what heals those wounds."

I came back from that retreat even more grateful for my parents and *on fire*. I loved coaching kids and adults, and as much as I enjoyed working one-on-one to effect positive and powerful change in people, I was becoming overwhelmed with intervention calls.

I realized something quickly: *The need is too great.*

Sure, my story and my energy and unconditional love had been helping certain individuals, but they weren't stemming the tide. They weren't touching the tsunami of suicidal ideation, depression, and rampant addiction in young people. I'd already been speaking, but even though I was crazy-busy being a dad, a teacher, a coach, a gym owner, and a nonprofit director, I was going to have to step up my game—again.

I realized two things were going to have to happen, if I were to leave the legacy my father and mother had given me:

1. I would have to speak to much larger groups of people who could spread the message immediately because kids and adults were dying every day. It had to happen right away.

2. I would need to train advocates old and young to become leaders in their homes, communities, and the world—utilizing the village effect of growing and nurturing each other; nurturing *more* Warriors in the Garden.

I was going to have to find these fellow students, peers, mentors, and recovering addicts with hearts to share. I couldn't stay in my comfort zone. I would have to stretch myself in ways I never had before.

Soon I was being asked to speak at a number of schools for their Suicide Prevention Week. I was very honored, although I wasn't

100% polished. I made mistakes, but I was passionate. Kids could tell I loved them from the way I spoke to them, and while I wasn't always politically correct, I was effective. How did I know? I made the administrators a little uncomfortable when they realized the power of transparency. Kids were coming out of the woodwork, both anonymously and straight-up out loud, about negative mental thoughts and ideas that the adults didn't know they were having. It was good news, because all of these feelings and emotions before had been in the dark, where they held too much power.

Here's the thing: until we talked about it openly like we did, these kids thought they were the only ones with the struggle. Before drug prevention, before study skills, before anti-bullying programs, we had to address the mental health of our little, miraculous humans. *They are giants in spirit, but they lack life and survival skills.* The power of transparent talk *plus* nurturing meant that the symptoms of addiction, failing grades, and bullies could then be addressed.

Instead of band-aids that taught kids they were either unworthy or too stupid to solve things, just like chess, positive rap songs about moms, and transparency in my classrooms, I realized we had to start turning these kids into empowered problem solvers.

Besides my summer camps and school, I started speaking anywhere people asked me to help save lives—from local church groups to athletic functions to schools, awards banquets, and funerals to huge stages.

One of the most epic days of my life was when I asked to be the keynote for True Blue, a leadership summit at Utah State University. All of the ambassadors and top students gathered once a year to get leadership training and motivation on that day. I asked Sophie to be a part of it. Along with a few of my nieces and nephews were 500+ students. It was surreal walking the halls to the ballroom, where life-sized posters with my name on them hung. When I came out dressed in my flat brim hat, white tee, and exposed tattoos, the loud crowd went silent.

"Let me guess some of the things you are facing this year in your education," I began, ticking off my fingers. "Trying to get the grades, trying to please teachers who expect your best, trying to juggle class schedules and homework, while trying to perform well to please parents who may be helping you pay for your education—or doing it on your own and not having a dime to waste, even as you try to make it economically in a recession on a student's budget." I took it in as they nodded and groaned, then I switched to the other hand.

"Then there's trying to find friends, trying fit in to large groups of strangers, trying to be significant in someone's life, trying to show up as the leader you are striving to be despite all of the political, economic, and climate crises you find yourself in that *you* never started, that you never instigated . . . but now must prepare to fix."

The students' eyes were wide. I noticed hands clutching pens until their knuckles were white.

Then I proceeded to tell my story—the short, dorky, freckle-filled, huge-eared, red-headed freak in school, the one bullied until he became a bully. I shared the star athlete with only one place to shine and it wasn't enough. I shared all my weaknesses, the false-bottomed rescues I was given, and then I shared losing Danny. Tears began to fall down some faces. I told them about my dark night of the soul when I handed my baby girl back to my mom, silently said my goodbyes, and went up on the mountain in Bountiful where I had that meeting with my Maker. More tears mixed with some confounded laughter at the words, "Is that loud enough?"

Then I shared the miracle of my real recovery, the miracle of learning that my diagnosis was a label for that day and not my life, and how I learned to lean into my pain instead of running from it. I shared the miracle of my daughter Sophie, what she had taught me, and what she was doing now as a Warrior in the Garden.

Delighted gasps filled the ballroom as Sophie ran all the way from the back and up on stage to jump into my arms. I swung her around, the biggest grin on my face as I thought about *what a miracle it all was—especially her.*

I held Sophie by my side as I taught principles of resilience. Then I added one more thing: "If you're ever in a place where you don't know where you're going . . . just remember that Utah State *kicked me out* in 1997!"

Suddenly there was a roar of applause and surprised laughter that rolled throughout the entire ballroom as they got the message. *You are not done. You are not your labels. And you are definitely not your fails if you keep going! You can get back up. No matter what anyone tells you, you can be a Warrior in the Garden.*

That day for me was a win. I had come full circle and could show these students that they could, too. Any failures could propel them *forward.* No matter where they were right now, they could lean in and allow life to propel them forward. I knew my message hit home when my cell phone was pinging with reactions:

I want you to know, your message resonated, Rob. I'm signing up for Psychology class next semester . . . I am NOT my diagnosis.

Wow, powerful breakthroughs! I'm reaching out to my therapist as soon as I leave campus.

Last week I almost took my life. I told myself just to hang onto one more week . . . that God would find me somehow. I feel like he did that during your talk today.

Guess what? It's been four months, but I just texted my parents . . .

Best of all that day, I could own myself in all my authenticity. I didn't have to pretend to be a single other person as I stood on that stage. I didn't have to wear a single mask or pretend to be a badass. As Sophie's face radiated love and pride, it was for me being me.

Word continued to spread as I worked in more schools throughout 2018, 2019, and further. However, after the pandemic of 2020 hit and students were struggling to get out of bed and go to school, I realized that it wasn't enough to engage students, as powerful as they were. I partnered with a couple of people, but we still were losing too many kids around us.

The old saying "It takes a village to raise a child" was all around me. I saw the miracles of that village effect when we engaged the whole community—school, parents, teachers—in the lives of our wrestlers. I also saw what happened all too often when there wasn't a mentor or guide at home or school.

I started asking kids to be each other's advocates. "Your job in this school is not just for you to show up and do your best every day, it's also to make sure your neighbor is around tomorrow, too. It's not about codependency—it's called 'caring.' It's a calling. It's vital now. We must be vigilant in taking care of each other today so there is a human race tomorrow."

A real test of this came when my team and I were asked to work with a charter school. I agreed on one condition—that we worked not just with the students but with the teachers, and had a session with the parents, too. The principal raised his eyebrow at me, but he and his team agreed. We worked with the students first, then the teachers. Some of the teachers were resistant. "I'm a math teacher, not a psychologist."

"You're right. And the good news is that you don't have to be psychologists," I said as I looked not only at him but around the room. "Still, you have the *privilege and honor* of being in the front seat of these kids' lives, to witness what is happening, and to act if red flags are hitting the field in front of you. Knowledge is power, and it might save a life. You're not a psychologist. You're a hero." The teacher blinked.

We had a night with the parents, and the next day back at school with the kids, everyone was speaking the same language of mental health. We noticed the teens' energy had changed immensely. Their walls were down, and they walked in warm, engaged, transparent, and vulnerable. Many of them had serious talks with their parents the night before and at breakfast. They were seeing the power of sharing with each other. They had become a team at home and school, accented by the teachers choosing to be engaged, and taking advantage of this growth and breakthrough.

When our time was done, instead of taking off, my partners for the day and I entered the lunchroom and started BSing with the kids, reinforcing what they'd been learning and engaging in. The discussions in front of all the kids were like the texts I often got after a speech—but here it was happening live, where they could all support one another.

Abruptly from across the cafeteria, a chant arose. It was my teaching buddy's name. "Bryan, Bryan, Bryan!" came the cheer. I turned to notice Bryan, who was actually quite shy, had turned a bright shade of red that could compete with my own pink skin on my best days. I *love it!* He was seeing the village effect firsthand. If I wasn't grinning, I would have been crying. Suddenly we were in the midst of selfies, which didn't stop until the bell rang.

I was in awe. For a school *to invest in their kids*, not just an assembly, was huge in itself. But to put up thousands of dollars to give them life skills, to give them pieces of the puzzle that made them better humans and more capable and caring students, was remarkable, and I praised the principal for it.

Bryan and I walked out, high as kites. Not because the selfies made us feel like rock stars, but because it could be considered *cool* to talk about something as important as mental health!

"You know what?" I said to him as we climbed into my truck. "I hope you will be working with kids forever, dude; you've got a gift." I looked at him squarely. "I just made myself a promise, too: I'll be speaking, consulting, and creating programs around the country for the next five, ten, or fifty years of my life."

That year my student Brendan was called to the Chile Santiago mission. He had to learn a foreign language. He had to leave his mom at home. He had to choose to be healthy in mind and body and spirit, and he said wrestling prepared him every step of the way to do that.

After my own spiritual experiences and my transformation in Nepal, I invited anyone I coached to focus on three things: mental health, physical health, and spiritual health. Like with my wrestling kids, I would invite them to call upon whatever higher power they believed in. And then I would ask them to wake up and show up that day, feeling good knowing that God would handle the rest on God's timetable.

"When we show up, the rest of the world shows up for us. It's not a perfect place of no pain, but it's a beautiful dance of rich experiences, love, joy, and triumph *when we don't run away.*"

Now, even my own family faces things when something comes up. Between my recovery, Dad's death, Nepal, and me waking up to what a freaking awesome human my mother is, we handle things as they come up. We don't even worry about a private setting anymore.

Recently, my mom, my sister, and I were at this poppin' place called "Plates and Palates." It was crowded, and amongst our savory soups, salads, and paninis, a hundred women chatted loudly and there was not a single other guy to be seen. In that setting, I shared with Mom what my last, greatest hurt in life had been—the one I hadn't been able to share in recovery. Then I told her how much I loved and respected her. My mom was crying over her tomato basil soup, and all three of us had an emotional and tender moment.

"Mom, I want you to know how cool it was that you sent me to Outward Bound to experience leadership opportunities. I look back and realize I have had the most insane life experiences to learn from—I just didn't utilize those tools in a timely manner. I promise you, I'm using them now, and then some . . . and it's all because of you and Dad." I looked over and noticed both my mom and my sister bawling.

Over paninis, Mom and I got to wipe off more than forty years of discoveries from the slate between us. This ongoing therapy was deeper than Family Day in recovery; it meant ongoing learning of new life skills and communication and doors opened to a mutual outpouring of love.

I wasn't that outrageous little kid in diapers and cowboy boots on the roof. I wasn't curled up in a ball anymore on her floor, either. I was a warrior. Now we could grow together in the latter half of our lives and enjoy the hell out of it—especially now that I realized that my mother was my unexpected warrior.

CHAPTER 30

WE NEED MORE WARRIORS IN THE GARDEN!

Recently, I was called in on a case where a kid came up missing. Fortunately, between the family, law enforcement, and other volunteers, the task force was able to find him and bring him home. After I listened intently for quite some time, I provided him some pertinent advice on how to make the most of the life he was living and stop running from his pain.

His parents, too, asked for help. It was a powerful process, but something that was so disruptive to the whole family and the whole community that frankly it sucked up a lot of energy from everyone involved in the crisis. I was so grateful my foundation could get involved . . . and it wasn't in supplying a headstone this time.

As I watched the fallout, I recognized the healing would not just take time but effort. On the other side of my Nepal experience with Drew, I knew what the other kids in the family would be facing and how vital it was to spread their love and attention to the whole family. For the rest of the community, I thought about what could be done in terms of prevention, education, and action.

We need more leaders to spread the word, to start a movement; we need to create more Warriors in the Garden.

Most kids, young adults, and parents that I work with are trying to survive. They don't always realize what an amazing world this is—*if* we're prepared to face it. I certainly wasn't at that kid's age. Most people are not taught how, and therefore not equipped to face the highs and the lows of a well-lived, breathtaking human life.

Even then, I continue to have people of all ages come to me, desperately wanting to *live*, not die . . . to *thrive*, not just survive. It can be taught. It can be learned. It can be shared.

Let's get real. As a society, we are facing high levels of suicidal ideation and chaos. Therefore, I have some tips to leave you, the reader. I hope you will not only take these into your heart and soul, but also into your family, into your community, and into the world at large because they are so desperately needed.

Become prepared. **Be** a Warrior in the Garden. Not only will you enjoy peace during peacetime, you will be prepared for battle during times of crisis—and most importantly, you'll know how to quickly de-escalate back to peace.

And prepare your kids. Teach them to be Warriors in the Garden. For parents and teachers of Warriors, please see Appendix II at the back of this book for even more tips, specifically for you.Imagine if our families knew how to do these things. Imagine if our world leaders knew how. Change happens one person, one kid, one family at a time. The following guides are a really great start. Turn the page!

TRAINING YOURSELF TO BE A WARRIOR IN THE GARDEN: A GUIDE FOR INDIVIDUALS

Be Your Best, Authentic Self

Every day you have choices, to go along with the crowd—in school, at work, or on social media. What most people don't realize is that everyone that looks like they've got it all together usually doesn't. Don't make choices based on someone else's opinion of you. It's not your business. Make choices that bring you joy. If you're at work or school and see people being bullied by the "popular" ones who are mean and nasty, just take a look around at the folks on the sidelines. They are probably a lot more fun to hang out with, who will accept you as you are, and who don't have to be rude, ignorant, or asses to make a name for themselves. (I can only say that because I was once that ignorant cuss.) What I found through life—and people choosing to live—is that it's much more important to be yourself. Making choices every day to care about you and what you care about will bring you closer to your passion for life and living than anything else. And when you're passionate, you will find authentic, lifelong friends along the way! Remember, you will never be the best copycat! The world needs the real you.

Focus On Your Mental Health—Every Day

In school, they focus on IQ—your intelligence quotient. Sure, it's important stuff, but memorizing test answers won't keep you alive if you don't know how to handle your emotions when you experience fails—like every single human on the planet experiences them! Get to know the language of your EQ, or emotional quotient. How are you doing today? What's going on with you? What is that emotion coming up for you? Can you name it? Where did it stem from? How can you lean into it and learn from it today instead of running from it?

There Is No More Failing—You Win or You Learn

Get into the mindset of a pro athlete or a successful, loving dad or the gal who just won that scholarship. They all "failed" in some capacity early on (or even later) in their endeavors by the world's standards. And yet, they each got back up, and learned from the experience.

Show Up. Show Up Every Day

So much pain is caused in life when we run away—physically, mentally, emotionally, spiritually. We have become a society that too often hides, or, worse, sleeps through life. Where I see the biggest change happening is when people begin showing up for themselves. Instead of drinking, drugging, sluffing, smoking, gambling, or shutting down, they start showing up for themselves. Can you imagine? Instead of waiting on the world to provide some miracle, they become the miracle! All it takes is waking up to yourself. Every day. Being present and awake and ready is one of the greatest gifts you can give yourself.

And one last note: Show up for whatever team you're on. Show up at home for your family, especially anytime something healthy is happening—connection, laughter, sports, vacations, and unifying experiences like pushing your limits and seeking adventure together. Show up day-to-day for your chores. They make you stronger and give you skillsets I didn't capture until my thirties. I would have been much more prepared for life if I'd spent less time arguing or running away and more time learning valuable life skills. Finally, show up for your teams at work and in sports. Giving your very best compounds all the good you're doing, and doors will open that will shock and surprise you and make you believe in miracles. It all has to do with you and the energy you bring.

Life Is Your Training Ground—Stop Comparing and Start Living

Every day when you wake up, there are stunning and miraculous opportunities for you to show up, step up, and to be more than who you were the day before. Competition can make you push harder, run faster, and train better, but your best competitor is yourself. Who are you becoming today that is one step further than you were yesterday? Maybe that's getting out of bed today. By next week, that becomes arriving on time, showing up for yourself, and hitting the gym! By next month it's being the biggest contribution you can be at work. By the following year it's celebrating all your wins and figuring out what the next challenge is that you're ready to tackle. It works. Comparison, which runs rampant in our society, is a killer of self-esteem and achievement. It's stupid, pointless, and painful. Competition with the guy or gal you were yesterday? Now that's the fun, the creativity, the passion, and the joy!

You Are Not Your Diagnosis

Just like when I took my psychology test and discovered I was not so many things that I had been diagnosed as, I'm seeing this happen to kids every day. If you don't have a diagnosis, hang onto this information for a friend or family member. If you do have a diagnosis of your mental health, I'm going to invite you to think twice about "chemical imbalances." Some of us feel deeper. For some, that's a real thing. But anxiety doesn't just pop up. It's something that you're afraid of that you haven't faced yet. If you're depressed, I can promise you something happened a long time ago that you didn't have skills to handle at that time—or even ongoing. Abuse, bullying, trauma. It doesn't feel good—and you don't feel good to yourself. You can start to get triggered every day.

Medication can numb your anxiety, but it doesn't teach you how to handle it. In fact, it can make you dependent, in a perpetual state of learned helplessness. If anything, I invite you to use it only for a short term while you develop skillsets to give you natural highs and natural balances in your brain. Develop tools for the next time you're triggered so every time you're taking out the trash. Eventually, you don't have to take that trash out anymore because there isn't any— you've learned skills in prevention and mental health.

Use Pain as Your Training Partner

No one gets away in this life without experiencing pain. It doesn't matter what color you are, what part of the world you come from, or what level of income you or your family has. Believe me, I know some really sad and depressed millionaires. Everyone faces pain! Now when you can grasp that concept that pain is present and it's meant to work for you, not against you, you start realizing how you can lean into it and learn from it. Pain is your greatest teacher! In training, it teaches your muscles how to become stronger, faster, better.

You as a human are designed to get stronger and better from that pain! In every other category of life—your mental fitness, your spiritual fitness, your fiscal or money fitness, your emotional fitness . . . using pain as your training partner will not only reframe your mindset—it will make you a badass! It wasn't until I made pain my friend and teacher, trainer, and partner that I truly began living. And what I'm witnessing from kids who don't know how to wrestle, or girls who don't know how to play volleyball, or guys who don't know how to recover from addiction is that leaning into your pain becomes your secret weapon to life. You become a warrior instead of a slave.

You become the hero of your journey—not the person still skirting pain at ninety, having never lived, and dying with regrets. It's all too real, and you don't deserve that. The next time something in life is kicking your ass, ask yourself, "What is this pain trying to teach me? What do I get to do differently?" Sit with it. Be with it. Learn from it. *Win.*

Use What You Are Learning to Help Someone Else

Just like Sophie, I'm seeing that even the youngest among us have lessons to teach. It doesn't matter if you're young or old, use what you are learning to teach and to benefit someone else. When I had my huge psychology class breakthroughs (and yes, therefore psychological breakthroughs), I used the knowledge immediately to benefit the people I was training. I caught became passionate, on fire because I saw that it works. There is a servant-leader inside of you. Everyone wants to be significant, to mean something to someone else, but when we keep trying to prove ourselves, we dig a hole. When we build someone else up with the things we are learning, we become a warrior-teacher, a warrior leader. Be that kind of badass. I'm telling you, the world needs more of them. The world needs you!

NURTURING KIDS TO BE WARRIORS IN THE GARDEN: A POWERFUL 4-STEP GUIDE FOR PARENTS AND TEACHERS

Our biggest failure with our children? Overprotection and under-preparation. We want to save our kids from the big, bad world—yet is hiding them from it the key? No, because reality is harsh, and it comes at them young. It just does. Training them for it is the key.

Based on my experience with youth, with young adults and with adults from all spectrums, I have some tips that will help you as parents to raise Warriors in the Garden. I promise, if you begin doing this for your kids, you will prepare them successfully for the world that does come at them! It also comes to them—in magnificent ways. Why not prepare them to face it young, to discover who they are—and who they are not—while they have you as a guide? Just do not be a safety net. Do not deny them their pain—their greatest teacher.

Some of what I write below may seem or feel harsh. It's okay. You're in training. You're waking up to your greatness. Let truth be your second-greatest teacher.

Step One: BE the Example of a Warrior in the Garden Yourself.

Stop hiding, burying your head in the sand, sleeping, drinking, drugging, gambling, road-raging, stuffing your mouth full of things that don't serve you and then expecting your kids to do something different. Do you really think they don't see it? Do you really think you are hiding anything from them? They know you and love you, and believe me, they see everything.

So what can you do? **Step one is to read and implement Appendix I, "Training Yourself to Be a Warrior in the Garden: A Guide for Individuals,"** above. Example is the best way to guide your kids.

Step Two: Be Present to Prepare Them to Prevent Pain and Walk Through Pain—Not Protect Them from It

There was a movie that changed my life—but probably not in the way you would imagine. I watched *Den of Thieves* with 50 Cent and a great cast of characters. There is a scene in which 50 Cent plays the dad, whose beautiful daughter is going out with a boy to her first prom. The kid walks in the door, pumped to see his beautiful date, and ready to get going. As the scene unfolds, I didn't just laugh at the kid's reaction to 50 Cent as he tucks the boy's gang colors down into his suit pocket where they won't be seen. I saw how he took him aside and introduces him to the big, scary, seriously badass group of gangster men who reinforce to the kid that he will get his daughter home safe by 11:30 . . . and doesn't even need to say the "or else".

But I also watched the daughter and the mom on screen. Even as the guys are laughing in the garage once the couple leaves, a huge truth came to me.

That was the dad I once was. I would have frightened and bullied the date to bring her home untouched and on time. However, knowing humanity, I also knew that girl would never trust her father again with a boy, would begin sneaking around him for natural teenage wants, and might end up in a worse situation—**because she would be overprotected and unprepared.**

Whose fault is it, I thought, when a girl is not taught red flags, not taught about her own decisions, not taught about a boy's natural desire, not taught about how to prepare herself? Is it her fault, the boy's fault, or the parents' fault?

I knew right then and there; it is the parents' fault. Boys should be taught and prepared about personal respect, self-respect, and boundaries, and girls should be taught about dignity, self-respect, personal boundaries, and what to do the moment a single red flag reveals itself so they can protect themselves. And remember from my example in the story: it doesn't just happen to girls.

This is true not only in dating, but in a thousand different scenarios your kids will face as preteens, teens, young adults, and as they become parents.

This was recently reinforced to me by the animals on our farm. I had to put my horse down. If you care about animals, it can be one of the hardest things you ever do in your life, but it is part of the natural circle of life. When the horse was down, I tried to put a tarp up to protect the rest of the animals on the farm from being affected negatively by their dead friend. Only they didn't like the tarp—in fact, they got really upset about it. Instead, one by one, many of the animals including other horses and goats came up and licked the horse tenderly. It was their way of saying goodbye. It was their way to have closure.

Stop overprotecting. Start preparing your warriors. Let them feel, know, and learn how to navigate within the circle of life.

Step Three: Do Not Treat Them as Their Diagnosis

Okay, this one may get me into hot water, because I know it is not politically correct. From what I'm seeing, nearly every kid is being diagnosed with an anxiety disorder, ADHD, and/or depression. That does not mean that label is who they are. Instead, it is reflective of where they are at when diagnosed—and even then, the diagnoses usually stem from coping skills—trying to cope in a world that is not cleaning up its own messes—including at home. Because of this, we're allowing the kids to wear their diagnosis like a freaking "get out of jail free" card—but on the game board of life, we're not empowering them to develop the necessary skills to move beyond it.

Tests at school are meant to prepare every student for college, but we're failing our children more each year. We should test our teachers on "student happiness" and have them get paid for *that*! Instead of teaching kids how to manage emotions at school or at home, we're teaching them what we learned—how to hide, how to numb, how to sleep, how to run away. It does them no good. I promise; I'm seeing it every day.

When I'm brought to a kid on the brink, I'll talk to him or her, and then I want to go into the home and find out what is going on there. Is Dad away or on another binge? Is the kid completely a latchkey kid? Is no one ever home and always working or doing drugs? It happens so much more than you could know. Is Mom single again and her boyfriend is trying to impose new rules? Kids can struggle even in a solid home. Loving a child so much that you take the consequences away from their actions is just as bad. These are puzzle pieces that affect every single kid. Chaos in the home means chaos in the individual kid.

I'm going to invite you to remember your job is not to be your teen's best friend but their parent. Be that example. Be that guide. Don't excuse your actions and don't excuse theirs—empower their actions! Teach them how to cope and deal differently than how they have been showing up. In all reality, a diagnosis is an opportunity to teach them how to turn coping mechanisms into superpowers.

Step Four: Life Is Hard; Asking for Help Shouldn't Be

There are millions more single parents now than there were when you or I was growing up. Parents who are doing their best but over-protect instead of empowering try to wear every hat their child needs: mother, father, psychologist, coach, teacher, friend, priest.

Don't do it. Take off the stack of hats. Call in the village and let the people around you who know more than you do about certain subjects help out. You do you. Support your child to do themselves. Teach them how to ask for support when they don't know some-thing. Chances are, they will Google a lot and figure it out. Even then, that can be a painfully long way to do something well. We used to live in a time of apprentices and masters. It's okay for you not to have mastered every great thing in life. Hire it out! Request assistance. Knowing how to learn from others—especially master-ful people in certain subjects—will help your child recognize that people have callings, passions, and different skill sets. It will help them accept the ones they do have and develop them—and forget about the rest. They can learn quickly from a Master.

Leonardo Da Vinci taught, "Poor is the pupil who does not surpass his master." He expected his protégés to rise far beyond him! We should do the same with our kids. Don't expect to know all the answers. Teach them a skill in figuring out how to ask the many other people who do in many categories. It will give them a grounded, well-rounded support system. They need a village to call their own. Then they will exceed in mastery in one or more areas of their own lives . . . and learn how to seek help in other areas when their own family deserves it. It's a skillset to ask for help. It's a skillset to receive. It's also a skillset to give. When someone comes to you for expertise with their child, please, I invite you to give freely.

ACKNOWLEDGEMENTS

To my most influential friends: Shawn Edwards, Dave Beck, Craig Jones, Jason Coombs, Tyler Burningham, Aaron Hoehne, Bryan Doty, Ryan Black, Bear Phelps, Kenny Oldwin, Levi Blundell, Porter Rasmussen, Ty Carlson, John and Tyler Flandro, Dustin Acord, Dusty Schick, Ryan and Justin Lassetter, Ryan (Winnie) Winquist, RIP, and Luke Palmer, RIP, and Natalie Allan, RIP, along with Spencer (Spinny) Carlson, Greg Raymond, Dave Kerr, Eric Pope, Dustin and Tacey Lawrence, Suni, Mike, Max, Luke Mason, Greg Gillian, Rick Turner, Monica and Brendan Lonecker, and Lincoln Duryea, Will Pace, Paul Sanders. Thanks for letting me be a part of your lives for so many years.

To the Davis County School District and every principal and coach that I have worked with. Each of you took a chance on me and let me work inside of your schools and give back. To all the teachers who let me speak in your rooms, faculty who supported my cause, and every student I ever worked with. Thank you from the bottom of my heart.

To every athlete I've played with or coached over the years, who have shaped my life and many more who loved me along the way. Thank you. You know who you are.

The gym I own, Empower Fitness, has brought me so much happiness and given me such an amazing opportunity to meet, connect and help so many, and I will be forever grateful for everyone who has been a part of that. Coaching,wrestling, volleyball, soccer, and MMA have given me family and supporters who have loved me on my journey. Thank you, and I hope you know I love you.

I'd like to include a special remembrance of Danny Low. Your friendship is the closest I've ever been to a male soulmate, and I'll never forget you. See you on the other side, brother, when it's time. Be waiting at the back door to heaven to sneak me in! I want to thank the entire Low family for loving me and allowing me into your family and letting me remember your son in every speech I give.

Tasha, thank you for continuing to care for me through the tough times of my addiction. I will love you and your family forever. To the whole Moss family, thank you.

To my recovery crew: Lacie Jay, Gentry Jones, Jameson Hedin, Bryan Hedin, Sheldon (Cowboy) Honey, Joey Polaro, Casey Scott and Dr. Matt Woolley, Randy Burton, Todd Sylvester, Lance Essihos and Chris Burns Thanks for holding space.

I'd like to acknowledge all my coaches and mentors over the years. I'll never forget the lessons you taught.

To former governor Mike Leavitt, thank you for stepping in as my surrogate father. I know my dad appreciates that. The time you've taken to mold me and apply the lessons my father taught hasn't gone unnoticed and means the world to me.

Angie and Levi, thank you for showing me so much love when you didn't have to. I love you and honor our coparenting relationship and friendship. I love you like my own. Levi, you're a godsend, and I would marry you. Angie lucked out for sure!

To my family, who suffered the most but never gave up on me and showed me unconditional love:

- Erin, you were the toughest sibling; you will never be forgotten. Rest in peace, ErrBear (02N). Hayley, I'm proud of you and see you as a strong young woman who has been through so much in your short time on this earth.

- To Danielle, thank you for your love and deep compassion for me in my darkest times and to Cade, Court, and Izzie. I love you.

- To Maegan for being my playpal growing up and support from afar during my dark times. And Brent, thank you for the tough love and support over the years. I appreciate our friendship. Ashley, Tanner, Paige, and Wyatt, I'm proud of and love all of you.

- To my brother Drew, I've apologized before, but . . . sorry again for the crap I gave you growing up. I am blessed to call you brother. I pray for many more years riding bikes in the desert together. Ashley, thank you for the years of compassion and Ryyan, Jax, Tyson, and Bo, you all bring light into my life. Don't ever forget who your Funcle is!

Uncle Russ and Aunt Barbara, thank you for loving my family, and stepping in as surrogate grandparents. To Grandma Shanna, Grandma Christine, Uncle Rob and Uncle Brett, Hal, Brian, Derrik: thanks for all the guidance. To Aunt Marsha, you have been a major pillar my entire life, loving me through thick and thin. You are forever in my heart. I love you. Also my late Uncle Wayne for being so invested in trying to get me to love education. I appreciate your efforts more than you know.

To Heidi, my beautiful wife. I never knew love like ours was even possible. You have lit a fire in me that can only be explained as my soulmate. I look forward to sharing stages, adventures, and growing old together, as well as sharing our stories to people all over the world. Kaden, Cole, and Miles, thank you for letting me be a part of your lives and giving me the family I've always wanted.

Now, to my dad, Dan R. Eastman. Thank you for showing me what it means to be a man, a father, and a man of service. I just wish I could have watered those seeds long before you passed. I hope I am now making you proud. You are the driving force behind my spirituality and I hope to hug you in heaven. I love you, Dad!

To Claudette Eastman, aka "Mama"—no words can ever begin to show the love I have for you. Only you and I understand the fullness of our journey together. I love and respect you and will be indebted to you forever.

To Sophie . . . where do I even start? You have been my reason for living, for recovery, and you have given me the gift of being a father. You've shown me just how much a father is needed in a daughter's life and a love that shines brightly in my soul. You will never know the fullness of my love as there are no words to describe my deep love for you.

And to everyone else who has ever supported me, including my social media family. Your love and support has not gone unnoticed. You are all a part of me writing this book. Thank you. To Bridget Cook-Burch and Hannah Lyon, thank you for helping me bring this wild journey to life and giving me the strength to know it was possible. I love you guys.

To all my haters, thank you for buying and reading this book.

I love you all! I know firsthand how it feels to be down. No matter if you love me or hate me, I'm still rooting for you. Keep your head up and keep moving forward.

GET INVOLVED

Now I have an important question for you. Has life felt too hard for you lately? Do you feel alone, isolated or need some support in becoming a Warrior in the Garden? You are where you are, and that's okay. Life is meant to be full of ups and downs. As you've seen by my story, there is always a way to climb out and become a Warrior. Life can be amazing when you're able to change your mindset and see the good even in the bad. Remember, you are worth it. I love you, even if I don't know you. Reach out. If you have a support system, reach out today. If not, then reach out to me; use the contact information below.

Ready for More? Contact Me! You Can Also Become a Part of the Team!

Are you ready to be your own Warrior in the Garden? I invite you to find me and my programs at www.RobEastmanCoaching.com. You can also find me on Instagram (@TattooedLifeCoach8) and Facebook (rob.eastman.5). I am here for you.

Do you want to get more involved in your community? Do you want to be part of the movement of recovery? Do you want to prevent suicide? Do you want to be one who stands as sentinel and nurturer during a crisis? Are you ready to advocate for others and teach the ability to create a rich and fulfilled life? Please join us or contribute to the Eastman Family Recovery Foundation, a 501(c)(3) organization.

ABOUT THE AUTHOR

Rob Eastman is a highly sought-after life coach, entrepreneur, speaker, author, wrestling coach, and youth mentor as well as an athlete and a father. His message resonates with a broad range of audiences, from youth to parents to high-profile corporate leaders . . . in other words, "K through Life."

Rob's personal story of overcoming bullying, mental health struggles, religious judgment, suicidal ideation, and addiction is incredibly moving and powerful.

Over Rob's thirteen years in recovery, he opened a gym to facilitate his clients' mental and physical health, coached junior high and high school athletes, and started Eastman Family Recovery

Foundation, a 501©(3) organization, to assist families dealing with mental health crises. During this time, he ran thirteen ultramarathons, was ranked in the top 150 in the world in obstacle racing, spent four years training in martial arts, fought MMA, and trained other warriors.

Through speaking engagements, one-on-one client interactions, group work, direct work with families, and life coaching, Rob motivates people to successfully change by overcoming their fears, coping with tough life events, making healthy life choices, and discovering who they truly are: Warriors in the Garden.

With specialized, real-world experience, Rob helps develop the mindset and strategies for people to climb out of any situation and take their life to the next level.

Rob invites you to reach out to him:

Instagram: @tattooedlifecoach8
Facebook: rob.eastman.5
Websites: RobEastmanCoaching.com and WarriorInTheGarden.com

PHOTO GALLERY

Most of the time, you would find me in cowboy boots, cowboy hat and a diaper. Lucky for you, this time I'm dressed (1980)

Drew and I hanging out with Dad (1982)

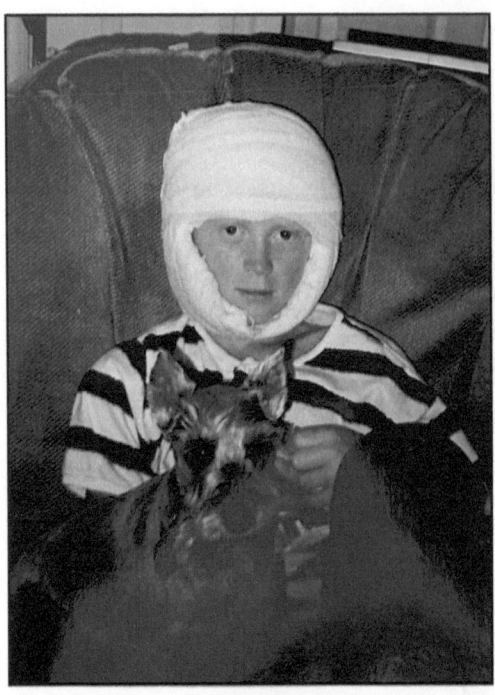

My head wrap after getting my ears tucked so kids would stop bullying me about them. I had the surgery before 7th grade (1990)

I needed to learn how to fight to keep the bullies away, and wrestling was the closest thing. 7th grade (1990)

One of the many news articles about my journey in my favorite sport and the only thing that gave me purpose and made me feel seen (1995)

Senior year of high school, still trying to find my place (1996)

One of the last pictures of Danny (next to Beetlejuice at Halloween) (1998)

Danny's tombstone (1999)

Recovering in Costa Rica
after Danny's death with
Outward Bound (1999)

Trying to be a father to a
newborn Sophie (2009)

Grandpa Dan and Sophie, she was his favorite (2009)

Dan and Claudette Eastman, one of the last pictures before he passed (2009)

A picture of Sophie where she spent a lot of time between the MMA gym and AA (2013)

One of my last MMA cage fights (2016) Photo Credit- Amanda Lynn Photography

Picture with Governor Leavitt and Lieutenant Governor Bell at the first fundraiser for my new foundation (2016)

Me speaking at a school about mental health and suicide prevention (2021)

Me taking a selfie in front of a packed crowd at one of my speeches (2022) Photo Credit- Jacom Stephens

One of my passions in life, coaching wrestling at a local high school, where I was head coach for four years (2022) Photo credit- Julie Mahana

At this choir event, Sophie surprised me. She had written a letter to her hero, and read the story about why she thinks I'm her biggest hero in front of 2,000 people. It was one of the proudest nights of my life (2022)

Me and Sophie sitting in the wrestling room at the high school after a tough day's practice. Sophie is the best example of a warrior in a garden that I know. We're doing everything to prepare her for what the real world has in store for her (2022)

REVIEWS

"I am an eyewitness. I saw the shattering struggles and the subsequent triumphs author Rob Eastman has written about in his book *Warrior in the Garden*. I saw Rob's pain and witnessed his parents' helplessness as their oldest son slipped into a vacuum of depression, alcohol, drugs, and insecurity. And then . . . I saw the recovery. Rob slowly overcame his addictions, focused his life by helping others. I have witnessed his emergence as a unique personage of hope and optimism, a tattooed teacher of wisdom, who speaks with an authenticity that demands attention and belief. *Warrior in the Garden* is a lifeboat for those in similar despair and their families."

—*Michael O. Leavitt, Former Secretary of the US Department of Health and Human Services, Former Administrator of the US Environmental Protection Agency, 14th Governor of Utah*

"Rob Eastman's narrative is a testament to seizing opportunities amidst adversity. He shares relatable stories, demonstrating that success can arise from mental health struggles and addiction through a resilient mindset. Eastman's journey shines a light on transforming challenges into triumphs, offering hope and inspiration. His emphasis on mindset shift and strategic determination showcases how such shifts can redefine life's course. Eastman dispels the myth that success is only for a select few, proving that, regardless of background, everyone can achieve. His story

motivates others to embrace change, nurturing resilience on the path to realizing untapped potential."
—Maresa Friedman, *Chief Strategy Officer at Strategy Solved*

"Reading *Warrior in the Garden* resonated on several levels. As a recovering alcoholic with 30 years of sobriety, I understand the roller coaster of addiction. Our choice either leads to a path of happiness or a path of misery. This book leaves the reader with a sense of inspiration and motivation, showcasing the realization that the only thing keeping you from being the best version of yourself is you."
—Kedma Ough, *CEO Superb Maids Portland*

"WOW!! What an amazing story of strength, perseverance, self-awareness and growth. As a recovering alcoholic myself, I am so grateful for this book sharing all the behind-the-scenes details of addiction, shining light, and bringing awareness that WE DO RECOVER!"
—Gentry Jones, *Certified Life and Recovery Coach*

"As humans, we all strive to be seen and heard. Rob Eastman has perfectly captured his personal journey to be seen and heard. I laughed! I cried! When a book can elicit emotions like that, then it's a winner in my book. But most of all, I loved the honesty in his powerful story."
—Misti Mazurik, *Director of Operations at RHG Media Productions*

"Robbie Eastman screams, cries, prays and swears out the telling of his decades of pain and addiction. You feel in this true-life drama his suffering, addiction, deceit, self-betrayal and the profound pain of long-suffering loved ones. Tragically, his community and schools wounded little Robbie because of his appearance and ADHD; he didn't heal soon enough to avoid decades of addiction. Yet, Rob

somehow found the inspiration and rock-solid determination to overcome it. Now he teaches others how to avoid or recover from what he went through. A painfully candid but compelling story of redemption. I heartily recommend it."
—*Greg Bell, Former Utah State Senator and Lieutenant Governor*

"This book illuminates mental health and mastery over life's challenges. It shows us how to be warriors of self-discovery and not lose ourselves in the face of life's battles. It gives the reader the insights needed to embrace resilience through personal struggles and unveil the authentic strength and vulnerability within each of us."
—*Baron Baptiste, New York Times Bestselling Author of Perfectly Imperfect (Hay House) and Journey Into Power (Simon and Schuster)*

"Raw and authentic, this book delves into the author's vulnerabilities, revealing a side we can all empathize with. It captures his evolution from addiction to resolute commitment, driven by the impact on his loved ones. Through personal transformation, the author poses a profound question: 'Is this the role model I want to be?' It's a testament to overcoming one's dark side. A beacon of resilience, the author's willingness to share his path inspires us to confront our own imperfections. As a survivor, I wholeheartedly recommend this book for its transformative message in a world that often shies away from self-examination."
—*Deborah Wiener, Intuitive & Inspirational Business and Life Coach*

"Rob Eastman is a compelling storyteller. Pulling readers into the world of a struggling and rebellious adolescent, *Warrior in the Garden* takes them on an emotional rollercoaster of joy and frustration as the protagonist finds his path and inspiration. A powerful read."
—*Maureen Ryan Blake, Bestselling Author, TV Show Host, and YouTube Expert*

www.ingramcontent.com/pod-product-compliance
Lightning Source LLC
Chambersburg PA
CBHW020432130626
46549CB00001B/104